"If there's one hockey book you want to buy . . . make it
Now Back to You Dick, by Dick Irvin."

– Hockey News

"Sometimes humorous, sometimes sad, always interesting –
this is a book that contains all sorts of emotions that the avid
sports fan can relate to."

– The Halifax Daily News

"Keep [this] book handy. It'll keep you occupied . . . during
Hockey Night in Canada intermissions."

– The Saskatoon Star-Phoenix

"Irvin's memoirs . . . are affectionate, witty and informative."

– TV Guide

" [Dick Irvin's] crisp style has become a benchmark for good
hockey broadcasting across Canada."

– The Globe and Mail

"**Now Back to You Dick** is a well-written book that adds to
the written history of the game.."

– The Vancouver Courier

Dick Irvin

Now Back To You Dick

Two Lifetimes in Hockey

An M&S Paperback from
McClelland & Stewart Inc.
The Canadian Publishers

An M&S Paperback from McClelland & Stewart Inc.

First printing September 1989

Copyright © 1988 Dick Irvin Enterprises Ltd.

Canadian Cataloguing in Publication Data
Irvin, Dick, 1932-
Now back to you Dick

(M&S paperback)
Includes index.
ISBN 0-7710-4354-6

1. Irvin, Dick, 1932-   . 2. Sportscasters –
Canada – Biography.   3. Hockey – Canada – History.
4. Irvin, Dick, 1892-   . 5. Hockey – Coaches –
Canada – Biography.   I. Title.

GV742.42.I78A3 1989   796.96′2′0922   C89-094033-9

Cover design by Peter Maher, adapted by Graham Ross
Cover photography by David Bier

Printed and bound in Canada

McClelland & Stewart Inc.
The Canadian Publishers
481 University Avenue
Toronto, Ontario
M5G 2E9

Contents

For Wilma, Nancy, and Doug,
my Three-Star Selection
every night.

Introduction

On April 11, 1932, the *Toronto Daily Star* carried this headline in its sports section:

> BABY SON'S ILLNESS CALLS IRVIN HOME.
> LEAFS COACH MAY NOT SEE SON ALIVE.

The coach was Dick Irvin. Two nights before, he had coached the Toronto Maple Leafs to a Stanley Cup victory over the New York Rangers. The City of Toronto honoured the new champions with a civic dinner on the night of April 11, but by then Dick Irvin was on a train bound for western Canada hoping to see his son alive.

I was the baby son, Dick Jr., so obviously he did.

That headline began my lifelong involvement with hockey. I spent the first twenty-five years of my life the son of a man who was elected to the Hockey Hall of Fame as a player and who went on to coach in the NHL for twenty-six consecutive years. Time marches on and I'd like today's generation of fans to learn about my dad, his contributions to hockey, and read some of the colourful stories he was part of during his great career.

During the past fifty years, while watching over 2,000

NHL games, I have seen every All-Star from Syl Apps to Wayne Gretzky. For the past twenty-seven years, I have been a sportscaster and hockey announcer, broadcasting over 1,500 NHL games. Along the way I have met most of hockey's greatest stars, listened to their stories, been part of a few myself, and had a lot of fun.

I'd like to share that fun with you in the pages of this book.

·················
Fear and Trembling in the Weight Room

Pierre Trudeau was the reason for a frightening moment in my career as a sports broadcaster. I have never met the man and he isn't much of a sports fan. But once we were in the same place at the same time, and it was kind of scary.

On May 21, 1979, the Montreal Canadiens defeated the New York Rangers to win the Stanley Cup at the Montreal Forum. Trudeau was Prime Minister of Canada and attended the game. Every once in a while during the previous few years, his office would call the Canadiens to advise them that the PM wanted to see a certain game. At the same time, they would ask if it was to be shown on national television. PMs are always at games that are being seen coast to coast. Somehow they don't seem too interested in games that are televised only in a local market.

PMs also always sit in the VIP box directly behind the Canadien players' bench, a location that just happens to be directly in line with the TV cameras positioned on the other side of the Forum. But on May 21, 1979, Trudeau had to sit on the same side of the building as the cameras. A federal election was taking place the next day and electoral laws forbid candidates from appearing on TV the night before.

The CBC wasn't about to breach those laws, so the PM had to change seats.

For many years, Brian and Mila Mulroney had season tickets located slightly to the right of the Canadiens' bench. Brian wasn't running for office in those days, so that night he was able to sit in his usual spot.

After the game, *Hockey Night in Canada* (HNIC) assigned me to interview some of the victorious Canadiens. The camera was set up in the team's weight-training room adjacent to the dressing room. It was a spot thankfully removed from the scene where supposedly grown men were gleefully pouring champagne over each other's heads, and over the head of any TV sportscaster who happened to pass by.

As I was interviewing Larry Robinson, I glanced toward the doorway leading to the dressing room and there was Pierre Trudeau, standing about ten feet away. He had been congratulating the champions and wanted to leave the Forum via a back-door exit rather than through the main lobby. The only way to that exit was through the weight-training room, but our TV camera was blocking his path.

That's when the scary part began for me. Larry was saying all the right things as a humble Stanley Cup winner, but I'm afraid I wasn't listening too closely as my mind raced to other matters. What a perfect set-up for a politician on election eve. I started to imagine the PM walking toward me and into camera range when the interview with Larry was over.

"Hi. My name is Pierre. What's yours?"

What was I to do? Could I turn him away?

"Sorry Prime Minister, but you can't come on with me coast to coast. There's an election tomorrow, remember?"

Somehow I knew I wouldn't be able to refuse the PM one last, albeit illegal, TV appearance before a couple of million undecided voters. Certainly the members of his entourage wanted that to happen. I could see their faces and while they were hopeful, my nerves were shaky.

The interview with Larry ended and the moment of truth arrived. I cued to fellow announcer Dan Kelly, who was in the *Hockey Night in Canada* studio waiting to interview Phil Esposito, took a deep breath, and waited for the PM to make his move. He did.

Trudeau had been staring rather vacantly into space waiting for the interview to end. He brightened as Larry walked toward him, shook his hand, then without so much as a sideway glance at the nervous TV interviewer clutching the CBC microphone, headed straight for the door, politely ducking under the camera lens even though he knew we weren't on the air. His minions trailed after him, obviously very frustrated. I was obviously very relieved.

Twenty-four hours later, the Trudeau camp must have been even more frustrated their boss hadn't made my life difficult in the weight-training room. On May 22, 1979, the ruling Liberal Party lost the election and Joe Clark became Prime Minister of Canada.

As I left the *Hockey Night in Canada* set that night, my nerves still intact after the near-miss with the PM, I thought of another experience involving sports and politics some fourteen years earlier. It happened on December 7, 1965, a date I remember because it was the day I signed the deal to purchase the first house I ever owned.

I was covering a news conference at a curling club near our apartment. The club announced it would be hosting the Canadian Ladies Curling Championship later that winter. Among the dignitaries present was our district's fairly new Member of Parliament.

Our MP was obviously out of his element at a sports gathering and nobody paid him much attention. When it was his turn to speak, he mumbled that he didn't know much about curling, wished everyone the best of luck, and was very relieved to disappear again into the woodwork.

(That was in sharp contrast to a curling club affair I had attended a few years earlier, when Lester Pearson gave a great speech. He then spent the afternoon curling with the boys and had a grand time.)

"You should have seen our local MP," I said to my wife Wilma, when I returned from the news conference. "Was he ever out of place. What a dandy he is."

Our local MP was Pierre Trudeau.

What did I know?

It Started with the Scrapbook

"*I*f it wasn't for your father you wouldn't have that job."

During my early years in the sportscasting business, complainers who didn't like my work used that phrase quite often. In reply, I would explain that my father had passed away four years before I became a broadcaster. But deep down I knew he truly was the reason I got my start in the business.

A lot of young sports fans contemplate careers in the media business. While I wasn't exactly young, I was doing just that when Canada's second TV network, CTV, began operation in 1961. When the new affiliated stations opened, so did a few jobs in the sportscasting field and, luckily, I got one of them.

CFCF-TV opened for business in Montreal in January, 1961. Brian McFarlane was the station's first Sports Director. We had played hockey against each other in college when Brian was an All-American at St. Lawrence University and I was a bench warmer for the McGill Redmen. He became a sportscaster upon graduation and joined CFCF from CFRB Radio in Toronto.

We met again at the Forum shortly after Brian began

working in Montreal. I was coaching a bantam hockey team and Brian thought it would be a good idea to have me appear on his Sunday afternoon program, *Sportsman's Club*, during Minor Hockey Week. Son of hockey's all-time winning coach and all that.

"Bring along anything you might have about your dad that we could talk about," he told me. So when I showed up at the station for my first TV appearance, I was carrying the "scrapbook."

I never saw my father play hockey. When I arrived, he was the thirty-nine-year-old coach of the Toronto Maple Leafs. But Dick Irvin is a member of the Hockey Hall of Fame as a player, not as a coach. So the story of his career on the ice unfolded for me as soon as I was able to comprehend what the scrapbook was all about.

It was made up of clippings about my dad's career from the time he began playing senior hockey through to his coaching years in Toronto, and I recall doing most of my reading from that scrapbook while sprawled out on our living-room floor in Regina. I particularly loved to read the headlines that featured Dad's name following one of his good games. Alongside one of the pictures of Dad, I scrawled in six- or seven-year-old handwriting: "The best hockey player that ever lived!"

My Grade Four teacher, Miss Traub, asked us to find a poem in a book at home to read to the class. Poetry was often used by old-time sports writers, so I dug into the scrapbook and came up with this one from a 1923 clipping in the *Regina Leader* when Dad was playing for the Regina Capitals:

"Swervin'", "Curvin'", or "Deservin'",
What in sixty rhymes with "Irvin"?
I give up; I'll call him Dick,
That rhymes with "quick" and "slick" and "hockey stick."

Miss Traub's brother played on that same 1923 team with Dad, so she was pleased with my choice, although I'm sure it wasn't quite what she originally had in mind.

Dad was born near Hamilton, Ontario on July 19, 1892. His father was a butcher who moved his family west to Winnipeg near the turn of the century. My grandfather had no use for hockey. "You'll never get anywhere chasing that little black thing," he used to tell his sons. But my grandmother was a fan. She started the scrapbook in 1912 when her nineteen-year-old son Dick began getting a lot of mention in the sports pages of Winnipeg newspapers.

My dad's main claim to fame during his playing career was his ability to score goals. He often told me about the hours he spent in the attic of their home on Atlantic Avenue, in Winnipeg's north end, shooting a puck or a ball at a doorknob. He used to say, half kidding and half serious, that he was the most accurate shooter of his time because of the hours he spent trying to hit the doorknob in the attic.

There's a story in the early part of the scrapbook about him scoring nine goals in one game. I know it was his favourite because it's a story he loved to tell me over and over again.

He began the 1913-14 season playing for an Intermediate team, but early in the season he was signed by the Monarchs of the Winnipeg Senior League. They reached the Western Allan Cup final series against Kenora, but on the morning of the first game Dad was ruled ineligible for further play. The rules stipulated that no one could be on an Allan Cup contending team who had played in another league that same season.

The *Winnipeg Free Press* described the news as hitting the city "like a thunderbolt." Dad was the Monarchs' top scorer. When the ruling came down, the Monarchs announced they wouldn't play without Irvin and forfeited the series to Kenora.

The Eastern Champions were the Toronto Rowing and

Amateur Athletic Club. They defeated Kenora to win the Cup and the Monarchs immediately challenged them. Toronto accepted, although they wouldn't go so far as to put their championship on the line. The teams agreed to a best-of-three series to be played in Toronto.

The Monarchs lost the first game 3-1. They won the second 9-2, and that's the game I heard about so often because Dad scored all nine of his team's goals. There's no doubt it was his favourite hockey accomplishment. And he got a kick out of the aftermath as well: the Toronto team refused to play the third game, saying too many of their players had been injured by the rambunctious westerners. Dad liked to think what really had been injured was their pride.

For many years, Toronto sports writers have named their own version of Canada's top athlete by awarding the Lou Marsh Trophy. Lou Marsh was a pioneer sports writer in that city and after Dad's nine-goal performance, he filed a special report to the *Winnipeg Free Press*, which read in part:

> The exhibition of Dick Irvin who scored every goal the Monarchs landed constitutes a record for hockey in this part of Canada. Nine goals from one man's stick is top notch hockey, is certainly "going some". Irvin was shooting dead on all night and his trickeries in front of the net, combined with his remarkable speed, took all the attention from Gordon Meeking who was the star of the first game. The local idol was not in it for a minute with Irvin.

Marsh's story wasn't the only big plug Dad got in print because of the nine goals. A few months later, he became the first, and maybe still the only hockey player to make it in Ripley's *Believe It or Not*.

Under a cartoon drawing of a hockey player, the caption read: "Dickinson Irvin, Canadian hockey star, scored all nine goals in a shutout game against Toronto, winning the Allan Cup."

But Ripley's readers could believe only part of it. The Cup wasn't on the line, and it wasn't a shutout.

The Monarchs played in the Winnipeg Senior League with teams called the Victorias and the 61st Battalion. In Dad's first full season, he was his team's top goal-getter. The scrapbook doesn't contain a list of the League's leading point men, but one article tells about Dad scoring seventeen of the Monarch's first forty-two goals in the 1914–15 season. The Monarchs were League champions, with Dad's older brother Alex their captain and best defenceman.

DICK IRVIN PLAYED REMARKABLE HOCKEY IN LAST NIGHT'S MATCH is one of the laudatory headlines about Dad in the scrapbook. The Monarchs defeated the Melville Millionaires in the 1915 Allan Cup final for the senior championship of Canada. DICK IRVIN CLOSELY WATCHED BUT BREAKS AWAY FOR COUNTER THAT WON THE CUP.

Other headlines from the amateur part of Dad's career include:

DICK IRVIN BEST GOAL GETTER IN AMATEUR HOCKEY.

TORONTO MANAGER SAYS DICK IRVIN IS WORLD'S GREATEST AMATEUR HOCKEY PLAYER.

Pretty heady stuff for a kid who was discovering his dad's career and learning to read at the same time.

That quote from the Toronto manager topped a story concerning a dispute that was getting some newspaper space comparing Dad's hockey abilities to those of Hobey Baker, an American from Princeton University who was being touted in the U.S.A. as the world's best player. The manager, Jimmy Murphy, saw both men play and jumped on Dad's bandwagon. Tragically, Baker never got the chance to play pro hockey. He lost his life in a plane crash just after World War One, at the age of twenty-four.

After the Monarchs' Allan Cup win in 1915, Dad played another year in Winnipeg, then turned pro, joining the Portland Rosebuds of the Pacific Coast Hockey Association.

The coach of the Rosebuds was Pete Muldoon, who would play a role in Dad's career at various times. Muldoon wasn't a Dick Irvin fan at the beginning and kept him on the bench for most of the first five games of the 1916–17 season.

In the sixth game, the team's top centre player, Tommy Dunderdale, received a match penalty. Muldoon had to use Dad. When Dunderdale was penalized, Portland was trailing Vancouver 2-1. Dad scored two goals in his first three minutes on the ice and the Rosebuds went on to win the game.

DICK IRVIN CRUSHES INTO GAME AND BEATS VANCOUVER 5-3 was the headline after that one. (Crushes?)

Muldoon still was not impressed. Dad sat on the bench for almost all of the Rosebuds' next game and at that point had pretty well made up his mind to return to Winnipeg and forget the whole thing. Then fate intervened and he became one of the few players, I'm sure, whose hockey career was saved because his coach suffered an injury.

The following day, Muldoon was crossing the street when he was sideswiped by a wayward Model T. The Rosebuds' business manager, Tom Scott, took over as coach while Muldoon recovered. He knew Dad was seriously thinking of calling it quits but prevailed on him to stay around for one more game, promising him plenty of ice time.

Obviously Dad was grateful. The final score of that game was 8-4 for the Rosebuds over Spokane. Dick Irvin scored five goals. Even Muldoon had to admit that the kid from Winnipeg deserved to be a regular.

More headlines from the Portland papers tell the story of Dad's first year in professional hockey.

TWO MORE GOALS FOR DICK IRVIN IN PORTLAND VICTORY.

THEY COULDN'T SUPPRESS DICK. (Has there ever been a headline telling us they couldn't "suppress" Gretzky?)

DICK IRVIN, FORMER 'PEG STAR, SENSATION OF COAST LEAGUE.

IRVIN REGISTERS FOUR GOALS AND PORTLAND WINS.

LIGHTNING ONLY THING FASTER THAN IRVIN.

The PCHA was considered on a par with the League in the East, the National Hockey Association, and the two League champions played off for the Stanley Cup. That year Seattle

At Year 2000:

The sky will not fall.

The water will not rise.

We will survive Y2K.

What is Y2K?

When computers were in their infancy and computer memory was a precious commodity, programmers used a form of shorthand to record years; for example, 1984 became "84." The Y2K "bug" is how computers will experience the arrival of year 2000 — "00" doesn't sequentially follow "99," and is therefore beyond their understanding. As a result, computers may become confused and malfunction.

How is John Hancock preparing for Y2K?

John Hancock has dedicated significant resources to a comprehensive program to identify, resolve, and test our computer systems (including both hardware and software), our building facilities, and the other elements of our business that are critical to servicing our customers and their accounts. Throughout the rest of 1999, we will complete testing the few remaining items and make sure that our tested systems stay year 2000 ready. Where appropriate, we are also conducting tests with our business partners and participating in industry testing. To be ready for the unexpected, we have developed detailed contingency plans for all aspects of our business.

I'd like more information.

Please visit us on the Internet at www.jhancock.com.

Please be advised that this is a designated "Year 2000 Readiness Disclosure" in accordance with the provisions of the "Year 2000 Information and Readiness Disclosure Act," 112 Stat. 2386.

John Hancock

John Hancock Mutual Life Insurance Company, John Hancock Variable Life Insurance Company
(not licensed in New York), Signator Investors, Inc., Member NASD, SIPC, Boston, Massachusetts 02117

MK00005 6/99

was the best in the West and defeated the Montreal Canadiens in the Cup final. The following season (1917–18) the
NHA became the NHL.

Dad finished his first professional season with thirty-five
goals in twenty-three games. He returned home to Winnipeg no doubt feeling he had honestly earned the money
they paid him, all $700 of it.

Players on championship teams these days usually are
given rings to mark their accomplishment. When the Montreal Canadiens won the Stanley Cup in 1986, each player
received a ring containing twenty-three diamonds because
the win was the twenty-third in the history of the franchise.

When the Winnipeg Monarchs won the Allan Cup in
1915, the players received a gift from the City of Winnipeg.
At a ceremony on the steps of City Hall each man was presented with his Allan Cup souvenir gift. Not a ring, not a
watch. Each player was given a motorcycle!

There is a great photo in the scrapbook of the entire Monarchs team, wearing hockey sweaters, sitting on their motorcycles. I don't know how many of them learned how to
ride their new machines, but Dad did. Following his season
in Portland, he returned to Winnipeg and joined the Fort
Garry Horse Regiment. A couple of months later, he was
overseas, involved in World War One as a motorcycle dis-
patch rider. He saw service in France, Holland, and Bel-
gium.

Returning from overseas, he moved to Regina to continue
his hockey career, first as a reinstated amateur and then
again as a professional with the Regina Capitals of the
Western Canada League. He joined them in the fall of 1921
and would continue to make his living in professional
hockey until his death thirty-six years later. That was the
first year of the Western Canada League, which joined the
NHL and PCHA in competition for the Stanley Cup.

There were four teams in the first Western League: Regina, Saskatoon, Calgary, and Edmonton. Dad scored twenty

goals in twenty games that year. He missed the first four games of the season because of an ankle injury suffered late in the fall when he stepped in a gopher hole while playing golf. He swore then he would never golf again, and he didn't, until we gave him a set of clubs for his fifty-ninth birthday.

Regina upset the League champion Edmonton Eskimos in the playoffs and then met the Vancouver Millionaires of the PCHA to decide who would travel east to play the NHL champions for the Stanley Cup.

It was a two-game total-goal series and the Caps won the first game, in Vancouver, 2-1. Dad scored the winning goal.

The teams then made the long haul by train back to Regina where, as one article put it, the fans were at a "fever pitch the likes of which has never been seen before in the Queen City."

I have a program from the game, which was played March 11, 1922. Advertisements taken by Regina business firms contained slogans like, "Regina is Proud of her Athletes!" and "Here's Hoping the Stanley Cup will find a Resting Place in Regina for 1922."

Sad to say, it didn't. The Millionaires won the game 4-0 with a player named Art Duncan scoring three of their four goals. Dad would gain some measure of revenge on Duncan by replacing him as coach of the Toronto Maple Leafs nine years later. But no doubt defeat on that March night in Regina was a bitter pill for him to swallow. It was the closest he would ever get to playing in a Stanley Cup final series.

By then Dad had decided to settle permanently in Regina. In 1923, he built a home for his parents at 2155 Angus Street. Most people can think of one house that was "home" during their youth and that one was mine. That was where I first listened to Foster Hewitt and skated on a backyard rink. That same backyard was where Dad kept pigeons and chickens, and raised Collie pups and Miniature Pinscher show dogs. Not exactly your normal city backyard. We lived there until our family moved to Montreal in 1951, when I was nineteen years old. I visited the old house many times in later years until it fell victim to progress, of sorts, and was demolished in 1985. I'm glad I wasn't driving down Angus Street the day they were tearing down the house my dad built at 2155.

Dad's mother continued to compile the scrapbook. A 1923 write-up of a game he played for the Capitals contains one of my favourite passages about Dad's hockey playing talents. It reads:

> Dick Irvin had a field day throughout the match and his stick-handling was beautiful to see. Dick scored twice and his machine gun shot was right in order and all of his drives were aimed straight for the net.

It's interesting to note how friendly writers were toward the players on their home teams. They wrote on a first-name basis – "Dick" and "George" and "Puss" and "Amby." I wonder if the journalists of that time were accused of being "homers" the way many of us are in the TV era today?

Another clipping showed how the Regina press protected its local sports heroes. Under a headline that read simply DISGUST:

> Dick Irvin missed an open net much to the disgust of the Regina fans, says the *Moose Jaw News* in its account of the game Tuesday night.
> Nothing that Dick Irvin can do will ever arouse disgust in Regina fans, least of all merely missing a shot on goal. Disgust is a dirty word to use in a case like this. Should Dick have a hundred chances on an open net and miss every time fans would put their hands affectionately on his shoulder and offer him their sympathies for his hard luck.

The Irvins were well ensconsed in Regina by the mid-1920s. The oldest of four brothers, Alex, had remained in Winnipeg working for the CPR. But Dad's two younger brothers, Chum and Pete, also moved to Regina. All three were active in hockey and baseball, Chum being considered the best catcher in semi-pro ball in western Canada.

There's one story from Dad's playing days in Regina that his mother didn't put in the scrapbook. Perhaps she felt it didn't belong with the glowing tales of her son's prowess as a stickhandler and goal scorer. But it's one Dad used to tell, one I know Don Cherry would have loved to hear him relate. (There have been many times when I have been reminiscing with Grapes wishing he and Dad could have known each other. When it comes to the story-telling part of hockey, they would have had a lot in common.)

One of Dad's big rivals in the Western League was Cully Wilson, who was playing for Calgary. One night they collided at centre ice and Wilson jammed his stick under Dad's jaw. Dad had the dangerous habit of skating with his tongue stuck out between his teeth. Mark Hunter is a modern player who does the same thing.

Wilson's stick drove Dad's teeth through his tongue and the blood was flowing freely. While Wilson was on his way to the penalty box, the Regina trainer tried to get Dad to go to the dressing room but he would have none of that. He had a score to settle.

When the referee dropped the puck to resume play, Dad skated directly to the penalty box and laid a two-handed cross check over Wilson's head. Again the blood was flowing freely, this time Wilson's, and a general brawl quickly ensued.

I must say I didn't always enjoy hearing Dad tell that story. I guess it didn't quite fit the image I had of him as a player. But there's a postscript to it and it's a dandy. It was told to me by my Uncle Alex.

The following summer, Dad was visiting Alex in Winnipeg. They were walking down an aisle in Eaton's department store and there, walking down the same aisle toward them, was Cully Wilson. . . .

As Uncle Alex told it, neither man broke stride and he was sure they were going to go at it right in the middle of the men's clothing department. When they got close, face to face, their eyes were blazing. But after a frightening couple of seconds, certainly for Alex, smiles started to replace the glares and the smiles turned into chuckles. Crisis over.

There isn't an organization called The Fraternal Order of Hockey Players, but it wouldn't surprise me if one was formed. Despite the fights and rivalries on the ice, very few players carry grudges off the ice. In the 1940's, Rocket Richard and a tough guy on the Rangers, Bob Dill, had two fights in one game in New York, then went out on the town together later that night. Modern day battlers John Kordic and Gord Donnelly fight almost every time Montreal plays Quebec. Yet they have posed together for a blue jeans ad and sometimes talk on the phone and compare notes between games. In the case of my Dad and Cully Wilson, they became teammates on the Chicago Black Hawks in the late 1920's. Not only that, they were roommates on road trips.

Life wasn't easy in the old Western Canada Hockey League. I suppose it's a perfect example for anyone who likes to talk about "the good, old days" and for anyone who wants to believe the game was rougher then. Dad once gave a newspaper reporter an interview about his playing days in Regina.

Saskatoon was the hot spot of the league. They had a real club with Newsy Lalonde, the Cook brothers, Harry Cameron and George Hainsworth. The fans were very warm too.

Bill Cook, Cameron and Lalonde cut our goalie Red McCusker down three times in one game. He was full of stitches.

Another night Red played goal with a tin helmet on. One end of the Saskatoon rink was called "the cat-walk." It was a rush section and looked right down on our goalie. The boys used to arm themselves with eggs and vegetables. Those who didn't chew tobacco and spit on the visiting goalies would throw down a barrage of garbage. You had to be tough. You had to love hockey to play in that league.

One of the toughest of the tough in those days was Edouard "Newsy" Lalonde. When he played for Saskatoon, Lalonde was nearing the end of a playing career that began just after the turn of the century. He was an original member of the Montreal Canadiens, a player who combined great hockey skills with a mean streak second to none. He was one of those players on the visiting club home team fans loved to hate.

Lalonde was the first star to play with the Montreal Canadiens. Like Rocket Richard in later years, Newsy had to fight his way through the League on his way to impressive goal-scoring records. Old write-ups tell us things like: "Lalonde knocked out Jimmy Gardner in the second period." In December of 1912, the Canadiens and the Montreal Wanderers played an exhibition game in Toronto to open a new arena. The game turned into warfare when Newsy boarded Odie Cleghorn. Odie's brother Sprague then clobbered Lalonde with his stick, cutting him badly. The Toronto police were on the scene and Cleghorn was hauled into court and fined fifty dollars. (Tiger Williams and Dino Ciccarelli can relate to that.) A year later, Lalonde was fined and suspended for a stick attack on Joe Hall, of the Quebec Bulldogs, who needed eight stitches to close the wound. Simply, Newsy Lalonde was a tough old bird.

Newsy lived in Montreal until he passed away and I got to know him in the latter stages of his life. He told me of a game he played in Regina when Saskatoon defeated the Capitals 1-0. Newsy scored the only goal of the game. "End to end through the whole team," as he described it.

When the game ended and the teams were leaving the ice, Dad skated up to Lalonde and shook his hand, congratulating him on his brilliant goal. "Never had that happen to me any other time," Newsy told me. "Your dad did something I never forgot."

In the mid-1960's, shortly after I joined *Hockey Night in Canada*, I received a rush call from the producers. They had received word that Newsy Lalonde was on his death bed. They wanted to put together a film tribute to run during the intermission of a game two nights later in the event he passed away. John Millar, the HNIC film archivist, hastily assembled shots of old photos of Lalonde and I went to his studio and voiced the sound track, written as though Newsy had died.

On Saturday night, two days after the obituary had been recorded, I looked down from the Forum broadcast booth while the teams were warming up and who was there leaning over the boards kibitzing with some of the players but Newsy Lalonde. A tough old bird, indeed.

In 1925, Dad was on the move again. After playing four seasons in Regina, he found himself back in his original professional hockey home. The owner of the Regina team, Wes Champ, transferred the franchise to Portland, Oregon. There must have been something in the air in that lovely west coast city that agreed with Dad because, after a couple of mediocre seasons in Regina, he had another big year in Portland. The team managed only twelve wins in thirty games, but he finished in a tie for the scoring championship with Bill Cook of Saskatoon. Each man scored thirty-one goals. There was no credit given for assists in those days.

That stay in Portland was like his first one, lasting only one year. The Western League folded after the 1925–26 season and the Portland franchise was purchased by two freewheeling, big spenders from Chicago, Tack Hardwick and Major Frederic McLaughlin.

The NHL had been a seven-team league. With the influx of players and franchises from the west, it grew to ten teams with two divisions, the Canadian and the American. The three new teams, the Black Hawks, the New York Rangers, and the Detroit Cougars were placed in the American Division.

The Canadian Division consisted of the Toronto St. Pat's, the Canadiens and Maroons from Montreal, the Ottawa Senators, and a team from New York called the Americans. So with the "Americans" playing in a League division called the Canadian, it's obvious that the strange and wonderful decisions we have all come to question when it comes to the operation of pro sports in fact had their beginnings a long time ago.

The Hawks played their first game at the Chicago Coliseum against the Toronto St. Pats and won it 4-1. The scrapbook contains a write-up by a reporter on his first hockey assignment. Some of the highlights of his story were as follows:

> ... Chicago's social, financial and business life were well represented at the inaugural game and the national pastime of Canada proved to be full of thrills, spills, rough work and clever defence on the part of both teams.
>   ... Hay snapped the vulcanized rubber disk into the net for the first point and the cheers that came from the spectators fairly shook the rafters.
>   ... Irvin zigzagged his way through the defensive lines and his keen eye and accurate shot sent the puck into the rival's net with such velocity that it bounced out and coursed its way to the middle of the rink.
>   ... "Even up the score in this inning boys," shouted Pete Muldoon, manager and coach of the Hawks.
>   ... Several players on both sides were fined two minutes.
>   ... Offside plays happened in all periods.

And so it went, as Chicago newspaper readers got their first taste of hockey reporting. And yes, the Chicago coach was the same Pete Muldoon who had kept Dad on the bench when he was a rookie forward with the Portland Rosebuds ten years before.

Dad was thirty-four years old when he arrived in Chicago to captain the Hawks in their first season in the NHL. He had an excellent year, finishing second to Bill Cook of the Rangers in the scoring race. Cook had thirty-seven points on thirty-three goals and four assists. Dad was one point back with eighteen goals and eighteen assists. The legendary Howie Morenz was third with thirty-two.

A couple of years ago, the NHL office in Montreal sent me Dad's player contracts with the Black Hawks. His salary for the team's initial season was $3,750. If the Hawks finished first, second, or third he was to receive an additional $250 (which he did because they finished third).

$3,750 is a paltry sum by today's standards, but in 1926 it wasn't all that bad. Ads in the scrapbook from Chicago papers of the time tell us that thirty-five cents was the admission at the United Artists Theatre to see Ronald Colman in his first talking movie, *Bulldog Drummond*. For that same thirty-five-cent-ticket price the State Lake had a stage show five times a day featuring "Jack Dempsey, In Person," plus a movie, *The Delightful Rogue*, starring Rod Larocque. Other ads show shaving cream at twenty-five cents a tube and shoes for $2.50 a pair.

In the wake of his good season in '26–'27, Dad was given a big raise the following year to $6,000. In addition, the team agreed to pay his expenses home to Regina at the end of the season.

Dad's second NHL season was cut very short by an injury that effectively ended his playing career. In a game in Chicago against the Montreal Maroons on December 27, 1927, Dad was bodychecked heavily by Red Dutton. He hit his head on the ice, and suffered a fractured skull. There are plenty of headlined stories about the accident in the scrapbook:

DICK IRVIN BADLY HURT IN CHICAGO GAME.
CAPTAIN TAKEN FROM ICE WITH SKULL FRACTURE.
CHICAGO CAPTAIN'S CONDITION GRAVE.
INJURY MAY END IRVIN'S CAREER.

For all intents and purposes it did end his career. Major McLaughlin felt he was "damaged goods," and insisted his salary be reduced to $4,900. He returned the next fall, but managed only six goals in thirty-nine games. The following season (1929–30), he attended the team's training camp but found the going much too tough. He was thirty-seven years old and suffered from constant headaches as a result of the skull fracture. So he ended his playing career, scouted for the Hawks that year, and became the team's coach in the fall of 1930.

At Christmas time in 1940, when Dad was in his first year coaching the Canadiens, I was with him at the Mount Royal Hotel, where he stayed in Montreal. Mother, my sister Fay, and I had travelled from Regina for the holidays.

Dad stopped in the lobby to chat with an old acquaintance and they talked and laughed for quite some time. I was standing alongside, very bored and impatient to get back to the room to play with the new toys Santa Claus had left when he had miraculously climbed through the window into our hotel room a couple of nights before.

"Who was that?" I asked when the conversation finally ended.

"Red Dutton."

"Red Dutton?" I shrieked in dismay. I had learned while reading the scrapbook that he was the villain who had checked Dad when he suffered his fractured skull.

"You really talk to Red Dutton?"

My dad and Dutton were a couple of tough competitors cut from the same mould when it came to hockey. They were fast friends, fractured skull and all, something the eight-year-old son of the recipient of that bodycheck found hard to believe.

When I arrived at the CFCF-TV studios carrying the scrapbook that Sunday afternoon January 29, 1961, I was headed for a live TV debut. Most of the shows on the fledgling station were done live including the one just prior to Brian McFarlane's *Sportsman's Club*. It was a scholarly type program called *Forum* and when I walked into the studio it had just begun. The special guest that day was the famed historian Arnold Toynbee. One of the panelists asking him questions was a former CBC-TV newsman turned politician, René Lévesque.

For some reason I wasn't at all nervous when Brian got around to interviewing me. We talked with some young hockey players about Minor Hockey Week leading up to the first commercial break. After that it was just the two of us, a pairing that has continued in front of the TV cameras for over a quarter of a century.

Brian McFarlane has an excellent feeling for hockey history and he was very kind to his guest that day. There was only one problem. He couldn't shut me up. Once I got into the scrapbook and stories about Dad, I just kept rolling right along. Brian, pro that he is, made no effort to cut me off or upstage me. That isn't always the case involving a veteran and a rookie in our business.

Non-broadcasting people who appear on TV always say they are amazed at how many people saw the show they were on. That was the case with me after my first appearance.

"You should think of getting into that business," was a comment I had from the father of one of the kids I was coaching at the time. Truth to tell, I had thought about it.

My interest in broadcasting went back a long way. When Dad would return home to Regina after an NHL season, he would go to the studios of CKCK Radio to be interviewed by sportscaster Lloyd Saunders. I would go with him and was always fascinated by the atmosphere around the station. I grew up listening to the radio and can still remember the nights my favourite shows were on. Jack Benny, Charlie McCarthy, and Fred Allen on Sundays. Lux Radio Theatre Monday. On Tuesday, it was Bob Hope, Red Skelton, and Boston Blackie. Wednesdays, *Mr. District Attorney*. Thursday was the night for Bing Crosby and the *Kraft Music Hall*. Friday, the Green Hornet and his faithful servant Kato fought the good fight against the bad guys. And of course Saturday night was hockey night and Foster Hewitt.

After I got into the hockey broadcasting business, my mother often recalled my young years in Regina when I would re-broadcast the Saturday night hockey games on Sunday morning. She always built a rink in our backyard and on Sundays I would be on it, all alone, doing the same things Syl Apps, Gordie Drillon, and my other hockey heroes had been doing the night before at Maple Leaf Gardens. As I skated around playing my imaginary game, I would holler out a play-by-play description complete with the obligatory "He Shoots, He Scores." Our crabby next door neighbour used to phone mother to complain about the noise her son was making on what she thought should be a peaceful Sunday morning.

I should mention that I did play some organized hockey. First, it was in the Regina Parks League at Rink 3, a municipally operated outdoor rink in our part of the city. That was followed by teams called the Central Collegiate Gophers, the Regina Pat Juveniles, the Regina College Cougars, the University of Saskatchewan Huskies, and the McGill Redmen. My hockey playing ended when my college days were over, except for a few late-night old-timer games with the Channel 12 Chickens during my first few years at CFCF. I like to remind people I am living proof hockey ability is not hereditary.

Dad and the Two Majors

Dad's first boss when he became a coach with Chicago in the National Hockey League was Major Fredric McLaughlin, who had risen to that rank while serving with the U.S. Army's Blackhawk Regiment during World War One. (The Regiment had been named in honour of American troops who quelled an Indian uprising in the Black Hawk War of 1832.) Dad's second boss when he coached with Toronto was Conn Smythe, who was a lieutenant in the First World War and a major in World War Two.

McLaughlin was the George Steinbrenner of his day. He hired and fired coaches with reckless abandon, although none of them ever came back the way Billy Martin has with Steinbrenner's New York Yankees.

After World War One, McLaughlin made a fortune in the food business, principally in the coffee trade, and opened a restaurant in Chicago which he named The Blackhawk. He married a famous dancer, Irene Castle, whose life with her first husband was depicted in a 1939 movie, *The Story of Vernon and Irene Castle*, starring Fred Astaire and Ginger Rogers.

When the Pacific Coast League folded, McLaughlin paid

$200,000 for the Portland Rosebuds franchise, moved it to Chicago, and renamed the team after his regiment and restaurant. The Hawks' first coach, Pete Muldoon, lasted one year. The second, Barney Stanley, lasted one year. The third, Herb Gardiner, lasted one year. The fourth, Bill Tobin, lasted one year. The fifth, Dick Irvin, lasted one year. In the first ten years he owned the team, McLaughlin hired and fired thirteen coaches.

The Major was a flamboyant, fast-talking character who provided the press with a lot of good copy. After the Hawks won nineteen times in the forty-four-game schedule their first season, they managed only seven wins in each of the next two seasons. McLaughlin attended every home game during these two disastrous years. Someone asked him why he kept going to the Stadium.

"I keep thinking some night they'll win and I wouldn't want to miss that kind of a thrill," was his reply.

When Bill Tobin coached the team in 1929-30, the Hawks won twenty-one games and made the playoffs. McLaughlin took a winter holiday in Florida that season and Tobin had to send him a telegram after every game. The Hawks went into a slump and after a few wires from Tobin describing losses, the Major sent one back.

"Don't send me any more hockey wires. I'm trying to get a rest."

McLaughlin, in his usual eccentric fashion, decided the Florida sun was better than watching his team play and remained there even during the playoffs. The Hawks played the Canadiens in the first round, a two-game total-goal series, and lost by a goal. Before the second game, in Montreal, Tobin received another weird wire from the Major.

"Don't use your stars tonight Tobin; save them for next season." Needless to say, the coach didn't read it to his players for inspiration before the game.

The following season, Tobin was out and Dad was in as coach. His first game ended in a 1-1 tie with the New York Rangers, in Chicago, on November 16, 1930. His career behind the bench in the NHL would continue for twenty-six years until his last game on March 18, 1956, a 3-2 win in Boston, when he was again coaching the Chicago Black Hawks.

Scotty Bowman passed Dad's records for wins in regular season and playoffs, but I am sure Dad's records for longevity will never be broken. Twenty-six years, 1,437 regular season games, 190 playoff games. Today when I mention to NHL coaches how long he lasted, their eyes glaze over and the usual reaction is "Twenty-six years?" They're just hoping to hang on to the end of the season.

With due respect to the heroes and legends of hockey's early days, the game must have been terribly slow compared to what we see now. Players often stayed on the ice until they were exhausted because line changes were made only during stoppages in play. When Dad became coach in Chicago, he started changing lines "on the fly" as the saying goes. He was the first coach to do this on a regular basis. Even then it wasn't anywhere near what we see today. In an interview about his coaching career Dad is quoted as saying, "We worked our defencemen in five-minute stretches my first year in Chicago."

If a five-minute shift on the ice was considered innovative, you can imagine how slow it must have been before that. What a difference there is today when coaches think nothing of thirty-second shifts for forwards and defencemen.

Another innovation Dad got credit for was forechecking. His Hawks of 1930–31 were the first team to work at a system of checking the opposition closely in their own end of the ice. His ideas of pepping up the game also worked at the box office. Crowds grew in Chicago to a point where one game against Boston attracted over 18,000 to the Stadium, a record at the time. The game was becoming a much better entertainment attraction.

"I disagree with those who claim the sixty-minute player of the past was greater than today's stars," Dad said in a story about his coaching philosophy. "A well-conditioned athlete can't give as good a show over a sustained period as he can when he is sent out for a few minutes, rested, then sent out again." Basic stuff today. But back then players hopping over the boards while the play was in progress, even every few minutes, was quite a change and the game became better because of it.

Dad was one win away from a Stanley Cup Championship his first coaching year in Chicago. The Hawks reached the finals against the Montreal Canadiens and, before crowds of 18,000 both nights, split the first two games of the best-of-five series on home ice.

Game Three in Montreal went into overtime, the Hawks winning on a goal by Cy Wentworth in the fifty-fourth minute of extra time. One more win and Dad would have the Cup in his rookie year as a coach. It looked like it was going to happen when his team opened a 2-0 lead in Game Four. But the Canadiens, led by Howie Morenz, came back to win 4-2. Emotions were running high that night. A fan threw a whisky bottle onto the ice, narrowly missing the head of the referee Bobby Hewitson.

So Dad's first coaching year boiled down to a winner-take-all fifth game at the Montreal Forum where the Canadiens prevailed 2-0 on shutout netminding by George Hainsworth and goals by Morenz and Johnny Gagnon. In later years, Dad would refer to that game as the biggest disappointment of his career; but it was a disappointment in some of his players rather than the final score.

In 1951, while our family was driving from Regina to take up residence in Montreal, we stopped at a fishing camp in northern Minnesota. One of the players on the 1930–31 Black Hawks, Helge Bostrum, was working at the camp and Dad wanted to pay him a visit. They stood beside the car reminiscing about old times and I was within earshot. They were talking about the 1931 Cup final.

"If those guys didn't go out and get drunk the night before that last game we would have won it," I heard Dad say. There was so much bitterness in his voice it obviously still hurt him to think about it twenty years later. I don't know who "those guys" were, but a night out on the town by some of his players on the eve of the season's biggest game hurt

Dad's chances for the Stanley Cup in his rookie season. In his twenty-six years as a coach, he imposed a curfew on his teams only two or three times. That night in Montreal wasn't one of them, but it was clear he wished it had been.

Major McLaughlin was at that final game. He and Dad parted with a "see you next fall." But they didn't see each other next fall. In late September, when he was making plans to get ready to leave Regina and travel to Chicago with Mother, who at the time was expecting me six months later, Dad received one of the Major's famous telegrams.

"As the directors desire to make a change, your services as coach will no longer be required."

That was it. One win away from a Stanley Cup, crowds filling the Stadium, yet the Major had struck again. So Dad stayed home in Regina, thinking his hockey career was over, until he received another telegram two months later. That one came from Toronto. It was signed by Conn Smythe.

Maple Leaf Gardens had opened for the 1931–32 season but the hockey team bearing the same name wasn't performing up to a standard to match Canada's newest and best arena. Conn Smythe, the dynamic owner of the team and builder of the Gardens, quickly became impatient as the Leafs sagged into last place. The season was less than two weeks old when Smythe made up his mind to fire coach Art Duncan. That's when he sent the telegram to Dad in Regina that read, "Stand by for long distance phone call." It came the next day.

"How would you like to coach the Leafs?" were Smythe's first words.

"What's wrong with the Leafs?" Dad replied.

"We've got the best team in the world. There's nothing wrong with the Leafs."

"What about Duncan?"

"He's gone. Do you want the job?"

Dad asked for a day to think it over and Smythe agreed. The next day, Dad called him and took the job. Three nights

later, he was in Toronto sitting near the bench while Smythe
coached the team against the Boston Bruins. The Leafs had
a 4-1 lead but the Bruins came back to tie the game. At that
point, Dad learned an early lesson about the way Conn
Smythe did business.

"You take over now, Dick," he ordered and walked away
from the bench. Dad got lucky as the Leafs went on to win
6-5. It was the start of his nine years as coach of the Toronto
Maple Leafs.

The Leafs were a colourful aggregation. In the line-up
were future Hall of Famers like King Clancy, Red Horner,
and the Kid Line of Busher Jackson, Charlie Conacher, and
Joe Primeau. Dad's first impression was that the players
were not in good physical condition. He fixed that with some
tough practices and the team began playing up to the poten-
tial Smythe said it had. The Garden's inaugural season
ended on the highest note possible, a Stanley Cup Championship. They defeated the Rangers 6-2, 6-4, 6-2 in the final
series. Some called it the "tennis final."

To reach the finals that year the Leafs eliminated Dad's
former team, the Chicago Black Hawks. Naturally this
gave him great satisfaction, particularly in the final game
of the series when Dad spotted Major McLaughlin and his
fancy show-business wife leaving their seats and heading off
into the night after the Leafs scored the goal that gave them
a 5-0 lead. Dad was later quoted as saying he felt "not one
iota of sympathy" for the McLaughlins as he watched them
flee from the scene in their team's hour of despair.

Dad coached the Maple Leafs through eight more seasons, reaching the Stanley Cup finals six times. Yet the win
in 1932 was his only championship in Toronto.

In 1940, the Leafs were in the finals against the New York
Rangers. A well-kept secret was that during that season
Dad and Smythe had pretty well agreed to part company
when the playoffs ended. Smythe was frustrated by the
Leafs "so close, yet so far" playoff record under Dad whom
he thought too sentimental when it came to handling his
players, especially veterans. I guess this is why Dad always

said the one thing he didn't like about coaching was that you had to hurt men you liked. He wasn't as tough as a lot of people thought he was.

The Montreal Canadiens were the worst team in the NHL that season, winning only ten times in forty-eight games. Attendance at the Forum was pathetic. The last time Dad coached the Maple Leafs in Montreal there were only 2,500 people at the game. The Montreal Maroons had folded in 1938. Conn Smythe and the rest of the League's owners were very concerned that the Canadiens might be on the verge of folding too. Smythe called the Canadiens' owner, Senator Donat Raymond, and asked if he would be interested in talking to Dick Irvin about coaching his team. The Senator said yes. So, while the Leafs were in the finals with the Rangers, it was pretty well set that Dad would be with the Canadiens the following season.

Dad's last game behind the Leafs' bench was played April 13, 1940. That was the night Bryan Hextall scored the Stanley Cup winning goal, in overtime, for the Rangers. It happened right in front of where I was sitting with Mother. (Dad had moved us from Regina for the last few months of that season and I had attended Grade Three at Davisville School.) There were tears in my eyes as I watched the teams shake hands. Now I like to say that I was in the building the last time the New York Rangers won the Stanley Cup. Not too many people still hanging around hockey can make that statement!

On the drive home after the game, Dad wasn't as upset as I thought he might be.

"Do you think you could cheer for the Montreal Canadiens?" he asked me. At the time that was unthinkable of course, but three days later I became an instant Montreal fan when Dad signed to coach the Canadiens, a job he would hold for the next fifteen years.

Dad maintained a great admiration for Conn Smythe to his dying day. He learned a lot about hockey and the way to handle players from Smythe and he had a lot of stories about their days together. One of his favourites was about a fiery Smythe pep talk delivered to the Leafs during a Toronto-Boston playoff series in 1933. The Leafs were down two games to one in the best-of-five series when Smythe ordered Dad to have the players assemble for a luncheon at Toronto's Royal York Hotel the day of the fourth game. Smythe sat through a deadly quiet meal with his dispirited team before going into an act Dad never forgot. Slowly getting to his feet and flinging his napkin down on the floor, the Leafs' ebullient owner opened fire at his men, one by one.

"There's your captain," he began, pointing to Hap Day who was due to be married when the season was over. "He's just hoping it ends soon so he can take off on his honeymoon. And look at Mister Clancy. He had to bring his mother here from Ottawa to keep his spirits up because he can't do it by himself."

Clancy tried to butt in with a reply, but Smythe paid no heed and kept rolling along.

"Conacher, I suppose you'll tell me your feet are sore. Jackson, you can hardly wait to head to your cottage. Cotton, something tells me you're turning a bright shade of yellow every time you should be going into a corner of the rink."

Smythe kept it up all the way down the roster, ending his tirade by picking up his napkin and throwing it to the floor again, and marching out of the room.

Dad always said it was the best pep talk he ever heard and no doubt tried to copy it in later years. It worked because the Leafs started to curse and swear at their owner the minute he left the room. Suddenly there was life in the team again, albeit in the form of anger directed at the man who signed their pay cheques. The ending to this one is obvious. Toronto came back to win the next two games and take the series.

Speaking of pay cheques, Smythe used to pay his employees in those early years of the Gardens by giving them a few shares of stock in lieu of some of their money. Dad owned some shares and had a few put in my name. When he moved to Montreal, he felt he should get rid of his Gardens stock out of loyalty to the Canadiens. It was likely the only stock he ever owned as he wasn't much into investments. I have often wondered what those shares would be worth today had he hung on to them.

My dad died May 16, 1957, a victim of bone cancer at sixty-four. He was home through his final weeks and, when able, liked to talk hockey with me. Two nights before he died, I asked him who he thought was the smartest hockey man he had known. Without hesitation, he replied, "Conn Smythe."

After a funeral service in Montreal, we took Dad's body to Toronto for burial at Mount Pleasant Cemetery. Conn Smythe organized a group of men who had played for Dad in Toronto to carry the casket to the grave site. It included Charlie Conacher, King Clancy, and Baldy Cotton. A good friend of Dad's, the Reverend Jack McBride, conducted a brief service. When it was over and we were turning to leave, Major Smythe spoke to me.

"Dick, I want you to understand that your dad saved the Montreal Canadiens. That franchise was going out of business when he got there. Without him the Canadiens wouldn't be around today. Don't you ever forget that."

In light of what Dad had said to me about Conn Smythe, especially the last time we talked about him, I haven't.

Fifteen Years
a Canadien

*D*ad was the last man to coach one NHL team for as long as fifteen straight seasons. Al Arbour coached the New York Islanders for fourteen years and Toe Blake handled the Canadiens for thirteen. Otherwise the coaching profession has, in recent years, been funnelled through a revolving door. If you don't get the name of the new man on the way in, catch it on the way out because most of them don't last too long.

When he arrived in Montreal, Dad was much more the boss of his team than had been the case in Toronto where Conn Smythe really ran the show. Smythe gave the pep talks, Smythe had the feuds with opposing coaches and managers, Smythe was the one whose name was in the newspaper headlines. In Montreal, for the fifteen years he coached the Canadiens, Dick Irvin filled all those roles.

Dad's time with the Canadiens is the best-known part of his hockey career, although when he arrived in Montreal he must have felt like most new coaches do today, hoping to last out one season. He inherited a rag-tag group of undisciplined has-beens and never-weres. He always said the Canadiens had only two bona fide NHLers when he took over the team, Toe Blake and Ray Getliffe. The team had been coached in the disastrous 1939–40 season by Pit Lepine, who had been a fine player in the 1930's, but who had little interest in the coaching side of the game. Ray Getliffe told me of a night when, after a trouncing on home ice, Lepine jauntily put on a coonskin coat, called out, "So long fellows, see you tomorrow," and sauntered out into the night with a smile on his face.

In Lepine's defence, he was really a temporary coach. Babe Seibert, a fine defenceman for years in Montreal, had been signed to coach the Canadiens that season but lost his life the previous summer in a drowning accident. Dad felt Seibert would have been a good coach and always said his career in Montreal was made possible by the Seibert tragedy.

A few years ago in the Forum press room, Toe Blake was talking with Jacques Plante as I happened to walk by. Blake didn't see me and I heard him mention "Dick Irvin." Toe is a great needler, so I gave him a verbal jab. "Still blaming your old coach for your troubles are you?"

Toe gave me a half-serious, half-comical stare and continued on with Plante. A few minutes later, Jacques came over to me.

"Toe was talking about your father all right," he said. "He was saying he had no idea what discipline meant to a hockey team until Dick Irvin became coach of the Canadiens." When Dad arrived in Montreal, Blake had been playing there for five years.

While he was the best player on Dad's first Montreal team, Toe was one of the first to fall victim to the new regime of stricter discipline. He had spent the previous summer in an army reserve unit and arrived at training camp with his waistline showing the effects of too many nights in the tavern with his army buddies.

"You can play for this team this year Mr. Blake," Dad told him when the players reported for the training camp weigh-in. "But if you look the same this time next year, don't bother showing up."

Dad coached the Canadiens for the first time on November 3, 1940 in a 1-1 tie with Boston at the Forum. Toe Blake scored the goal for Montreal.

Big crowds didn't suddenly materialize when the 1940–41 season began. Tommy Gorman, the General Manager and a real character, tried to give away the tickets they couldn't sell. But slowly interest started to pick up. There were some promising newcomers on the team including Elmer Lach and Ken Reardon, two kids from the west who would have careers leading to the Hockey Hall of Fame.

In Dad's third season in Montreal, a twenty-one-year-old rookie, Maurice Richard, joined the team. I have a vivid memory of the first time I saw him play, because he broke his leg.

On December 27, 1942, the Canadiens played the Boston Bruins at the Forum. It was during one of our Christmas visits to Montreal and Mother and I were sitting just behind the Canadiens' bench.

Early in the game, Richard scored twice for the Canadiens on Bruins' goalie Frank Brimsek. Ironically in later years, when Richard was hockey's greatest goal scorer, he would mention Brimsek when asked which goalie was the hardest for him to score on.

About midway through the game, Richard received a terrific body check from veteran Bruin defenceman Johnny Crawford. He fell to the ice with one leg buckled beneath him. The Canadiens' team doctor, Dr. Walter MacKay, was sitting next to Mother. The instant Richard hit the ice, he said to Mother, "That man has a broken leg," bolted from his seat, and went directly onto the ice to aid the fallen rookie.

Richard was playing in his sixteenth NHL game and the two goals he scored were the fourth and fifth of his career. But he was through for the season, a fact that didn't draw too much attention from the press or the fans.

The Canadiens won the game 4-2. Afterward in the dressing room, Dad and some of the veteran players were talking about the rookie who had broken his leg. Toe Blake was doing a lot of the talking and was demonstrating how Richard was in the habit of carrying the puck too close to his feet. By doing that his eyes were looking down too much and he was wide open for an old pro like Crawford to cork him one when given the chance.

Dad felt Richard had a lot of promise because of his attitude if nothing else. The Canadiens had a few rookies around at that time and on game night the coach would tell a couple they wouldn't be in uniform. The game before the one in which he was injured, Richard was told he was one of the designated sitters.

When a crusty old coach like Dick Irvin told a young rookie he wouldn't be playing, the usual thing for the rookie to do was maintain a stiff upper lip and quietly find a place to sit to watch the game.

There are many versions in print as to what happened in the case of young Richard. Dad always said he wheeled around, went out the door, slammed it loudly behind him, and went home.

No doubt there were a few open mouths in the dressing room when the kid did that to the old coach. For his part, the old coach was silently impressed. He liked that kind of a reaction.

Maurice Richard was back at the Canadiens' training camp in the fall of 1943. Early that season, he was put on right wing alongside centre Elmer Lach with Toe Blake on left wing. The Punch Line was born and for long-time fans of the Canadiens, as the old cliché goes, the rest is history.

Butch Bouchard was another newcomer who broke in with a lumbering, crude, but effective style. Dad had high hopes for Butch and the first time Bouchard was to play in Toronto, he told the press they would be seeing a youngster who was going to become one of the game's all-time great defencemen. That night, Butch stumbled all over the ice from start to finish and the Leafs made mincemeat of him. Dad was embarrassed, but Butch did turn into one of hockey's all-time best defencemen and he too made it into the Hall of Fame.

The Canadiens made the playoffs in each of Dad's first three years in Montreal and became the best team in the League his fourth season, 1943–44. A combination of circumstances made this so. Many of the best players were serving with the armed forces so the product was slightly watered down. Maurice Richard had become "The Rocket" and the team finally had a good goaltender. After suffering through his first three years with goalies like Bert Gardiner, Paul Bibeault, and Wilf Cude, Dad finally had a decent netminder when Bill Durnan joined the team as a twenty-nine-year-old rookie.

Durnan was the best goaltender in Canadian senior hockey, but had always resisted when approached by NHL teams. Tommy Gorman finally broke down his resistance and Durnan joined the Canadiens for the 1943–44 season. He played eight years, and won the Vezina Trophy seven times.

Bill Durnan was the only ambidextrous goalie in NHL history, the only one to play half a game holding his stick in his right hand, and the other half holding it in his left hand. When the opposition started a rush toward the Canadiens' zone, Durnan would stand in the middle of the net with both hands on his stick. If the play swung over to the left wing, he would put the stick in his right hand. Right wing, left hand. That way he always had his catching hand covering the open part of the net. Obviously, his hands were his most important weapons and he very seldom used them to catch pucks in practice in order to avoid injury. That often upset some of his teammates when he'd let a high hard one go by in practice, especially if bets were riding on the scrimmage between the Reds and the Whites. No way could Durnan have worn one of the big trapper gloves today's goalies use to catch the puck. And no way would any of today's goalies want to wear the thin five-finger mitts Durnan wore so he could catch the puck and handle his stick with both hands.

Fairly early in the 1943–44 season, Maurice Richard became known as "The Rocket," still the most recognizable nickname in hockey history.

Almost every Montreal hockey reporter in that era claimed credit for coming up with the nickname "The Rocket." The man who actually did was one of Richard's teammates, Ray Getliffe.

Getliffe, a defensive forward, was never on the ice at the same time as Richard, so he had a great ice-level view of him in action. When Richard began to emerge as a star alongside Lach and Blake, he prompted Getliffe during a practice to remark, "That kid can take off just like a rocket."

A few nights later during a game, Richard made a great play and Getliffe said to his mates on the bench, "There he goes again, just like a rocket." The players picked up on it and young Richard was being called "Rocket" in the dressing room long before he was referred to by that name in print.

Ray Getliffe was a scratch golfer during his hockey career and today is one of Canada's top senior golfers. In 1960, I ran into him after he had been an official at an International Amateur Tournament in Ottawa.

"I've just seen a kid who is going to become the greatest golfer in the world," he told me.

Obviously, Ray still had a good eye for young talent. The young kid was Jack Nicklaus.

The Canadiens finished in first place in the 1943–44 season and were unbeaten in twenty-five games on home ice. Richard, in his first full season, scored thirty-two goals. After a 3-1 loss to Toronto at the Forum in the first playoff game, the team rattled off eight straight victories to win the Stanley Cup.

They played Chicago in the finals and easily won the first game in Montreal, and the next two in Chicago. Back at the Forum, Game Four seemed like a mere formality. Instead, it turned into one of the best remembered games in the Canadiens' history.

By the time the third period began, the Hawks had a 4-1 lead. With the next game slated for Montreal some fans began to think the Canadiens were rolling over in order to get another home game. Cries of "Fake!" began to ring through the Forum. (The only bright note for the Canadiens had come when Durnan stopped Virgil Johnson on a penalty shot.)

I have no idea what kind of a speech Dad gave his players during the second intermission. Likely the fans' reaction stirred them up far more than he could. In any event, in the third period the Punch Line took over and produced a remarkable comeback.

Elmer Lach tallied to make the score 4-2, and it remained that way with less than five minutes to play. Then The Rocket exploded for two quick goals, both very spectacular, and nobody in the Forum was crying "Fake!" any longer.

Doug Smith was the Canadiens' radio broadcaster and the game was carried coast to coast by the CBC. I was listening in Regina and Smith was magnificent as he called the winning goal scored by Toe Blake in overtime.

"Toe Blake . . . Toe Blake has scored! The game is over, the Cup is won, Toe Blake has scored on a pass from Butch Bouchard and the Montreal Canadiens have won the Stanley Cup for the first time since 1931, thirteen years ago, and this is April 13, for those of you interested in numbers."

Indeed it was the Canadiens' first Cup victory since the 1931 series when my dad had come so close to coaching Chicago to a victory against Montreal. Now he had his second Stanley Cup. He had been coaching in the NHL for fourteen years.

By the time he was into his second season, Maurice was really Rocketing. It was 1944–45, his "fifty goals in fifty games" season. Lach, Blake, and Richard finished 1-2-3 in point scoring. Bill Durnan played all fifty games and allowed forty fewer goals than any other team in the NHL. The Canadiens lost only eight times in the regular season, yet in the playoffs were upset in the first round by the Maple Leafs.

On December 28 of that season, Richard had the biggest point night of his career. I was able to watch him do it from the best seat in the Forum, a spot on the end of the Canadiens' players bench. I was twelve, and we were on another Christmas visit to Montreal.

The story of Richard's great performance that night started before the game when he told Dad he didn't think he would be able to play against the Detroit Red Wings. It had been moving day for the Richard family and he said he was worn out from carrying furniture up and down stairways. Dad, no doubt upset at his star for this kind of a routine on the day of a game, told him to "give it a try."

Some try.

The Rocket was so tired all he managed to do was score five goals and add three assists as the Canadiens thrashed the Red Wings 9-1.

I recall three things from that night as I sat on the bench while hockey history was being made. The NHL modern-day record for points by one player in one game was seven. Richard was tied for the record when, late in the third period, Toe Blake scored. Dad was yelling, "He gets an assist, Richard gets an assist!" as the referee skated by the bench on his way to the PA announcer. The assist was awarded, and the Rocket had the record.

After one of his goals, maybe the fourth or fifth, Richard came off the ice to a standing ovation and sat down right beside me. I was really shook up, figuring that everyone in the Forum was looking at their hockey hero, at the same time wondering what the twelve-year-old kid sitting beside him was doing there.

The Red Wings were coached by Jack Adams, long one of Dad's adversaries. They traded barbs and insults for years, a feud that perhaps began in Regina in 1922 when the Vancouver Millionaires defeated the Capitals, depriving Dad of his only real chance to play in a Stanley Cup final series. Adams had played on that Vancouver team.

Late in that game at the Forum twenty-two years later, his team being soundly whipped, Adams was a dejected figure sitting on the Wings' bench. Dad had Elmer Lach skate over to him before a faceoff and say to him, "Irvin wants to know if you'll concede." Adams lept to his feet and started hollering at Dad – a bit of by-play hardly anyone noticed what with the euphoria over Richard's performance rampant throughout the building.

To this day a lot of hockey people get a kick out of that story. Don Cherry thought it was hilarious when I told him a twelve-year-old kid was allowed to sit on the bench of an NHL team during a game. What would happen today if a coach wanted his twelve-year-old son to sit on the players' bench?

Forget it. Things were a bit looser then than now.

One other note from that night: while Richard fans were ecstatic over their hero's performance (a performance that has been chronicled in all histories of the Canadiens), one point is never mentioned.

The Detroit goalie was Harry Lumley, who became one of the best. But that night Lumley was a raw rookie in one of his early NHL games. On December 28, 1944, he was only eighteen years old.

A few days after Richard's eight-point performance, I made my first road trip with the Montreal Canadiens. It was obviously turning into a pretty exciting Christmas holiday trip for a Grade Eight kid from Davin School in Regina.

People today find it strange that Dad was able to coach the Canadiens while still maintaining his home in the West. A lot of these same people complain the NHL season is too long. In those days, it wasn't. Dad would leave for training camp in late September or early October and be home again by the end of March or early April. Often, he would travel home for Christmas or we would travel east. It was during our trip east for Christmas 1944 that I made my first hockey road trip.

The first stop was in Boston and before the game Dad let

me stay in the dressing room until the players went on the ice. In those days, teams would warm up and then immediately begin the game, unlike today when the ice is resurfaced between warm-up and face-off.

I figured coaches gave fire-and-brimstone pep talks before every game, the way Pat O'Brien did for Ronald Reagan and the rest of the Notre Dame football team in the movie *Rockne of Notre Dame*. I felt this especially had to apply to my dad because the legendary college football coach of the 1920's, Knute Rockne, was his inspiration when it came to his coaching career.

When Dad played for the Black Hawks, they trained at the Notre Dame campus in South Bend, Indiana, and he actually watched Rockne put his football team through practice sessions. Inspired by watching one of sport's all-time best, Dad started thinking that one day he might want to coach a hockey team.

Knowing this, I figured his every pre-game talk would be Rockne-like, so that night in Boston I huddled in a corner of the room waiting for what surely would be a ten or fifteen minute highly charged oration.

Time moved along and Dad wasn't saying anything. Then a bell rang, the signal for the team to go on the ice. That's when he finally spoke.

"The captain's line will start. Bouchard and Lameroux on defence. Bibeault's their goalie so, remember, shoot high. Let's go." That was it, the whole thing. So much for Knute Rockne.

The game dealt me another blow, of sorts, thanks to some rabid fans in the Boston Garden.

I sat right behind the Canadiens' bench. In those days, visiting players weren't protected by a glass between themselves and the fans as they are today. The game had barely started when a group of very tough-looking individuals began bombarding my father with a barrage of insults.

"Irvin, you're this . . . Irvin, you're that . . . Irvin, why don't you take those frogs of yours back to a fish pond."

It was the first time I had heard French players referred

to as "frogs." The whole scene was so unexpected and Dad was being called so many horrible names, it was all I could do to fight back the tears as the game wore on.

What I didn't know was that Dad enjoyed it. In Detroit, where the scene was just about the same, Henry Ford II used to join in from his seat just behind the visitors' bench. Ford spoke to Dad and told him he was the only coach who sat on the side of the bench closest to the taunting fans. "You're the only one we can have any fun with," Ford told him.

That night in Boston, the Canadiens had a 5-3 lead, but The Rocket, who was on his way to his fifty-goal season, hadn't scored.

"Hey Irvin, where's your *stah?*" they started to yell as the game neared its conclusion and the Bruins were on the way to defeat. Then, with a couple of minutes to play, The Rocket did score. For the first time that night, Dad turned to his tormentors.

"There's your *stah!*" he hollered, giving his best imitation of a Boston accent. There was no reply. . . .

After the game, Dad left the team in Boston and we took an overnight train to New York where he conducted a one-day tour of the city for his twelve-year-old son. We went to Yankee Stadium, Madison Square Garden, the Empire State Building, and Radio City Music Hall, where the movie was *National Velvet* starring another twelve-year-old, Elizabeth Taylor.

We took a train out of New York late in the afternoon, joined up with the Canadiens' train at Albany, then travelled to Toronto for the second half of my first road trip.

Before the Toronto game, a photographer got Dad to pose with me for a picture.

The game went badly for my heroes who were soundly beaten 4-2. I sat on the players' bench again that night, certain the only reason the Canadiens were losing to the underdog Maple Leafs was because I had distracted Dad from his job. Surely his players were off form because he had left them in Boston so I could have my trip to New York.

Mother and Fay joined us in Toronto and the next day we headed back to Regina. It was then that Mother told me Dad thought having his picture taken before a game was bad luck.

I was truly crushed. Now I knew for sure it was my fault the Canadiens had lost to the Leafs. It was a terrible burden for a twelve-year-old to carry as his life returned to normal in the midst of a cold prairie winter, far removed from his dream world of the Boston Garden, Radio City Music Hall, and the players' bench of the Montreal Canadiens.

The 1943–44 season was the first of four straight first-place finishes for the Canadiens. They won the Stanley Cup that season and again in 1946. They lost to Toronto in the semi-final upset in 1945 and in the finals in 1947.

The following season (1947-'48), the Canadiens' fortunes changed. Toe Blake suffered a broken leg in January and never played again. The Rocket and Durnan had sub-par seasons and, while Elmer Lach won the scoring title, the Canadiens finished in fifth place, four points behind the New York Rangers. It had been Dad's eighteenth season as a coach in the NHL and it was the first time his team missed the playoffs.

Naturally, the rabid fans in Montreal didn't take kindly to their team's season-long slump. When things were going from bad to worse, one of them called all the local newspapers and said he would burn down the Forum if Irvin was coaching in the next home game. The team was on the road at the time for a game in Toronto. Bill Durnan organized a visit to a hat factory where the players all bought red fedoras. When they skated onto the ice at Maple Leaf Gardens that night, they were wearing the red hats and holding their sticks as if they were fire hoses. The story had received a lot of play in the Toronto press, so the fans knew what the boys were up to and got a great charge out of it. The team was in trouble, but the players obviously weren't siding with those who thought it was all the fault of the coach. Three nights later, at the next home game, they didn't wear the hats and the Forum wasn't burned down.

A couple of weeks later, following a loss on home ice, the players and Dad tried a new strategy in a game in Detroit. They had outshot the Red Wings on a Saturday night in Montreal by a wide margin, but still lost the game 5-1. It was that kind of a season.

On the train to Detroit for a return game the next night, they figured if they couldn't win while getting a lot of shots, they'd try to win with hardly *any* shots. They decided the defencemen wouldn't cross centre ice and the forwards would shoot at the Detroit net only when completely in the clear. It almost worked.

The game was tied 0-0 in the third period when Murph Chamberlain, a tough-checking Montreal forward nick-named "Hardrock," was stopped on a clear breakaway. The Red Wings scored on the return rush and won the game 1-0. When it was over, the Canadiens had taken only twelve shots on goal.

In those days, newspapermen rarely travelled with the team and there hadn't been any on the trip to Detroit. When the game stats came across the wire, it seemed as though the Canadiens had hit rock bottom and there was a great hue and cry in the papers the next day that the team had totally collapsed. Just twelve shots on goal! A real disgrace. When he returned home, Dad tried to convince the writers it had been planned that way, but nobody really believed him.

Dad was well-known as a pigeon fancier. When the season was over and the Canadiens were out of the playoffs, one of the Montreal papers had him pose for a picture sitting on a park bench feeding some pigeons. The caption read: "At least these guys like me."

The picture of the Canadiens' 1944 Stanley Cup team shows twenty men. There are fifteen players, three trainers, one coach, and one General Manager. The picture of the Canadiens' 1986 Stanley Cup team has forty-two smiling faces, thirty belonging to players. Times have changed, and so have payrolls.

When the Canadiens missed the playoffs in 1948, Frank Selke was in his second season as General Manager. The roster was still pretty thin and there wasn't much depth backing up a team with a fair number of aging stars. The Canadiens paid the price in '48, but by that time Mr. Selke had started building a farm system for the future.

The makings of Dad's final good Montreal team were underway by the late 1940's. In the three years following the 1948 debacle, players like Bill Durnan, Ken Reardon, Murph Chamberlain, and Glen Harmon were gone from the scene. Among the new breed moving in were Doug Harvey, Tom Johnson, Bernie Geoffrion, Floyd Curry, and Gerry McNeil, the goaltender who replaced the legendary Durnan.

The Canadiens played the New York Rangers in the first round of the 1950 playoffs. Durnan, his nerves shot, decided to retire after a 4-1 loss in the third game of the series in New York. Dad always said the moment when Bill told him he was through was one of the most emotional of his career.

Dad had a long talk with him to make sure he wanted to go through with it. Durnan was adamant. Dad then called in McNeil, the team's back-up goalie (who was a standout with the Montreal Royals of the Quebec Senior League), so Durnan could offer some advice to his rookie replacement.

Realizing that McNeil's presence meant he was truly passing the Canadiens' goaltending torch to younger hands, Durnan began to cry. So did Gerry. Finally, Dad shed a few tears. Not your average scene at a meeting between a coach and a couple of his players.

McNeil won his first start, thanks to an overtime goal by Elmer Lach. But the Canadiens lost the next game as the Rangers eliminated them in five games. The following season, they made the finals, something the Montreal Canadiens would do for ten straight years, a record that has never been broken.

Dad had five more years left in his Montreal coaching career, a period that provided him with some of his highest highs and lowest lows.

Certainly in the 1951 playoffs there were examples of both extremes. The Canadiens eliminated the Red Wings in the first round, a mammoth upset after Detroit had finished thirty-seven points ahead of them at the end of the regular season. Then it was a case of going from high to low as the Maple Leafs defeated the Canadiens in a five-game final, every game decided in overtime.

The teams split the first two games in Toronto. Sid Smith scored the winner for the Leafs in the first game. The Rocket gave the Canadiens the win in Game Two with his third overtime goal that year. The Leafs won two bitterly fought games at the Forum, Ted Kennedy and Harry Watson scoring the winning overtime goals.

Game Five is the best remembered from that series. The Canadiens had a 2-1 lead with less than a minute to play in the third period. The Leafs pulled goalie Al Rollins and Tod Sloan scored the tying goal. (Years later, Frank Selke would criticize Dad's choice of players for the crucial faceoff that led to Sloan's goal.)

So into overtime they went for the fifth straight game. It didn't last long. In the third minute of play, Howie Meeker passed the puck from behind the Canadiens' net toward Leaf defenceman Bill Barilko, who had scored only eight goals in sixty-eight games that season. Barilko, a rugged type of player, literally left his feet as he blasted a slapshot toward the Canadiens' net.

There is a great photo of that moment showing Barilko in mid-air, Gerry McNeil down on the ice with the puck going into the top part of the net, and Cal Gardner, Butch Bouchard, Meeker, and The Rocket all watching the goal go in. A great hockey moment frozen in time by the camera lens, with some imagination needed to complete the picture. Foster Hewitt described it on radio, but there were no TV cameras in Maple Leaf Gardens. That kind of coast-to-coast coverage was still a couple of years away.

The Canadiens were beaten by Detroit in four straight games in the 1952 Stanley Cup final after getting there thanks to The Rocket's all-time greatest goal.

Maurice Richard scored 544 regular season goals and eighty-two more in the playoffs. Ask any Richard devotee to name the greatest of those 626, and he would likely answer, "The one he scored against Boston after Leo Labine knocked him out."

On April 8, 1952, the Canadiens and the Boston Bruins played Game Seven of the Stanley Cup semi-finals at the Forum. In the second period, Richard tried to leap through the Bruins' defence. He was knocked down and as he fell to the ice Labine landed on top of him. Richard's head hit the ice with a sickening thud. The man who had knocked out several opponents with his fists had himself been KO'd.

Six stitches were needed to close a deep cut over his left eye and it took about an hour for The Rocket to return to the real world. When he did, it was late in the third period, the game tied 1-1.

Even though it was obvious he wasn't quite back to normal, The Rocket insisted to Dad that he was able to play. With about four minutes left in regulation time, Dad put him back on the ice alongside Elmer Lach and Bert Olmstead.

I was sitting in the press-box area keeping statistics. Dad had me record who was on the ice when the goals were scored, the number of solid bodychecks delivered and by whom, face-off wins, and anything else he considered important for any particular game. Toe Blake, then coaching Valleyfield in the Quebec Senior League, was standing just behind me. I must have looked distressed. Toe said to me, "Don't worry Junior. The Rocket will score."

About thirty seconds later, that's exactly what happened. Those of us who think it was Richard's greatest goal still remember it as if it had been scored yesterday. I sometimes wonder how I would have called the play-by-play.

"Less than four minutes to play.... They're still tied 1-1. ... Are these teams headed for overtime here in Game Seven? ... Bouchard in the corner to the right of McNeil feeds the puck to Richard who is finally back in action, blood still dripping from the cut over his eye.... Chevrefils forechecking for the Bruins.... Oh, a good move by Richard on Chevrefils.... Here comes The Rocket to the Boston blue line ... he swings to the right side ... around Quakenbush.... He's cutting for the net.... Armstrong tries to check him ... Richard ... jams the puck through Henry ... HE SCOOORRRES!!!"

Doug Smith and Michel Normandin were calling that game and I have no idea how they described it. Somehow, I don't think any of us would have been able to come up with anything that did justice to that one.

In the euphoria that followed, I jumped up and began hugging Blake who was cheering just as loudly as the rest of us. Then I tried to write down the names of the players who had been on the ice when the goal was scored. My hand was shaking so much I gave up trying. I figured if the Canadiens held on to win, Dad wouldn't be interested anyway. They did. He wasn't.

There was a "what if" aftermath to The Rocket's greatest goal as far as Dad was concerned.

The two defencemen The Rocket found the toughest to get around in those days were Frankie Eddolls, an ex-Canadien then with the Rangers, and Gus Kyle, a former Mountie who left the force to play pro hockey.

Kyle was a plodding type, slow-moving but solid, who for some reason had the knack of being able to stop The Rocket more often than not. He was with the Bruins in 1952, but Boston coach Lynn Patrick benched him for the final two games of the series. Kyle normally played left defence alongside Bob Armstrong. In Game Seven that spot was filled by Quakenbush.

Dad always wondered what might have happened had Gus Kyle been playing left defence for Boston instead of Bill Quakenbush when Maurice Richard scored his greatest goal.

When Maurice Richard scored a goal at the Montreal Forum, the cheer that followed was just a bit different than any sound that building has ever known.

I'm still convinced of that all these years later. While they enjoyed many a glorious moment on home ice, great Canadien scorers like Béliveau, Geoffrion, Shutt, and Lafleur could never quite match the response The Rocket got when he put the puck in the net.

He played with such flare, his spectacular goals coming with such suddenness, that we came to expect it from him all the time. When our hopes were realized, it gave the moment a special meaning.

Dad always claimed Maurice couldn't describe most of his goals after the fact. They usually came as the result of his spontaneous reaction to a situation and the puck was in the net before Richard, and certainly the goaltenders, really knew what had happened.

It was typical of The Rocket that when he was approaching a major scoring milestone, he kept everyone in suspense. When the 1952–53 season began, he needed six goals to reach a career total of 325 and surpass the record held by Nels Stewart. So what did he do? Richard played the first six games that season without a goal.

Then he scored five in three games, equalling Stewart's record with two goals in Toronto, October 29. After that, it was suspense time again, going three games without a goal.

Life magazine had assigned a photographer, Hy Peskin, to follow The Rocket and record goal number 325. Hockey had never received much coverage in that prestigious American publication so it was a bit of a breakthrough.

Peskin clicked away every time Richard was on the ice through the three games when he didn't score. He was at the Forum, positioned beside me in the catwalk, on November 8 when the Canadiens played the Black Hawks.

Early in the game, Richard had two fine scoring chances, but Chicago goalie Al Rollins stopped him. Elmer Lach was also on the brink of a career milestone that night and in the second period scored the 200th goal of his great career.

The fans responded well for Elmer, but Richard's 325th was what they had come to see. After Elmer's goal, Dad left the same line on the ice, Bert Olmstead on left wing alongside Lach and Richard.

Less than a minute after Lach scored, Richard let go a fairly soft shot from about thirty feet in front of the Chicago net. Olmstead had been knocked down in the crease area. The puck was loose in the crease, there was a scramble for it, and it slowly rolled over the goal line.

Bert Olmstead may have touched the puck, but at that moment there was no way anyone but Richard was going to get credit. There was bedlam in the Forum and tears in The Rocket's eyes when referee Red Storey presented him with the puck. Fans littered the ice with programs and it was five minutes before play could be resumed. Everyone was ecstatic, everyone but my neighbour in the catwalk, Hy Peskin.

After following Richard for almost four full games, snapping pictures every time he touched the puck, Peskin had missed the big moment. His camera had run out of film just after Lach's goal and he was reloading when the Rocket's record breaker was scored.

Once again, no exposure for hockey in *Life* magazine.

In the 1953 playoffs, Dad took the biggest gamble of his coaching career, and won. The Canadiens were favoured to defeat the Chicago Black Hawks in the opening round, but, after a 4-2 loss on home ice, were down three games to two heading back to Chicago for the sixth game. On the afternoon of that game, Dad called home.

"I'm putting my job on the line tonight," he told me. "I'll be fired if we lose."

He had decided to make four line-up changes. In place of Paul Masnick, Dick Gamble, and Paul Meger, he switched to veterans Ken Mosdell and Calum McKay plus a rookie, Lorne Davis. But his biggest move was in goal where he replaced McNeil with Jacques Plante. Plante had played in just three regular season NHL games and had spent the season with the Canadiens' farm team in Buffalo.

"I'll never forget it," Jacques told me many years later. "I was walking through the hotel lobby in the morning and your Dad called me over. 'You're playing tonight and you're going to get a shutout' was all he said to me and he walked away."

Plante's penchant for coming out of his net to handle the puck was well known even then. When he joined the Canadiens, everyone thought that Dad would make him stop doing it. Instead, Dad said Plante's unorthodox style would help revolutionize the way goaltenders played the game. He was right, and Jacques went on to become one of the greatest of all time. But that night in Chicago he was a very nervous, untried rookie.

"My hands were shaking so much I could barely tie the laces on my skates," Jacques told me. A few minutes later, he began a performance that was certainly an omen of things to come in his career.

A couple of minutes into the game, a veteran Chicago forward, Jimmy McFadden, broke in alone on the Canadiens' nervous rookie goalie. I can imagine what was going through Dad's mind as that scene unfolded. McFadden leaned into a wrist shot aimed at, as I might have said had I been broadcasting, "far corner, stick side." Plante did the splits, kicking out his right foot and deflecting the puck off his skate into the corner of the rink. A few minutes later, The Rocket scored when he broke in from the blue line and the Canadiens went on to win the game 3-0. Jacques Plante had made his coach look like a genius by doing exactly what he had been told to do, get a shutout.

Back in Montreal, with Plante again in the nets, the Canadiens won easily and advanced to the finals against Boston. A Montreal-Detroit final had been eagerly sought by hockey fans, but the Bruins spoiled that, upsetting the Red Wings in the other semi-final.

The Canadiens won the Cup in five games, with Elmer Lach scoring the Cup-winning goal, in overtime. Many years later, Elmer told me a story that kind of spoils the drama we always associate with moments like a Stanley Cup winning goal, especially in overtime.

Boston's great centre, Milt Schmidt, was a close friend of Lach's. The two men, and their wives, spent time together at their summer cottages during the off-season. When the overtime began that night, Elmer and Milt were lined up for the faceoff, but they didn't have their sticks on the ice. Instead, these two supposed hard-nosed and bitter rivals were having a little social chit-chat.

"Milt asked me if I had any thoughts as to where we might take the wives that summer," Elmer said as he told me the story while we were golfing a few years ago. "I didn't have any idea at the time and we wondered when we could get together to talk it over. Bill Chadwick was the referee. He finally told us to quit the small talk so he could drop the puck to start the overtime."

A minute and twenty-two seconds later, Elmer scored the biggest goal of his career. The Canadiens won the game 1-0 and the Stanley Cup was back in Montreal after a seven-year absence.

There was a great photograph snapped right after Lach's shot went into the net behind Sugar Jim Henry. Taken by the late Roger St. Jean, it shows Lach being joyfully embraced by Rocket Richard. Both men have *both* feet off the ice. In his exuberance, Richard actually broke Elmer's nose when their heads collided, but at that moment Lach didn't feel a thing.

Milt Schmidt is also in the picture, sitting on the ice looking forlornly at the two celebrating Canadiens. Those of you
familiar with the picture have no doubt thought all these
years that Milt was sad because the Canadiens had just
beaten his Bruins to win the Stanley Cup. Now you know
the real story. He's looking that way because Elmer couldn't
tell him where they would be taking their wives on their
summer holiday. . . .

The Canadiens rivalry with the Detroit Red Wings domi-
nated Dad's last two years in Montreal. The teams were the
class of the NHL and games between them produced terrific
hockey and great entertainment. They played each other
fourteen times during the regular season, adding to the
intensity of the rivalry. In Dad's last two years with the
Canadiens, they played Detroit in the Cup final and both
series went the full seven-game distance. That meant
twenty-one games each season between the teams and, believe me, it was just great for the fans.

Dad loved games between the Canadiens and the Red
Wings. He said he wished they could play each other sev-
enty times. He felt we'd see the greatest hockey in the world
if the two teams could play without a referee. Both ideas
were intriguing, if unworkable. With players like Terry
Sawchuk, Gordie Howe, Ted Lindsay, and Red Kelly on one
side against the likes of The Rocket, Doug Harvey, Elmer
Lach, Boom Boom Geoffrion, and Jean Béliveau on the
other, most fans would have gone along with either idea.

But Dad would experience a lot of disappointment in his
last two seasons in Montreal when it came to the final
crunch between his team and Detroit. The Red Wings won
the Stanley Cup both years, 1954 and 1955. Like his days
with Toronto, it was again a case of "so near, yet so far."

The 1954 series was particularly heartbreaking. The Red
Wings were ahead three games to one when the teams
headed back to Detroit for what everyone thought would be
the Cup-clinching game. After the Wings had won the

fourth game 2-0 at the Forum, I ventured into the Canadiens' dressing room expecting to find Dad at his gloomiest. Instead, he was surprisingly enthusiastic. Gaye Stewart, a long-time NHLer, played that season for the Canadiens' farm team in Buffalo and was in Montreal on a standby basis for the final series. After the fourth game, Dad had decided he wanted to use Stewart the next night in Detroit, but by that time Gaye had left the Forum.

"I want you to find Gaye Stewart," he ordered me. "Tell him to get on a plane in the morning and fly to Detroit. I think he's staying at the Windsor Hotel."

I found Stewart at the Windsor and delivered the message. Dad had a hunch he would play well, supplying some playoff experience and, more importantly, a rested pair of skating legs. Stewart did just that, taking a regular turn and playing a strong game. The Canadiens stayed alive with a 1-0 win on an overtime goal by Ken Mosdell.

Two nights later, the Canadiens evened it up with a 4-1 win at the Forum. But the series was to end on one of Dad's low notes as the Wings won the Cup in the seventh game on Good Friday night, in Detroit. That was when Tony Leswick's harmless looking shot caromed into the Canadiens' net off the arm of Doug Harvey in overtime.

In the aftermath of the winning goal, with fans pouring onto the Olympia ice to help their heroes celebrate, only a few of the Canadiens stayed around to shake hands with the Red Wings. Dad wasn't one of them and, the next day, he and his team were severely criticized by the Detroit media for what was considered poor sportsmanship.

"They had just picked a lot of money out of my pocket. I was hardly in the mood to shake hands," was Dad's answer.

About twenty-five years later, I was at the Olympia for a CFCF Radio broadcast. In a room where employees gathered, I was chatting with several people about the good old days when one gentleman spoke to me in a rather nasty tone of voice.

"You ought to be ashamed of your father the way he acted after Tony Leswick scored his goal."

At first I thought the old gent was kidding, but he wasn't. After all those years, he was still mad at Dad for not shaking hands at the end of the 1954 Stanley Cup Finals!

That handshaking business in hockey is a rather strange ritual when you come to think of it. There have been some players, Doug Harvey was one, who wouldn't shake hands with the other team win or lose. And if hockey players are poor sports when they don't do it, why doesn't anyone get upset when the World Series ends? Have you ever seen baseball players lined up at home plate shaking hands when it's all over?

The next year, 1955, it was the same story: a loss to the Red Wings in the seventh game of the final series at the Olympia. But that year there was another story – the one about the Richard Riot.

Every March 17, someone breaks the mood of St. Patrick's Day to write or broadcast that it is the anniversary of the Richard Riot at the Montreal Forum. For me, March 17 is the anniversary of the night I got hit smack in the face with some smoke from a tear gas bomb.

The bomb was the most publicized part of a very bizarre week in the city of Montreal. What happened was that the previous Sunday, during a game in Boston, The Rocket had gotten into a fight with Bruins' defenceman Hal Laycoe. During the melee, Richard struck linesman Cliff Thompson. In his ruling on the affair, NHL President Clarence Campbell wrote that Richard "punched linesman Thompson two hard blows in the face." He went on to say that he was satisfied Richard did not strike Thompson, "as the result of a mistake, or accident."

The referee, Frank Udvari, gave Richard a match penalty. Dad, Kenny Reardon (then a Canadiens' front office executive), and Richard attended the hearing held in Campbell's office a couple of days later. Dad always maintained that the game officials didn't tell the whole truth and nothing but the truth when they gave their side of the story.

Campbell listened to the evidence, then suspended Richard for the three remaining regular season games, plus *all* games in the playoffs.... Columnist Andy O'Brien put it best when he wrote that the decision put the city of Montreal in a "state of stun."

The Rocket, Montreal's greatest hockey hero, had been having a fine year. He was in first place in the scoring race and appeared set to win a title that had eluded him so far in his career. At the same time, the Canadiens were neck and neck with Detroit in a battle for first place. Hockey fever, indeed Richard fever, had never been hotter.

Campbell's announcement was made on Wednesday, the day before a Canadien-Red Wing first-place showdown at the Forum. Pickets denouncing Campbell and his decision paraded outside the Forum all day Thursday and there was an uneasy atmosphere both inside and outside the building at game time.

When the game began, Richard took a seat directly behind the Detroit goal, a spot about forty feet away from where Campbell sat. There had been controversy about Campbell attending the game, but he showed up anyway. For some strange reason he arrived late, halfway through the first period. By then, the Red Wings had a 2-0 lead and the Canadiens were in total disarray. Campbell's conspicuous entrance stirred up an already restless crowd even more.

The first period ended with the Wings ahead 4-1. Campbell, again for some strange reason, chose to remain in his seat during the intermission. With Forum guards surrounding him, fans heaped verbal abuse on the NHL President from all parts of the building. One leather-jacketed man convinced the guards he wanted to shake his hand, so they let him through, whereupon he slapped Campbell across the face. The Forum erupted in cheers and there was a feeling of further ugliness yet to come. Then, the tear gas bomb exploded, almost at the spot where Richard had been sitting during the first period.

I was witnessing all this as I sat in the press box keeping

stats for Dad. The press box had been relocated to a level running across the south end of the Forum. Clarence Campbell was sitting directly below that area.

I remember seeing the smoke rising and people at ice level scattering. Like a lot of others in the press box, I thought it was just smoke. A few seconds later, we found out otherwise.

As I leaned over the edge of the box watching the smoke slowly rise in our direction, I was hit by it smack dab in the kisser. Every time I see a movie or watch a TV news clip showing people left helpless and bawling because of tear gas, I can readily relate to the scene. It does indeed leave you helpless and it certainly left me bawling.

That was the end of things inside the Forum. The game was called and awarded to Detroit. Police ordered the rink evacuated and the ugliness spilled onto the streets of Montreal where the fans were joined by hundreds of thrill seekers streaming out of every tavern within ten miles of the place. They started smashing windows and lighting fires, and the infamous Riot was underway.

Some deeper thinkers than I claim the events of March 17, 1955 were a major beginning to what happened in the political arena in Quebec during the province's turbulent era of the 1970's.

When Dad left the Forum that night, I thought he would want to get out of the area as fast as possible. Instead, he asked me to drive him around where the trouble was going on. Rather than being upset and gloomy, as I expected him to be, he seemed strangely serene and content.

Frank Selke later wrote that Dad had lost his ability to control Richard's violent temper. That didn't square with the fact that The Rocket was having one of his best seasons leading up to the incident in Boston. But Dad (who always insisted his greatest star played his best hockey when he was angry) may have felt he had goaded Richard once too often. Certainly, he had been very much a part of the events leading to the chaos raging in the streets of Montreal that night. As he surveyed the scene, I'm sure he knew there was no way he could continue coaching the Montreal Canadiens after that season.

The next day, the *Montreal Herald* carried a picture of Dad holding the remnants of the bomb container. The caption under the photo quoted him as saying, "I've seen The Rocket fill a lot of rinks. This is the first time I've seen him empty one."

Pretty good line. But I've read many times since then that it upset his boss Mr. Selke and especially the Canadiens' owner, Senator Donat Raymond. They were thinking seriously at the time of replacing Dad with someone else. That quote apparently helped them make up their minds to do it when the season ended.

It doesn't upset me too much to think of the Riot and the events leading up to it as costing Dad his job with the Canadiens. What does upset me is that it cost him his last chance to coach a Stanley Cup winner.

Campbell had to do something but, despite my admiration for him, I've always felt he went too far in adding the playoffs to Richard's suspension. It worked out to a total of fifteen games.

The Canadiens had led the Wings by two points in the race for first place going into the final week of the season. They had to play their final three games without the Rocket, two of them against Detroit. The Red Wings won both and the Canadiens finished the season in second place.

In the playoffs, they eliminated Boston in five games and took the Wings the full seven-game distance before losing the final contest. Jean Béliveau has always claimed the Canadiens would have beaten the Wings had Richard been playing.

In the 1987 Stanley Cup Final, goaltender Ron Hextall of the Philadelphia Flyers landed a vicious two-handed slash with his stick across the legs of Edmonton player Kent Nilsson. Hextall received a five-minute major penalty and finished the series. Only then did the NHL suspend Hextall, banning him from the first eight games of the following season.

I wonder what the ruling would be today if a player, top rank or otherwise, slugged a referee just before or during the playoffs. Somehow I can't see a fifteen-game suspension.

Dad's career with the team did come to an end after the 1955 Cup final series. Maybe Frank Selke (as Conn Smythe had before him) decided that Dad was lacking something because of all the close finishes that had failed to produce a Cup victory. Certainly, Dad had acted rather strangely in the final weeks of his last season in Montreal. What we didn't know at the time was that he was suffering from the early stages of the cancer that would take his life two years later.

He coached one more year, in Chicago, where his job was to regroup a bad hockey club and try to get it into the playoffs. Again, close, but they didn't make it.

Dad had coached in the NHL for twenty-six years. His teams had reached the finals sixteen times, but had won the Stanley Cup only four times. And yet, right to the end of his career, he maintained a tremendous love for the game and an enthusiasm for his job. I used to wonder how he was able to do it through so many bitterly disappointing experiences in the Stanley Cup Finals. But maybe he had a secret weapon going for him.

Maybe it was the Unseen Hand.

The Unseen
Hand and Other
Tricks

*D*uring his fifteen years as coach of the Montreal Canadiens, my dad became very fond of the "Unseen Hand." It was a catch phrase that got a lot of publicity, one he used to explain the many unexplainable things that can happen in a hockey game. A deflection, a hit goal post, an injury to a key player, a bounce of the puck that went against his team, all of these and more came under Dad's definition of the "Unseen Hand."

It followed him around as the years went by. Fans on the road would yell: "Hey Irvin, will you blame the Unseen Hand tonight?" when his team was on the short end of the scoreboard.

Dad enjoyed inventing oddball sayings to describe what happened in certain games.

"We won because we had a lot more hits than they did." He liked the word "hits" rather than "bodychecks." Or he might say, "There are no wet sweaters in this room tonight." That would be after a loss when he thought his team hadn't worked hard enough.

The "Unseen Hand" arrived early in his coaching days in Toronto. In the 1933 playoffs, the Maple Leafs and the Boston Bruins played what was then the longest game in NHL history. (It still ranks as Number Two.) The teams were in the sixth period of sudden-death overtime, tied 0-0. Boston's great defenceman Eddie Shore tried to force a whistle to allow a tired Bruins forward line to leave the ice: he attempted a pass that would have been offside. But the puck was intercepted by a Leaf forward, Andy Blair. He passed it to Ken Doraty, a little winger out of Regina who had rarely been on the ice until late in the fourth overtime period. Doraty scored on Bruins' goalie Tiny Thompson and the marathon was over.

A few years later, Toronto sports writer Ted Reeve interviewed Dad about his career and asked him about that game.

"Why would a game like that end on a mistake by one of the greatest players in hockey, leading to a goal by a seldom used sub?" Reeve wondered.

"Hard to figure," replied Dad. "Maybe at a time like that there's something like an unseen hand that decides who will win and who will lose." From then on the "Unseen Hand" became part of his hockey vocabulary.

Perhaps it was already on Dad's side many years earlier – although he didn't know it at the time. During his heyday as a top goal scorer in amateur hockey in Winnipeg, a wise guy started needling him from the sidelines during a Monarchs' practice.

"If you're so hot Irvin, try and hit the bell," he taunted.

The bell that rang to end the periods was hanging on a wall behind one of the nets. Dad wound up and fired a shot that hit the bell, dead centre. Honest. There's a write-up and a cartoon in the scrapbook to prove it.

The most bitter blow dealt Dad by the Unseen Hand had to be Tony Leswick's Stanley Cup winning goal, in overtime, in the seventh game of the Canadien-Red Wing final in 1954. It was a great series of pure, unadulterated end-to-end hockey between the NHL's two best teams.

The Canadiens had come back to even the series after being down 3-1. And they should have won Game Seven too.

Only an amazing performance by Detroit goalie Terry Saw-chuk (still my pick as the best I've ever seen) prevented the Canadiens from winning in regulation time. The Canadiens outplayed the Wings all night, yet the score remained 1-1 at the end of the third period.

Early in overtime, Leswick, a defensive forward whose main job was to cover The Rocket, lobbed a shot toward the Canadiens' net while the teams were changing lines. Doug Harvey was standing in front of goalie Gerry McNeil and tried to block the shot with his arm. But he didn't get all of it. As we like to say on the air, the puck "changed direction," deflected past McNeil, and the Red Wings had won the Stanley Cup.

Shades of the Leafs and Bruins in 1933: a great defence-man and a forward not known as a goal scorer, both involved in high hockey drama. The Unseen Hand, indeed.

Danny Gallivan was one of a group of media men who sat with Dad in his train compartment that night as the Canadiens returned to Montreal. The mood was sombre until Dad, up to then the most sombre of all, pulled out a pocket calendar and began to study it.

"Well gentlemen," he finally said, "training camp begins exactly five months from tomorrow." The mood in the compartment wasn't as sombre after that. Danny often tells that story to show how Dad could put the past behind him, especially the unpleasant past.

But the Unseen Hand didn't prevent my father from being a very tough loser. I didn't live with him during a complete hockey season until the final four of his fifteen years in Montreal. But once we moved east from Regina, I quickly learned about life with father when father is a hockey coach.

I'm sure there haven't been too many coaches get as gloomy as he did after a loss, especially one in which his team had played poorly or he felt he had coached poorly. His depression, marked mainly by almost total silence around the house and at the dinner table, would usually last one day. We never looked forward to him arriving home from a road trip if the Canadiens had been beaten the night before.

In those days, teams didn't get time off at Christmas as they do now. On Christmas Eve, 1952, the Canadiens lost 2-0 in Toronto. Dad came back in a terrible mood. We had Christmas dinner at the home of former Regina friends, Dorothy and Charlie Morrow, who had recently moved to Montreal. It was a disaster. Dad barely spoke all night, carrying his gloominess over a bad game just a bit too far.

In the 1987 Wales Conference Final between the Canadiens and the Philadelphia Flyers, the Flyers won the fourth game in Montreal to take a three-to-one lead in the series. After the game, along with my daughter Nancy and son Doug, I ran into the Flyers' coach, Mike Keenan, sitting by himself on the visitors' bench. I introduced him to the kids and saw that he was still shaking with excitement.

"What's the matter coach?" I asked him. "You won the game. You should be relaxed by now."

"No way," Mike replied. "I get like this every time we win a big one. Takes me hours to settle down."

I could relate to that. Dad always had a tough time getting to sleep following a win, especially in an important game. He would be talkative on the drive home and would stay up reading or watching a late show trying to unwind.

A loss was a different story. The drive home would be quiet – with a Capital Q. Once home, Dad would head straight for bed and be sound asleep about a minute after his head hit the pillow. You'd think it would work the other way around. I could never figure it out.

I guess I'm not describing Dick Irvin Sr. as a laugh-a-minute guy, but, believe me, he could stir up some fun. His all-time best stunt happened because of the great Detroit-Montreal rivalry in the early 1950's.

Following a particularly bitter game between the teams in which Maurice Richard played a big role in the bitter-

ness, the Red Wings' General manager Jack Adams blasted
The Rocket. Adams was nicknamed "Jolly Jawn," but he
wasn't very jolly after watching Richard ream a couple of
his Red Wings.

"Richard is no hockey player," Adams fumed to the press
after the game. "He's nothing but Irvin's hatchet man."

The magic words were "hatchet man."

The Canadiens' assistant trainer then was Gaston Bettez,
a favourite of Dad's, who was very agile on skates despite
being somewhat rotund in build. The next time the Canadiens played in Detroit, it wasn't Richard who was Irvin's
hatchet man, it was Gaston.

Dad told Gaston to bring his skates on the trip. Before the
game at the Olympia, he had him dress up in a French-
Canadian outfit, complete with toque, knickers, and a Canadiens' sweater with a crude number nine stitched on the
back. A false beard completed the costume. Dad made sure
the Red Wings were on the ice warming up before he sent
the Canadiens out of their dressing room. When they hit the
ice, The Rocket was still in the room while Gaston Bettez,
the Quebecois lumberjack, hurtled onto the ice brandishing
a very illegal hockey stick that had a cardboard axe-blade
taped on the end.

The Detroit players were startled as Gaston wheeled into
their end of the ice swinging his axe-hockey stick as though
he were felling imaginary trees. He swooped past Gordie
Howe and Ted Lindsay brandishing his weapon. They got a
kick out of it, but goalie Terry Sawchuk didn't and swung
back at Gaston as he cruised in front of the goal crease.
After a couple of circles through the Detroit team, Gaston
bolted off the ice and down the corridor into the Canadiens'
dressing room. Dad had The Rocket ready and sent him out
on the ice a few seconds later. The crowd, always totally
anti-Montreal, loved it. Adams apparently was outraged,
but Dad didn't bother going near him to find out.

Picture that today. The coach responsible would likely be
censured by the League for damaging the image of the
game.

Detroit was Dad's favourite spot to pull stunts and he got another chance following the final game of the 1952-53 season, a game that had no bearing on the final standings. What was pertinent was Gordie Howe's goal total for the season. Forty-nine. The magic number then was fifty and had been reached only once, by Maurice Richard. The Richard-Howe rivalry was intense and naturally the Red Wings were anxious to see their Number 9 equal or pass the record held by the Canadiens' Number 9, especially since the Canadiens were the visiting team.

Gordie's bid for number fifty was the whole story and the Olympia was jammed. Normally Bert Olmstead had the job of checking Howe. But Dad knew Howe would get extra ice time that night, so to help Olmstead he assigned Johnny "Goose" McCormack, who was clearly a defensive specialist: in his previous fifty-eight games The Goose had managed to score just one goal.

Olmstead and McCormack were given very basic orders: go wherever Howe goes. They were told to forget about the puck, just stick with Big Gordie. Even though the game meant nothing in the standings, the air was electric inside the Olympia.

When the game began, Howe was on right wing for Detroit and Richard on right wing for the Canadiens. There had been fire in the Rocket's eyes all day as he wrestled with the horror of seeing his arch-rival reach the fifty-goal mark or, worse still, get another one to break the record. The game was barely underway when Richard bolted across the ice and nailed Gordie with a vicious check that earned him a charging penalty. Dad kept him on the bench for most of the game after that. Meanwhile, Olmstead and McCormack had begun playing "Me and My Shadow" with Gordie.

They followed their instructions to the letter. Wherever Howe went, so did they. When Howe was standing at the Canadien blue line playing the point on the power play, one of them was standing right beside him. If Gordie was deep in the Detroit zone while the play was moving up ice, one of them was right there with him.

Howe played forty-eight minutes that night and managed to shake loose from his shadows for only one good shot on goal. Gerry McNeil, the Canadien goalie, came up with a big save.

When the final buzzer sounded, the Canadiens had won the game 2-1 but they couldn't have cared less. Howe hadn't scored and that was all that mattered. As the teams were leaving the ice, Dad grabbed The Rocket, steered him to centre ice, and held up his arm the way a fighter's arm is raised to signal victory in a boxing ring. Adams and the Red Wings weren't exactly thrilled about that one and no doubt were even more chagrined the next day when a picture of that moment appeared on the front page of a Detroit paper. The caption read: STILL THE CHAMPION.

The Red Wings, first-place finishers that season, were upset in the opening playoff round by the Boston Bruins. Dad quickly claimed that the picture of The Rocket on the front page had been a downer for the Red Wings and a factor in their quick exit from the Stanley Cup scene.

I like to think that Dad played a part in the ultimate success of Maurice Richard. I know he said many times the reverse was true. Certainly, they had one thing in common. The Rocket and his coach were tremendous competitors who hated to lose.

On the eve of the 1954–55 season, the Canadiens attended a dinner given by Molson's to introduce the film of the 1954 Stanley Cup playoffs. Dad sat through it until the Cup-winning play (Tony Leswick's fluke goal) began to unfold. At that point, he jumped out of his chair and headed for the nearest exit. I was right behind him. As I got to the door, I glanced back for one last peek at the screen. Right behind me was The Rocket. He couldn't stand to watch it either.

It's been said that Dad lost his job with the Canadiens because, eventually, he couldn't control Richard's violent temper (with the final straw coming in 1955, in Boston, when The Rocket hit the linesman). That may or may not have been the case, but certainly The Rocket was no shrinking violet from the very day he entered the NHL.

Every time Richard got into trouble (and there were many), Dad defended his actions. He would often say The Rocket had to fight his way through the League season after season.

So how about this opinion? That Maurice Richard has to rate as the best fighter in the history of the NHL. . . .

Before fans of Dave Schultz, Chris Nilan *et al.*, start disagreeing, consider this: Richard knocked out four tough guys, including one he actually KO'd twice in the same game.

I don't mean he pinned them to the ice. I don't mean he was winning a fight when the linesmen finally separated him from his opponent. I mean knockouts, one punchers: the other guy not just groggy or bleeding – but out *cold*.

He did it to John Mariucci of the Black Hawks: Mariucci was standing in the penalty box while Richard was standing on the ice.

Then there was a guy named Bob Dill, nicknamed "Killer," who was KO'd by Richard on the ice at Madison Square Garden. When he woke up, he was sent to the penalty box along with The Rocket. In an attempt to restore his image in the eyes of the gallery gods in New York, Dill decided to start round two. One punch later, he was out cold again. Richard often said that punch might have been the best he ever threw.

Early in the 1951–52 season, he knocked out Bill Juzda of the Maple Leafs. He liked to nail guys with tough nicknames. They called Juzda "The Beast." I have a great set of still pictures taken of that incident. In one shot, referee Bill Chadwick is giving Richard the thumb, tossing him out of the game. At the same time, you can see Juzda hollering something at The Rocket over Chadwick's shoulder. Then the next picture shows Juzda face down on the ice, turned completely around, out cold.

Another of The Rocket's one-punch victories was when he KO'd Ted Lindsay in a playoff game in Detroit, in 1951.

The Red Wings had finished first with 101 regular-season points. The Canadiens were third, with sixty-five. Surprisingly, the underdogs won the first two games in Detroit. The first went into a fourth overtime period, The Rocket scoring to win it. The second game went into a third overtime period, and The Rocket scored again.

Back in Montreal, it was a different story. The Red Wings evened the series with two wins.

In the fifth game, the Wings were leading when Lindsay and Richard tangled as they often did. Push led to shove, which led to punch and suddenly Lindsay was flat on the ice, out cold. The Canadiens came back to win the game and Dad was widely quoted when he said The Rocket's punch had turned the tide.

The Canadiens went on to win Game Six two nights later, one of the biggest upset playoff victories in the team's history.

One last word about Bill Juzda. Like all Richard fans, I enjoy remembering his goals and KO's. But Bill had a last laugh on me, after a fashion.

The first NHL building to install plexiglass around the boards was Maple Leaf Gardens. It was advertised as being unbreakable. Then along came The Rocket and he broke the plexiglass.

There is a well-remembered photo taken of the incident. Richard can be seen falling to the ice right after the tip of his skate has hit the glass, causing it to shatter. A Toronto player, Vic Lynn, is also in the picture looking totally shocked.

A few years ago, Danny Gallivan and I were broadcasting a game at the Forum when the glass was broken. While repairs were being made, we reminisced about the photo of Richard breaking the glass in Toronto. I pointed out that it had happened when he had been bodychecked by Vic Lynn.

The following summer, I was at the St. Charles Golf Club in Winnipeg broadcasting a tournament for CTV. Bill Juzda was working as a volunteer marshall.

The minute he saw me, Bill wasted no time assuring me I had been wrong on the broken-glass story. *He* had hit Richard with the bodycheck, not Vic Lynn. And he was right.

After that had been established, we had a great chat about the old days. But I didn't mention those pictures I have of him, Bill Chadwick, and The Rocket. . . .

One night when he was at the peak of his career, Richard got into a terrible fight at Maple Leaf Gardens and was thrown out of the game. As he was stomping down the corridor leading to the dressing room, a Toronto policeman on the scene made a move toward him as if he wanted to conduct some official business.

At the same moment, Conn Smythe, the equally fiery and controversial owner of the Leafs, came down the hall. Smythe immediately saw what was happening.

"Don't touch that man," he yelled at the policeman. "He's the greatest hockey player in the world."

In the early 1950's, the argument over who was the best player in the NHL centered around Maurice Richard and Gordie Howe. But Dad sometimes thought neither one deserved the accolade. He felt that some nights Doug Harvey deserved to be called "the best."

Harvey won the Norris Trophy as the NHL's best defenceman seven times and was voted to the first All-Star team ten times, still a record for defencemen. He had the talent to slow the game down to his pace, to dictate the flow of play because he could dominate it with skillful puck-handling and tremendous hockey sense. But his style led some people (even some of his own teammates) to criticize him for being too nonchalant.

In the summer of 1952, the Canadiens played a softball game against the inmates at St. Vincent de Paul Penitentiary. I went along as the bat boy. Harvey, a fine ball player, was the catcher. During the game, he got into a fierce nose-to-nose argument with the home-plate umpire. A couple of Harvey's teammates mumbled behind his back that maybe he should try being as aggressive on the ice. But they were duly put in their place when they found out the umpire was serving a life sentence for murder!

Great as he was, Harvey could drive a coach up the wall with his nonchalant approach to the game. He would often carry the puck dangerously close to his own goal crease, so much so that Dad threatened him with a hundred-dollar fine if he ever did that and the other team checked him and scored. After that, the players referred to the goal crease as "Doug's hundred-dollar zone." Harvey's tendency to lapse into a lackadaisical style finally resulted in him being benched for the only time in his career. And I knew about it a couple of days before he did.

During the first week of February, 1953, the Canadiens were in a mini-slump. They had been tied 0-0 on home ice on a Saturday night by the Bruins. The next night in Boston, they blew a two-goal lead and lost.

The following Tuesday, my dad's boss, Frank Selke, and Mrs. Selke were at our house for dinner. As always, the two men running the Canadiens talked about their team and on this night they were not happy.

I was all ears. They weren't long into their conversation before it became obvious the player they thought deserved the main share of the blame for the mini-slump, especially the loss in Boston, was Harvey. They felt that careless play on his part had resulted in both the tying and winning goals for the Bruins. The Canadiens' next game was at the Forum, against the Maple Leafs, two nights later. Before Mother had served dessert, Dad and Mr. Selke agreed that the NHL's top defenceman would pay for his recent sins. For the first time in his career, Doug Harvey would be benched.

I was a McGill student at the time, not a sports reporter, and for two days carried around what surely was a pretty good media scoop. At the same time, I was sure Dad and Mr. Selke would change their minds and not make such a shocking move in such a big game. Obviously, I misunderstood the motives of two of the toughest task masters in hockey history.

When the game with the Leafs began, Tom Johnson and Butch Bouchard started on defence. Harvey was on the bench. Johnson and Bouchard got a lot of ice time that night because Harvey stayed on the bench for the full sixty minutes.

It took the fans a while to catch on to what was happening. They were in a good mood after Dollard St. Laurent scored to give the Canadiens an early 1-0 lead. But by the time the second period was winding down, the Canadiens still ahead 1-0, the fans started hollering for Harvey.

In the third period (just after one guy sitting about two rows behind my mother yelled, "Come on Irvin. Play Harvey you stubborn old bastard!"), The Rocket scored a typical Richardian goal and the fans joyously erupted as they always did at a time like that. For the few minutes remaining in the game, the fans forgot about Harvey, Gerry McNeil held on to his shutout, and the Canadiens were 2-0 winners.

The next night, the Forum was booked for an indoor tennis exhibition starring Jack Kramer and Frank Sedgeman. There wouldn't be ice available after ten in the morning, so Dad gave the Canadiens a day off.

I was playing for the McGill Redmen and we practised at the Forum each day at noon. For that particular Friday, our coach, Rocky Robillard, had called a practice for seven in the morning. When we arrived, the Forum ice wasn't empty. Doug Harvey was on it, in his Canadien uniform, skating around by himself shooting pucks into the empty nets.

Doug asked Rocky if he could work out with us and of course he did. And I found myself in a rather embarrassing situation. The Harvey benching was receiving more attention that morning from Montreal's media than the final score of the game. So at seven in the morning, there was Harvey, obviously upset, and on the ice with him was the son of the guy who, a few hours earlier, had caused him the greatest embarrassment of his career.

It crossed my mind that maybe hockey's top defenceman might feel like throwing a bodycheck or two at his coach's 145-pound son. Thankfully, that didn't happen. Doug skated with us at about half speed and we still couldn't get the puck away from him when he decided to hang onto it for a while.

The only time he put out a bit extra was when he skated up the ice and fed me a perfect pass, which sent me into the clear for a shot on goal. Naturally, I blew it and Doug, a great needler, threw a couple of good ones at me.

I arrived home a couple of hours later, just as Dad was getting out of bed.

"Guess who was on the ice when we got to the Forum?" I asked him.

"Bet it was Harvey," was his quick reply.

I don't think Dad was too surprised. Despite what some critics said about Doug's apparent lack of enthusiasm, Dad always felt that he was a lot more uptight, nervous, and caring than he would let on. His solo appearance on the ice at the Forum the morning after that humiliating night before helped confirm Dad's theory.

In the game against Detroit the following night, Doug took his regular turn and didn't miss a shift the rest of the season. He was voted to the first All-Star team and the Canadiens won the Stanley Cup – with Doug playing his usual key role in the victory.

During those couple of days when the "Harvey Gets Benched" story was a hot topic, I don't recall Doug being quoted or publicly complaining. It's a different story today, what with players crying to the media about lack of ice time or complaining that their coach hadn't prepared them for a certain game. It's something that hasn't gone unnoticed by people who have been around hockey for a lot of years.

"I couldn't coach today. Punch couldn't coach today. Your father couldn't coach today." That was what Toe Blake told me a few years ago, when I caught him in one of those "things aren't what they used to be" moods. Toe was complaining about the apparent disregard for discipline in today's game. But perhaps today's players wouldn't enjoy playing under an old-school regime any more than the old-school coaches would enjoy trying to handle today's players.

Players of the past were subjected to much more "psychology" from their coaches than is the case today. In 1949, a World-War-Two movie was released called *Twelve O'Clock High*, starring Gregory Peck. It's one of my all-time favourites and I have seen it at least a dozen times.

Twelve O'Clock High is the story of an American bomber squadron in Britain plagued with morale problems because the commander is too easy on them, too nice a guy. He is relieved of his command and Peck, his replacement, sets out to improve morale by ramming strict discipline down the throats of his men. He commissions one plane to be manned by the worst of the lot and tells its captain, "If there's a bombardier who can't find his plate with his fork, you got him. If there's a navigator who can't find the men's room, you got him." Naturally, Peck turns things around to help win the war.

Dad saw the movie when it first came out and loved it. A few mornings later, he cancelled the team's practice and took his players to a private screening. Instead of listening to him that day, the Canadiens sat through *Twelve O'Clock High* listening to Gregory Peck and, their coach hoped, learning something about the value of discipline.

Another memorable line in the movie was, "I don't believe in bad luck. There's always a reason."

It wasn't long before there was a new sign in the Canadiens' dressing room. It read, "There's Always A Reason."

A few years ago, I told this story to Bob Gainey of the Canadiens. Bob asked, "Do you think that would work today?" I knew from the tone of his voice he was certain it wouldn't.

I'm not so sure men like Toe Blake and Dick Irvin couldn't coach today's players, but certainly in years gone by there was a much different relationship between coach and player.

For example, when Dad first coached in Toronto, he shared a hotel room with one of his players, King Clancy. It was King who answered the phone when Dad got the call telling him I had just been born.

When Dad commuted between Regina and Toronto, he would drive there and back accompanied by a couple of Maple Leafs who lived in the Regina area. Ken Doraty and Murray Armstrong were two who shared the driving, and likely the expenses, in this fashion.

Sometimes players, and their wives, visited the Irvin home in Regina during the summer. There is a picture in our family photo album of Busher Jackson and Dad showing off ducks they have shot with a three- or four-year-old Dick Jr. standing between them. That was when Busher was playing for Dad in Toronto. After Dad left the Leafs, Turk Broda and his wife stayed with us, even though the two men were then in opposing hockey camps.

When Dad was with the Canadiens, players like Ken Reardon, Elmer Lach, and Glen Harmon would visit us in Regina and eat meals cooked by my mother. One time, Dad even suggested a date for bachelor Reardon with the good-looking daughter of one of his pigeon-fancier friends. I don't know if Reardon took him up on it.

When the Canadiens travelled through Western Canada during their training camp in 1948, about half the team came to our house for lunch on the day of an exhibition game in Regina. They hung around to listen to a World Series game on the radio and I recall proudly telling my school mates that the great Rocket Richard was there and had fallen asleep on our living-room floor!

During a game in the late 1940's, Dad was rescued by his players from the strong arm of the law. It happened in Detroit when Dad became very upset with the work of the referee. When the period ended, instead of going to the dressing room, he walked onto the ice and waited at the gate leading to the referee's room to let the guy in the striped shirt hear from him at close range. Jack Adams, the Red Wings' manager and no friend of Dad's, saw what was happening and ordered the police at the Olympia to take Dad into custody, which they tried to do. When word of this reached the Canadiens' dressing room, the players, led by Reardon and The Rocket, stormed out into the lobby and grabbed their beleaguered coach out of the clutches of the local gendarmes. (I found myself thinking of this incident as I watched the Jim Schoenfeld and Don Koharski "dough-nut" circus during the New Jersey-Boston 1988 playoffs.)

When we moved to Montreal in 1951, I had a few weeks to kill before starting classes at McGill. Dad would call one of his players and ask him to take me golfing. There was likely more ordering than asking, so I was picked up, taken golf-ing and driven back. It was quite a thrill for a teenaged Canadien worshipper to play golf with the likes of Elmer Lach, Gerry McNeil, and Glen Harmon. I don't imagine they were too excited, but I was their coach's son and I guess they felt they had no choice in the matter.

I'm not trying to claim that every man who played for him thought my dad was the greatest guy, and the greatest coach, of all time. Far from it. But there was a different, and closer, bond between player and coach in those days.

Dad loved to spar with newspapermen from other cities. Once, when a group of Toronto reporters were in the Cana-diens' dressing room, he pointed to the spot where Maurice Richard's equipment was hanging.

"There's The Rocket's jock strap, gentlemen," he pro-claimed with a flourish. "Take a good look at it because it's the closest you'll get to a great hockey player this season."

The Toronto reporters always looked to Dad to provide them with good quotes and that one was duly reported.

When Jean Béliveau was with the Canadiens for three games while he was still playing senior hockey in Quebec City, one of the games was scheduled for Boston. Dad sent a telegram addressed to Boston hockey fans care of Herb Ralby, the Bruins PR man.

"Montreal Canadiens playing at the Garden Sunday night," it began. "They will be there with the world's great-est player, the world's greatest centerman and a young man who someday will be the world's greatest player. Don't miss them."

Dad was referring to, in order, The Rocket, Elmer Lach, and Béliveau. The wire made the papers and the fans were on his back from the start of the game. But the "Unseen Hand" was on his side that night. The Canadiens won 4-3 with Béliveau scoring twice.

Today's NHL teams almost always practise the morning of a game. That never happened when Dad was coaching. Instead, the players would report to their home rink for a meeting on game morning, or to the coach's suite in the hotel if they were on the road. Most of the time there wouldn't be much said. Dad basically wanted the players to show up to make sure they were out of bed. But once in a while, he would try something different to rouse his troops into thinking seriously about the game to be played that night.

Once, when the team was in the grip of a dreadful scoring slump, he brought one of the goal nets into the dressing room. On the ice a net doesn't look all that big, but it certainly does within the confines of the dressing room. The players were expecting a pretty good going over. Instead, all Dad did was place the net in the centre of the room and put a puck on the floor in front of it. A puck is a couple of inches high. A net is four feet high and six feet wide.

"O.K. boys," he said, "why is it you're having such a tough time putting that little thing into that big thing?"

Then he walked out of the room, leaving the players to figure out the answer for themselves.

Another time, he was lecturing them on the art of scoring. He had a hockey stick in his hand, and there was a puck lying on the floor.

"This is what I mean," he said and fired the puck at the open end of a trash can that was tipped over on the other side of the room. The puck drilled right into the can, dead centre. With a hushed group of young players now figuring that maybe their sixty-year-old coach knew what he was talking about after all, Dad gently placed the stick up against a wall and left the room.

"Couldn't have done it again if I'd tried for an hour," he told me afterward. "The Unseen Hand was with me."

There is no doubt Dad's unseen partner was with him more than against him during the twenty-four years he coached in Toronto and Montreal. Coaches succeed when they have the right players to work with and certainly Dad had his share of good and great ones with the Maple Leafs and the Canadiens.

But all good things must come to an end and he finished his career coaching his worst team, the 1955–56 Chicago Black Hawks. There was one bright note: his contract. It was worth $20,000, the most money he ever made in one year during his lifetime in hockey.

After Dad was told by Frank Selke that he would be replaced as coach of the Canadiens following the Richard-Riot-marred end of the '54-'55 season, he was contacted by Jim Norris, the Black Hawks' owner. Dad could have stayed with the Canadiens in some kind of off-ice capacity but, as he put it, "Something is telling me to go to Chicago."

So he went back to where he had started his NHL career, taking over a poor team that had managed only thirteen wins in 1954–55. There was a slight improvement and the Hawks were in playoff contention until the final few weeks of the season, but then they faded, and finished in last place with nineteen wins.

In Dad's last two seasons with the Canadiens, the team lost a total of forty-two games. In 1955–56, his team in Chicago lost thirty-nine. One of his theories was that when a superstar has a bad night, he's still pretty good. When an average player has a bad night, he's fair. But when a poor player has a bad night, he's nothing. There were several superstars on the Canadiens. There were no superstars on the Black Hawks, only a lot of average and poor hockey players.

One of the thirty-nine losses was to the Canadiens at the Chicago Stadium when Rocket Richard won the game with two goals in the third period. Afterward, a newspaper reporter not normally on the hockey beat spoke to Dad.

"How come Richard was able to score those goals?" he asked. "You coached him in Montreal. Don't you know how to stop him?"

"What sport do you usually cover?" Dad asked.

"Baseball," was the reply. "I follow the Cubs."

"OK," Dad said, "suppose the Cubs are playing the St. Louis Cardinals. The Cardinals have runners on second and third, one out, and Stan Musial is coming to bat. If you were the Cubs' manager, what would you do?"

"I'd walk Musial," answered the reporter, saying exactly what Dad wanted to hear.

"Well, young man," he said, "in this sport you can't walk The Rocket."

By the time the Hawks' training camp began in 1955, the bone cancer that had started to take its toll during his last year with the Canadiens had really set in. However, with the help of various forms of medication Dad was still in reasonably good health. The one thing he couldn't do was skate, so he had to watch the practices from the seats.

One day, the referee scheduled to work a scrimmage didn't show up. Dad wondered out loud if there was anyone around who would fill in. A sixteen-year-old blond kid who was there for the Junior try-out camp jumped up.

"I'll do it, Mr. Irvin."

And so he did, with efficiency, handling face-offs and calling offsides with no trace of nervousness. That's how Bobby Hull made his first appearance on the ice with the Chicago Black Hawks.

Dad was in and out of hospital a couple of times during the summer of 1956. He went to training camp, but after a week he knew there was no way he could do the job. He was too ill. On a Saturday morning, he met with the Hawks' General Manager Tommy Ivan. In a tearful moment for both men, Dick Irvin retired from the game of hockey.

Dad's last public appearance came a couple of weeks later, when members of the 1932 Stanley-Cup-winning Toronto Maple Leafs were introduced at centre ice before the Leafs' first home game of the season. I think that was the only time he ever wore a tuxedo.

A few nights later, NHL President Clarence Campbell came to our house and offered Dad a job as a goodwill ambassador for the League. Dad accepted, but he was unable to work at any time after that.

Red Fisher had just started covering hockey for the *Montreal Star*. One afternoon a few weeks after Dad retired, he came to our house to interview him. Dad was feeling good that day and took a liking to Red, giving him more than enough quotes for a good story. The one Red best remembers was the last one. Workmen were cutting down trees along our street, including one in our front yard.

"See that tree?" Dad said, pointing to the window. "It's been standing there for seventy-five years. Now, in one day. . . ."

He made a sweeping motion with his hand, a motion that meant the tree was coming down, its life at an end – as he knew his was. He passed away five months later at the age of sixty-four.

The Right Place at the Right Time

*T*he saying "timing is everything" sums up the way I landed the two jobs I've had as a sports broadcaster.

After twenty-five years of commuting between his NHL job in the winter and his home in Regina, Dad decided to move the family to Montreal. We left Regina on his fifty-ninth birthday, July 19, 1951, and spent a very pleasant month on a leisurely motor trip east.

I graduated from McGill in 1953 with a Commerce degree and went to work for W.C. Pitfield, an investment dealer. But an interest in broadcasting stayed with me. A few months into my first job, I called Al Cauley, a sportscaster at CJAD Radio in Montreal, and asked him about my chances of getting into broadcasting.

"You'll have to start out in a small town," Al told me. "That's where you do everything; play the records, read the news, and sweep the floors at night. You don't make much money, but you learn a lot. You keep changing jobs, going to larger centres each time and if you're good, and lucky, someday you could end up in Montreal or Toronto."

I was a twenty-two-year-old bachelor, living at home, with

free access to every Canadiens game at the Forum. Life was good, too good to go through that hassle. So much for my ambition to be a broadcaster.

I did change jobs. After a year with Pitfield, I spent six years with Shell Oil and was working for a small stationery supplies firm, Wheatley and Wilson, when Brian McFarlane asked me to bring the scrapbook to CFCF.

When the scrapbook and I appeared with Brian on *Sportsman's Club*, he was looking for an assistant. There were plenty of experienced sportscasters in Canada who would gladly have moved to Montreal. But there was one reason none of them did. CFCF, non-unionized at the time, was offering only seventy-five dollars a week for the job.

A few weeks after I appeared on Brian's show, we sat together at a Canadiens game at the Forum.

"Ever thought of being a sportscaster?" he asked me, careful not to mention that the position open at CFCF was worth only seventy-five dollars per week.

"I could be interested," I replied, careful not to tell him just how interested I was. Following my appearance on his show, and mindful of some encouraging words I had received in its wake, I bought a tape recorder. I spent a lot of time in the basement pretending I was a sportscaster.

There was no doubt Brian was interested in my services, although after having spent a couple of months as a one-man sports department, I'm sure he was interested in anyone who might even remotely fill the bill. He invited me to the station a few times to watch him prepare shows and, just like the days when I accompanied Dad to the CKCK Radio studios in Regina, I was fascinated.

We talked about an audition, but it didn't happen. Finally, Brian admitted that I was just a bit too green, even though I had told him I would work for the money being offered if I got the chance.

"If you want to look into a smaller market, I'll be glad to put in a good word for you," Brian said, by way of ending my initial hopes of getting a job at CFCF.

A few days later, I was to meet a friend for lunch but he called to cancel at the last minute. So I decided to call on Doug Smith. It was the smartest business move I ever made.

Doug Smith was a westerner from Calgary who had come east to broadcast Montreal Canadiens games on CFCF Radio in the early 1940's. He had written to Dad, then coaching the Canadiens, asking if he could help in any way. Dad put in a good word or two that helped Doug land the job. By 1961, he was out of the hockey broadcasting business and was working as a TV commentator on the CBC and producing network radio shows of major international sports events, including the Olympics.

"Can you write?" was Doug's first question when I told him about the CFCF situation. "Nobody gets anywhere in this business unless he can write."

Doug was living proof of that. To this day I have never heard anyone write better sportscasts and sports editorials than Doug Smith. But could I write? The question set me back a bit.

I thought back to my meagre writing experience, all of it, at Central Collegiate in Regina when I was sports editor for both the monthly school newspaper and the school yearbook. Most of my prose then was along the lines of: "The girls' basketball team, while finishing third, still managed to play some very exciting games. . . ." Nevertheless, I plucked up my courage and mumbled, "I think I can."

"At twenty-nine, you're too old to start in the boondocks," he said. "But you're just the guy McFarlane needs right now. He's new here and you know the way around sports in this city. Leave it with me. I'll see what I can do."

When I got back to my office at Wheatley & Wilson, there was a message for me to call Doug Smith. I was sure he had decided to hire me as his assistant, but that wasn't the case.

"The timing was perfect," he told me when I immediately returned his call. "You weren't out of my door a minute when Brian phoned. I steered the conversation around to what was happening at CFCF and gave you a big plug. I think you'll hear from him very soon."

It was a long afternoon as I waited in vain for Brian to call me. But when I walked into the house after taking the 5:10 train home from downtown, the phone was ringing.

"Dick, this is Brian. I was talking with someone today whose opinion I respect and he mentioned your name. He thinks you might be able to fit into our set-up here, so we've decided to give you an audition. If you're interested, I could set it up for next Wednesday morning."

Was I interested? Could Gordie Howe play hockey?

My newly purchased tape recorder got a real workout during the few days leading up to the following Wednesday morning. At Brian's request, I had written out a three-minute sportscast which I delivered to a camera while trying to convince myself I was still in the basement talking into the tape recorder.

Following the sportscast, Brian slid into a chair beside me and I interviewed him for another couple of minutes. I think I asked him to tell me how he got his start as a sportscaster. When it was over, Brian whispered to me, "That was great. You're exactly who I've been looking for."

I doubt someone with knees shaking and breath coming in short gasps could deliver an audition that was "great," but that was the word he used. Later that afternoon, with my knees still shaking and my breath still short on power, I received another phone call from Brian McFarlane.

"I've shown the tape to the bosses here and they want to hire you. Could you start next Monday?"

I asked for time to check with my employer, a marvellous man named Len Wheatley.

"If this is what you want, go right ahead. If it doesn't work out, you can come back here anytime," said Len.

I would have taken him up on his offer had it been necessary, but it wasn't. On Monday, May 8, 1961, eight years after I had graduated from McGill University with a Bachelor of Commerce degree, I began my career as a twenty-nine-year-old sportscaster at seventy-five dollars per week.

I was at the right place at the right time again a few years later when I joined *Hockey Night in Canada*. But before that I made a somewhat controversial HNIC appearance as a guest. At least it seemed that way judging by the reaction of some viewers in Saskatoon. On November 27, 1965, the Detroit Red Wings played the Canadiens at the Forum. I was the official scorer for games in Montreal, which means confirming who scored the goals and assists and compiling the official game score sheet for the NHL. The scorer had a seat adjacent to the TV broadcast booth, a spot I had occupied since Mr. Selke asked me to become the Official Scorer in 1958.

At the end of the second period, Keith Dancy, the colour commentator alongside Danny Gallivan, asked me if I would go on TV with him after the game to select the three stars. Naturally, I said yes to my first opportunity for a coast-to-coast on-camera spot.

During the game, Gordie Howe scored the 600th goal of his career. Otherwise, he was having a very ordinary night. The Canadiens were ahead by a goal when Howe drew a five-minute penalty for high-sticking J.C. Tremblay late in the third period. That killed any chance the Wings had for a comeback and the Canadiens held on to win 3-2.

Keith interviewed me in the broadcast booth. I can't remember who I picked as the stars of the game, but Howe wasn't one of them.

He asked why I hadn't selected Gordie on the occasion of his 600th goal. I replied that I thought he had played a very un-Howe-like game and that the major penalty had hurt the Wings when they were trying to tie the score.

A couple of weeks later, the Forum forwarded some mail for me. There were four or five letters, all from the Saskatoon area, all criticizing me as a Canadiens "homer" for not picking the favourite son of Floral, Saskatchewan as one of the three stars.

I wasn't surprised to learn that Gordie had a devoted following in the West. But I was a bit surprised to learn how serious hockey fans are about the nightly Three-Star selection. Since then I have received many letters from people all over Canada accusing me of being a "homer." It comes with the territory.

My interviewer that night, Keith Dancy, preceded me on my two main broadcasting jobs.

Keith was a sportscaster on CFCF Radio in Montreal for many years, and I have worked for CFCF since the day I got into the business in 1961. Keith was also Danny Gallivan's colour man during the early 1960's.

While he worked for *Hockey Night in Canada*, Keith performed one job that was quite amazing. The games would start at the Forum at eight o'clock, but the telecast wouldn't begin until 8:30. During the first intermission, they would show highlights of the first period with Keith describing the play in the past tense.

Sportscasters do that while showing highlights on newscasts, but Keith called the play *live*. When the game began, so did the video-tape machine, and he would do the play-by-play commentary like this:

"The face-off took place just outside the Canadiens' blue line. Béliveau fed the puck back to Laperrière who passed it along the left-wing boards to Gilles Tremblay. Tremblay crossed the blue line and fired a shot. Bower made the save, but couldn't clear the rebound. Béliveau moved in close, picked up the puck, and scored."

Think about it for a moment all you sportscasters out there, myself included. That wasn't easy. Yet Keith pulled it off every night without a hitch.

Keith Dancy eventually gave up his on-air duties and became a very successful executive in the business side of broadcasting in Canada, no doubt following a principle he preached while working at CFCF. He would sign off his nightly radio sportscast with the phrase, "A good sport always wins, if he loses with a smile."

The CBC had televised hockey exclusively since 1953, but, in 1964, the CTV Network began showing games out of Toronto and Montreal on Wednesday nights. In those days, the broadcast crew was hired and paid by MacLaren Advertising. When the CTV show went on the air, MacLaren was able to use the same announcers.

Two years later, the Saturday night CBC Montreal show had Danny Gallivan as the play-by-play commentator, Dan Kelly as his colour man, and Frank Selke Jr. in the studio hosting the show. Kelly was a full-time CBC employee working in Ottawa and the Corporation refused him permission to work on the opposing network. This meant a colour man was needed to work with Danny on the Wednesday night shows. Guess who was, once again, at the right place at the right time?

By then Brian McFarlane had left CFCF and returned to work in Toronto. I was CFCF's Sports Director and wasted no time saying "yes" when asked by MacLaren if I would like to work alongside Danny on Wednesday nights.

My first CTV telecast was a game between the Canadiens and the Chicago Black Hawks, on October 26, 1966, with my good buddy Ralph Mellanby sitting in the director's chair. Not only was that my first *HNIC* experience, it was also the first for Ralph Mellanby. Ralph was working at CFCF as a Producer-Director, and we had teamed up on all the station's sports shows during its early years. At one point, we were churning out a weekly series called *Montreal Minor Hockey*, taping three games in one afternoon. At the same time, we were producing a weekly quiz show called *Know Your Sports* and, to make sure we had something to do on Thursdays, they had us doing a weekly football show with Jim Trimble, the Head Coach of the Montreal Alouettes. Our close association would continue at CFCF and then at *HNIC*, where Ralph rose to become Executive Producer – until he joined CTV as Producer of their world feed at the 1988 Winter Olympics in Calgary.

Those early times, when we often worked seven days a week, were likely the best thing that happened to us in our careers. The team of Mellanby and Irvin learned a lot about the TV sports business in a very short time. Today, when I tell younger sportscasters about the work load we carried, and the fun we had doing it, they look at me as if to say "Were you crazy?" Maybe we were. Certainly we were over-worked and underpaid, but I'm glad it happened that way, and so is Ralph.

I don't recall too much about our first Wednesday night CTV hockey telecast except that I interviewed Bobby Hull at the beginning of the program. But Ralph certainly remembers the night as one of his scariest experiences. Everything had been put nervously in place and all seemed ready when, ten minutes to air time, there was a power failure at the Forum and suddenly nothing was working.

"What do we do now?" one of the technicians asked Ralph.

"Pray baby, pray!" was his reply.

Maybe they did, and maybe it worked, because one minute before show time the power came back on.

I sat back when the show ended to watch the credits and see my name on *Hockey Night in Canada* for the first time. It was there all right – sort of. Under the heading "Commentators" were the names of Danny Gallivan, Frank Selke Jr., and "Dick IRWIN."

Danny spotted the spelling mistake and said, "Great to be famous, isn't it?"

During my first season on CTV, I would occasionally appear on the Saturday night CBC program. This was done with the permission of both the CBC and my full-time employer CFCF, a CTV station. In 1967, the NHL expanded from six to twelve teams. One of the new teams was the Oakland Seals, and Frank Selke Jr. was hired as its General Manager. That meant there was an opening on *Hockey Night in Canada*'s CBC production. And guess who just happened to be around when that happened?

Dan Kelly moved from the colour commentator position to become host of the Saturday show and I was again very

quick to reply in the affirmative when asked if I would like
to become Danny's broadcast partner on Saturday, as well
as on Wednesday.

By this time, Ralph had joined HNIC on a full-time basis
and I knew he put in more than one good word on my behalf.
Also in on this one was Bud Hayward, my boss at CFCF. Bud
was a hockey fan and one of my biggest supporters, which
wasn't a bad thing considering he signed my pay cheque.
By then, it had edged up slightly from the seventy-five-
dollar-per-week figure.

"We've got to get you on those hockey telecasts," Bud
would say to me, so when the opening came he was all for it.
Thankfully, so was whoever was in charge at the CBC.

A couple of years later, the Canadiens wanted to expand
the English-language coverage of their games on radio. At
that time, it consisted only of CBC broadcasts of away games
on Sunday night. CFCF Radio jumped at the chance to do it,
and guess who was hanging around the station, very available to become the play-by-play man? My broadcast of a
game between the Canadiens and the Oakland Seals, in
Oakland, February 4, 1969, was the start of a radio series
that reached its twentieth anniversary season in 1987–88.

I've been asked many times how I can work full-time for a
CTV station and freelance every Saturday night for six
months on the CBC. It likely has been the longest-running
situation of its kind in Canadian broadcasting and quite
unique, although in recent years there has been a fair
amount of talent moving between networks and local stations on the French side of the business. I know that when
other broadcasters have requested permission to work on
another network, and have been refused, they've asked
"What about Dick Irvin?"

Well, what about him? Each season when I receive a contract from *Hockey Night in Canada*, I ask CFCF if I can
sign it. So far, the answer has always been yes. Without
gilding too many lilies, let me say that for over twenty years
now I have been one very lucky hockey announcer.

One last word about my start in the sportscasting business. When it appeared that I wasn't going to get the job at CFCF, I inquired about openings in the West. I was put in touch with Wilma Dobson, a one-time public- and high-school classmate who was working at good old CKCK Radio in Regina. Wilma wrote to tell me there were possibilities at Saskatchewan stations in Yorkton, Prince Albert, and Weyburn. I then wrote back to thank her for the information and tell her I had been hired to work in Montreal.

One year later, I was in Winnipeg visiting my uncles, Pete and Alex, and learned that Wilma was there, working at CKRC Radio. The smooth-talking bachelor from the East called up his former classmate and talked her into meeting him for lunch.

To paraphrase one of Winston Churchill's oft-quoted remarks, a year later Wilma and Dick were married, and I have lived happily ever after.

Danny and Dick – the Best of Times

When I joined Danny Gallivan as his colour man on *Hockey Night in Canada*, there was only one microphone in the booth. That's the way Danny wanted it. He held the mike and gave it to his partner only when he wanted him to say something. That situation didn't last too long after I got the job, but it showed that *HNIC* was in the dark ages just a bit longer than it should have been.

For the first several seasons I was there, we worked with what are known as hand mikes. Danny had used that kind of equipment during all his years as a play-by-play broadcaster. When progress reared its ugly head and we had to change to the head-set mikes that almost all other sports broadcasters were wearing, he balked strongly. I could see his point. Years of holding a microphone in his hand didn't make the transition to one wrapped around his head easy to deal with. They were trying to take away a very integral part of his job – his hand-held microphone.

After much discussion, Danny compromised. He would agree to wear the head-set mike, if they would let him hold a dead mike in his hand and in front of his mouth as he had done in the past. It was settled that way and led to a very hilarious moment the first night we were wired for sound in the new fashion. The Canadiens were playing the New York Islanders and, during the play by play, Danny forgot all about the new equipment.

"Face-off in the Islanders' zone . . ." he began to broadcast. Suddenly, he had to clear a tickle in his throat. For years, he had handled such situations by holding the hand mike at arm's length, away from his mouth, and coughing out the tickle. So that's what he did, completely forgetting that his hand mike was only a prop – and that the one positioned in front of his mouth was live. The whole country heard his *"Hrumph - hrumph - hrumph"* loud and clear. It's the only time I've ever had to take off my head set and walk away for a minute. I was laughing so hard there was no way I could have said anything. Danny gave me a puzzled look, shrugged, and carried on, totally oblivious of what he had done.

He kept holding the dead mike for the next year or so. Whenever we did a game on the road there wouldn't always be a mike available, so he'd hold a pen or pencil or something else that would serve as his security blanket. One time in Boston, a cameraman situated beside us watched Danny for a while in total confusion.

"How come he does that?" he asked me during an early commercial break.

"When you're the best in the business, you can do it any way you want to," was my reply.

I never knew Danny's age until 1967.

"Two things started in 1917," he said one night. "The NHL and me." The League was celebrating its fiftieth birthday that year and so was Danny. It is well known that he is a Maritimer. So we used to tell people we had the country represented from both ends, Danny from the East and Dick from the West.

Danny first broadcast from the Forum in the 1940's when he accompanied an amateur team from his home town for a game in Montreal. Russ Taylor, who was to become a long-

time Montreal sportscaster and an original Expos broadcaster, along with Dave Van Horne, was working as the
technical director on Danny's show. A couple of years later,
Doug Smith, the Canadiens' play-by-play man, became ill.

"Why don't you bring in that chap Gallivan from the Mar-
itimes?" Russ asked Walter Downs, the producer of the Canadiens' radio broadcasts. They did, and that's how Danny
Gallivan got to broadcast his first NHL game. He often told
me the story of his visit to the Canadiens' dressing room,
where he went to meet Dad to pick his brains a bit about his
team. Dad immediately got Danny's name wrong.

"*Gavilan,*" he said, pointing at his players. "Take a good
look at them now, because when the game starts they'll be
skating too fast for you to recognize them." Irvin the psy-
chologist was at work again, on both his team and the rookie
announcer.

When the 1952-53 season began, they were together again.
Doug Smith had left the hockey business and Danny's great
job the night he filled in as Smith's replacement earned him
the position on a permanent basis. Dad and Danny enjoyed
each other's company from then on, even though Danny had
to endure Dad calling him "Gavilan."

The Canadiens won the Stanley Cup that season. It was
Dad's last and Danny's first, and certainly an omen of
things to come for the talented broadcaster from the Mari-
times. The Canadiens won the Cup in six of his first eight
seasons in the broadcast booth, and when he retired after
thirty-two years on the job they had won it sixteen times.
There is nothing a broadcaster can do for a hockey team as
far as winning or losing is concerned. But a team can do a
lot for a broadcaster and his career. Danny and I are living
proof of that. Again, a case of being in the right place at the
right time.

Danny's arrival in Montreal coincided with the beginning
of the televised version of *Hockey Night in Canada.* Network ratings peaked at playoff time and the Canadiens
reached the Stanley Cup finals in each of Danny's first eight
years on the job. Early impressions run deep. The Cana-

diens were the dominant team on the tube in the beginning of televised hockey and Danny Gallivan was their voice. It was a perfect match. Danny became the most popular hockey broadcaster in this country and, even though he has been retired since 1984, I feel he still is the most popular hockey broadcaster in Canada. Certainly none of us on the air now can match him in this regard.

What made him so great? While he is quick to admit that, like all young broadcasters of his time, he patterned his work after Foster Hewitt, Danny gave Canadian viewers and listeners a different style. The sound of his voice was electric, and he was broadcasting a winning team. His knowledge of the game ran deep, and he always came to work totally prepared to do a broadcast. He had done his "homework" as we say, something I quickly learned to do once I joined him in the booth.

And, of course, there was his vocabulary. I don't know what the reaction of viewers would be today to a new broadcaster who started using words like "spinnerama," "paraphernalia," and the most famous Dannyism of them all, "a cannonading shot." Old-fashioned by today's standards? Perhaps. But as long as it was Danny coming up with flowery words and phrases the fans loved it.

"Bossy failed to negotiate the puck through the plethora of players in front of the net" was one he came up with late in his career. Mickey Redmond was working in the booth with us that night. He looked at me and I looked at him. "Mickey, I think that means there were a lot of players standing in front of the net," I said, and we all had a laugh, Danny included.

Danny's ability to analyze a game as the play was in progress was amazing. A colour man's job begins when the play stops. I would spot a situation I wanted to mention but very often, by the time the whistle blew, Danny would have analyzed it during his call of the play by play.

Danny had little patience when it came to stretches of dull hockey and didn't waste any time in letting everyone know how he felt.

"Not much in the way of scintillating action so far," he might say, four or five minutes into a first period. I'd think to myself, "Come on Danny. Give them a chance." And he also never quite got accustomed to the commercial interruptions that became more frequent as the years went along. One night, a fight broke out on the ice when a commercial was running.

"We've had a lot of action during the time we were away for you know what," was the way he phrased it when he got back on the air. The sponsors had the HNIC phones ringing early Monday morning after that one.

He also wasn't too thrilled giving the in-period commercial cues. That job fell to me early in our association and was one reason I worked in the booth as well as the studio during the five or six years I served as both colour commentator and host of the Montreal-based shows. I called that the "Upstairs, Downstairs" phase of my career. I would have to stay in the studio until the game had almost started. By the time I reached the booth, they would be two or three minutes into the play. Then I would leave the booth with about three minutes remaining in each period to get downstairs in time to be set as the intermission host.

One night, the Canadiens defeated the Red Wings 4-2 and I actually didn't see *any* of the six goals. They were all scored in either the first two or the last two minutes of a period. We had time to fill at the end of the telecast and I was told by the director I would have to comment on a highlight package of all six goals.

"What goals?" I answered. "I haven't seen one all night."

When I did get to see them on the replay, we were on the air, live from coast to coast. My commentary contained no embellishments. Just the facts, folks: goal scorers, assists, and times. In our business that sort of thing is called "faking it."

The HNIC presentation of Canadiens games became known, particularly in Montreal, as the "Danny and Dick Show." Most sportscasting play-by-play teams spend a lot of time together, especially on the road, but Danny and I rarely did. We seldom worked road games, except during the playoffs. Our socializing was done mainly in the broadcast booth, live on air, with the hockey game dictating much of what we said to each other. And despite what most fans thought, our attempts at one-upmanship with trivia questions were always spontaneous, never rehearsed.

Despite frequent protests from HNIC producers, Danny seldom attended the pre-game meetings during his last several years on the show. There was no real reason he had to be there. The meetings, which take place about three hours before game time, deal mainly with show openings, intermissions, and post-game possibilities; areas which rarely involved Danny. But he was always on hand when the teams went through their workouts the morning of a game, and he was always totally prepared to do what they paid him to do, call the play by play.

In thirty-two years with HNIC, Danny Gallivan missed only three or four broadcasts due to illness. During the playoffs in Chicago in 1971, he came down with a severe cold and sore throat. Ralph Mellanby went to his hotel room during the afternoon of the game and found Danny surrounded by almost every brand of throat spray and cough medicine known to man.

"I'll try to make it, Ralph," Danny croaked, while Mellanby was saying to himself, "No Way."

At the pre-game meeting, Ralph told me and Brian McFarlane we were a two-man team.

"Dick, you will do the play by play," he said, words that sent a few shivers up my spine in anticipation of a debut for a Stanley Cup final game. "Brian will be both host and colour commentator. Danny won't be here."

Brian taped the show opening and, five minutes before air time, the original team on CFCF's *Montreal Minor Hockey*, including Ralph in the Director's seat, was all set to take their act coast to coast.

The TV broadcast booth in the Chicago Stadium is located in the midst of the paying customers. One minute before air time, Danny suddenly appeared, making his way through the crowd and down the stairs, looking pale and shaky, but reporting for duty.

"Danny is here," I told Ralph over our intercom.

"I don't believe it," was his reply.

I did all the talking through to the National Anthems before Danny took over. His "Good Evening Ladies and Gentlemen" sounded like it came out of a broken down foghorn. But a minute or so later, his call of the action was sounding a lot more like Danny Gallivan, and he finished the game with his usual flying colours.

Seven years later, Danny's voice did give out during a playoff game and he didn't give us any advance warning that he was in trouble. We were at the Nassau Coliseum doing a game between the Canadiens and the Islanders. His voice seemed fine through the first period and during an on-camera chat we had during the intermission.

Two or three minutes into the second period, right after an offside call, he said, on the air, "Dick, this throat of mine isn't working very well tonight. You take over."

He then removed his headset, sat back, and lit a cigarette. Just like that I was into my first bit of *HNIC* play by play. In those days, we worked as a twosome, so I flew solo the rest of the game.

I thought it went pretty well, and the bosses told me the same thing. So I was somewhat disappointed when they had Bob Cole take the first flight out of Newfoundland the next day to fill in for Danny until he was ready to return. My TV play-by-play career was back on hold until Danny retired six years later.

Danny Gallivan had a job that was the envy of every other hockey broadcaster. He only had to do the play by play of the games themselves. He rarely did interviews and at no time did he have to lug a tape recorder downstairs after a game and do interviews for use on radio or television the next day. In fact, in his thirty-two years broadcasting Canadiens games, he was in the team's dressing room only two or three times. While I feel Danny missed something in not getting to know some of the players, it certainly kept him in a position to be as objective as one could be under the circumstances. Sure, he was called a "homer" by non-Montreal fans. Conversely, I know the team tried at various times during his career to get him to be more of a cheerleader. Danny flatly refused, which he had to do considering he worked on a national broadcast.

When the 1979 playoffs began, it was announced that *Hockey Night in Canada* and the U.S.A. Cable Network would share the telecasting of the final series. The play-by-play commentary was included in the sharing arrangement, which meant Danny would split the job with Dan Kelly.

Like most of us in our business, Danny was very protective of his territory. He expressed his displeasure with the idea from the beginning and, as the playoffs continued, Danny and the producers were involved in an ongoing struggle. Danny insisted he wouldn't work thirty minutes a game as they were asking him to do if the Canadiens made it to the final round, which they did.

The discussions continued until the day of the series opener between the Canadiens and the Rangers, in Montreal. Danny held firm and, true to his feelings on the matter, refused to work. So Dan Kelly did the play by play for both the CBC and U.S.A. I worked as the colour man and Bobby Orr was the analyst.

The morning after Game One, it was Danny Gallivan, not hockey players, whose picture was on the front page of the *Montreal Gazette*. It showed him sitting at home, watching the game on TV. He stayed there for the balance of the series.

Danny's stand didn't harm his career with *HNIC* and he was back doing business as usual the following season. A few years later, after he had retired, he called me to express his concern over a situation I had been put in by the producers of the show.

"I wouldn't work tonight if I were you," he told me.

"If I were you I wouldn't work either," I replied. "But I'm

Dick and you're Danny. They still treated you like a legend after '79. If I don't show up tonight, they'll treat me as an ex-employee tomorrow."

Danny finally became an ex-employee of HNIC following the 1984 playoffs and, in typical Gallivan fashion, he didn't give us much notice.

The Canadiens were eliminated by the Islanders in the Conference Final that year. Before what turned out to be the deciding game in the series, at the Nassau Coliseum, Ralph Mellanby told me if the Islanders won the game Danny and I would work the New York-Edmonton final which would open in New York the following Tuesday.

Danny and I rode home on the Canadiens' charter flight after the game. There was the usual small talk and series rehashing until it was time to go our separate ways in the parking lot. One of the subjects discussed was the upcoming Final series and, as always, Danny was full of ideas on what might happen.

"See you next Tuesday," I said.

"No you won't," he replied. "That's it. I've done my last game."

He had been bothered by a cold and I figured that, plus fatigue, had prompted a temporary depression that would be long gone by game time Tuesday. I was wrong. Danny wasn't at the Islanders-Oilers opener. He had indeed done his final broadcast.

A few weeks later, his retirement was officially announced. Danny, in many ways a private man, had his own reasons. When I talked to him about it, he would only say, "It was time."

He has enjoyed his retirement, especially meeting hundreds of his fans at sports banquets across the country. He doesn't come to the Forum very often, but he still follows hockey closely, listening to radio games, watching TV games, and reading every scoring summary in the paper.

The Danny and Dick Show lasted seventeen years. We had a great run. It will always be the high point of my broadcasting career.

Telling It
Like It Was

When the sales people responsible for signing up sponsors for *Hockey Night in Canada* head out into the market place, I'm sure they try to convince prospective clients the show has a great coast-to-coast impact.

It certainly does, but it's not something new. It goes back as far as hockey has been broadcast on a national basis, which means back to the days of Foster Hewitt.

Hewitt wasn't the first man to call the play by play of a hockey game on radio. The legend is his, but a broadcaster in the West, Pete Parker, was in fact the first. He called a game in Regina between the Regina Capitals and the Edmonton Eskimos on March 14, 1923. (My father was playing for the Regina team, so I can proudly claim that the Irvin name has been a part of hockey broadcasting, one way or another, since Day One.) Hewitt was on the air in Toronto a couple of weeks later and was of course at the microphone when games were first carried on a national radio network.

Foster spent the major part of his hockey broadcasting career as a voice - not as a voice with a face. But even though he was working long before the advent of television, his impact on the game, and the Canadian radio business, was staggering. He began doing NHL games on a regular basis when the Toronto team, then known as the St. Pats, played in the Mutual Street Arena. Foster's facilities were primitive, so when Conn Smythe opened Maple Leaf Gardens in 1931, it included the famed "gondola," which Foster would soon make almost as well known as the Gardens itself. As the network for his radio broadcasts spread outside the Toronto area, visitors to the Gardens would look for the gondola as soon as they entered the building.

Foster played a role in building the Gardens and in so doing got his first real indication of the power of his radio broadcasts. He was doing games from Mutual Street, during the planning stages of the Gardens. He mentioned on the air that Frank Selke Sr., then Smythe's top assistant, had written a book about the Leafs. Money received for the book would go to the Gardens' Building Fund. Amazingly, 90,000 orders poured in. The commercial impact of hockey broadcasting had begun.

Hewitt spent most of his radio career doing a solo broadcast, without benefit of a colour commentator. Like Danny Gallivan, he had a great ability to call the play by play and analyse the game at the same time, giving radio listeners a very vivid "picture" of what was happening on the ice. But I'm sure there were times when a colour man would have added immeasurably to the broadcast; like the night of April 3 and the morning of April 4, 1933. That was when a semi-final game between the Leafs and the Boston Bruins lasted from 8:30 p.m. through to 1:45 a.m. before Ken Doraty scored the winning goal for Toronto, the same game that prompted my Dad to come up with the phrase, the "Unseen Hand." The teams played 164 minutes and 47 seconds and Foster broadcast the entire game by himself. He claimed he called the last hour of the game "in a daze," hardly knowing what he was saying. I'm not surprised.

Three years later, in Montreal, the Maroons and the Detroit Red Wings played an even longer game; it lasted 176 minutes and 30 seconds. It was broadcast on CFCF radio, but there were two men working it, Charlie Harwood on the play by play and Elmer Ferguson doing the colour. Halfway through the second overtime period, Fergy mentioned how nice it would be if someone would supply them with some liquid refreshment. A few minutes later, a chap showed up, saying he had been listening in his apartment across the street from the Forum, and offered the thirsty announcers a couple of cold beers. I don't know about Harwood, but Fergy gladly accepted.

Although he was Canada's Number One media personality during the 1930's and 40's, there was a pretty good chance Foster Hewitt could have entered a crowded room at a sports banquet and only a few people would have recognized him. Once he started to talk, it would have been a different story. When the TV age of *Hockey Night in Canada* arrived, the recognition factor became quite different for the Gallivans, McFarlanes, Hodges, Wittmans, and the rest of the cast of characters wearing the blue coats on Saturday nights.

When I first joined the show, I didn't get too much reaction from people in Montreal. They had been watching me on CFCF-TV for half a dozen years. But when I travelled to other parts of the country, I was amazed at the "instant recognition" that goes with the territory of a show like *Hockey Night in Canada*. A few people would call me by name. But more often it was, "Aren't you the guy who does the hockey?" or "Hello Danny!"

The first hockey types to experience instant recognition weren't announcers. They were players.

In 1934, Dad was coaching the Toronto Maple Leafs. Following the playoffs, the Leafs and the Detroit Red Wings scheduled a series of exhibition games in Western Canada. Dad knew how many fans there were in the West, and how thrilled they would be to get a close-up look at teams from the NHL.

The Canadian Pacific Railway provided two private cars on a train travelling west and on the first stop a very strange thing happened.

When the train pulled into Jackfish, Ontario, there was a large crowd waiting at the station. It had been advertised that the players would get off the train for a few minutes and sign autographs. A lot of autographs were signed all right, every one by a Toronto player.

The Leafs were surrounded by fans. The Red Wings were left standing on the platform all by themselves. It was a scene that would be repeated at every stop of the trip.

Dad and Frank Selke were in charge of the Toronto entourage and it was Mr. Selke who first realized why the Leaf players were so much in demand, while the Red Wings seemed to be virtually ignored: Foster Hewitt and his *Hockey Night in Canada* radio broadcasts. The Toronto players were familiar to everyone. Hewitt, not bashful about leaning the way of his home team, had made the Leafs into national heroes. The Leafs were on the air every Saturday night. The Red Wings might have been their opposition on a radio game only a couple of times that season.

The next year, the Leafs and the Chicago Black Hawks made a similar trip and the reaction across the West was pretty much the same. It was obvious to a man like Frank Selke that they were on to a pretty good combination, hockey and the airwaves.

Before Pete Parker and Foster Hewitt began broadcasting hockey games on the radio, the only link between the players and the fans was via newspapers and magazines. Judging from the old Irvin scrapbook, the players had their pictures printed often enough to result in hockey heroes of that era being recognized by a lot of people when they walked down main streets, winter or summer. Certainly, fans were eager for news and went to great lengths to get it.

When the Winnipeg Monarchs were playing in Melville, Saskatchewan in the Allan Cup final of 1915, hundreds of fans in Winnipeg braved below zero weather as they stood outside the local telegraph office to get the story of the game as it was in progress.

Scoring plays would come across the wire from Melville. The telegraph operator would then step outside and, using a megaphone, announce the news to the crowd. Newspaper stories the next day told how the crowd reacted to every bit of information, and how they "cheered wildly" when the final score was flashed and their Monarchs had won the Allan Cup.

Newspaper reporting was of course a lot different than it is now. Today, most game stories are filled with quotes, so much so that in many cases a fan interested in the ebb and flow of a game can find little of that in the next day's story. The print people defend this style of reporting by claiming people have seen the game on TV. But those who have adopted this style never change it for the games that aren't on TV. There are a few too many reporters on the beat today, print and electronic, who haven't spent much time learning how the game is played. There's more gossip than hockey knowledge in their reporting.

The ink-stained boys back in the old days weren't like that. Here's how the *Regina Leader* reported a 1923 game between the hometown Capitals and Calgary. After a lengthy bit of reporting, which didn't include a single quote from a player or a coach, the final half of the paper's game coverage came under the heading "The Game in Detail" and began like this:

They were off promptly at 8:30 with referee Skinner Poulin in charge. Oliver secured from the face-off but his pass to Stanley was offside. Hay checked Barney on a good play and went down with Irvin. The Calgary defence turned them back. Dutton got as far as Moran and went down with Stanley. The latter shot and Laird made a good save. Oliver and Martin played a snappy combination and Foley passed to Oliver who got a nice goal in 1:22.

And so it went for almost three full columns, a complete, written play-by-play description of the game. The writer must have been scribbling furiously from start to finish. The write-up of that particular game ended with this:

> As the minutes went by the Calgary team attacked like famished tigers but they could not break through the local defence. The Regina team shot the puck to the other end at times to gain time and, try as they might, Calgary could not break through the cordon of athletes which stood in front of the Regina net.

Not only was that reporter busy with his pencil throughout the game, he managed to come up with some very descriptive phrases along the way. These included "Regina attacked with vehemence" and "Laird stopped a hot one." It was mentioned that a dispute over a delayed penalty was "settled amicably." Readers were informed that a play "foozled at the Calgary defence." And I love that bit about the Calgary team attacking "like famished tigers." The team's nickname was the Tigers.

The detailed descriptions of games were done, of course, without the benefit of TV replays. Today, there are monitors in every press box around the NHL and when goals are scored or controversial plays shown again the newspaper reporters give the replays their undivided attention. In many ways TV has made their jobs both easier, and more difficult. They can't use flights of fancy to embellish descriptions of the way goals were scored or saves were made, as their predecessors often did.

Incidentally, the final score of that Calgary-Regina game was 1-1. After Oliver opened the scoring for Calgary, Irvin tied the game for Regina.

Dad's favourite story about recognition in the 1930's involved the Conacher brothers, Charlie and Lionel.

Charlie played for him in Toronto as the right winger on the Kid Line alongside Joe Primeau and Busher Jackson. He was a scoring champion during that era and had the hardest shot in the game.

Lionel played hockey for the Montreal Maroons at the time. A brilliant all-around athlete, Lionel Conacher was named Canada's Athlete of the Half-Century in 1950.

The brothers travelled west for a hunting trip late one summer and joined up with Dad in Regina for a duck-hunting expedition. They were told where the best spot was for that sort of thing, but at the same time were warned that the farmer who owned the land never allowed hunters on his property. In fact, he often stopped people with a very basic tactic. He'd point a loaded rifle in their direction.

During the drive into the country, the boys discussed the situation and decided they'd give it a try. They turned into the farmer's property and were heading up the road toward the house when, sure enough, out came a grizzled old gentleman carrying a rifle.

They stopped the car, got out, and, with the rifle slowly being raised in their direction, heard the farmer tell them they were not welcome on his property.

Charlie was wearing a Toronto Maple Leafs leather jacket. The farmer wasn't quite finished saying his piece when he spotted the Maple Leaf crest emblazoned front and centre on the jacket.

"What's that?" the old gent asked, pointing the rifle toward the crest.

They told him.

"Who are you guys?"

They told him. Down went the rifle, out came a handshake, and for the rest of the day three of the NHL's best-known personalities had the run of the property where no one else was allowed to hunt. The old gent turned out to be a great fan of Foster Hewitt's Saturday night radio broadcasts.

I have a couple of pictures taken that day. One shows the

Conacher boys with their arms draped over the shoulders of their host. The other shows Charlie in a rather strange situation.

The hunting dog they had with them decided he didn't like the water in the pond where some of the ducks had landed. So with the dog refusing to do his thing, Charlie took off his clothes and swam out to retrieve the fallen mallards.

In the picture, Charlie still doesn't have any clothes on, but a duck he collected is strategically positioned. It never would have made *Playgirl*.

•••••••••••••••••••
Irvin, You're a Homer!

Danny Gallivan; Vin Scully; Curt Gowdy; Dave Van Horne: a few big names in sports broadcasting with whom I can claim to have something in common. We have all been accused of being "homers." It's nothing new.

In the 1930's and 40's, Foster Hewitt would begin his coast-to-coast Saturday-night radio broadcasts from Maple Leaf Gardens by saying, "Hello Canada, and hockey fans in the United States and Newfoundland." The game would be either at the end of, or late in, the first period. My mother, listening in Regina, claimed you could tell by Foster's voice if the Maple Leafs were winning, losing, or tied. She said he would be bouncy if they were ahead, subdued if they were behind, and somewhere in the middle if the game was tied. Mother would call it before he gave the score and, truth to tell, she was usually right.

Once I got on the air with *Hockey Night in Canada*, I learned very quickly that viewers hear exactly what they want to hear. The first playoff series I worked as a colour commentator involved the Canadiens and the Boston Bruins. I received two letters written after the opening game. One, from Port Hope, Ontario, accused me in no un-

certain terms of being totally and utterly a Canadiens' fan.
The other, written in Montreal, berated me for favouring
the Bruins and not giving my home team the credit it deserved. Same game, same words, heard two different ways
by two different listeners.

I did the play by play of Montreal Alouette football games
on CFCF Radio from 1965 to 1972. During that time, I joined
Hockey Night in Canada and a combination of those two
jobs provided my favourite "you're a homer" story.

During a football trip to Edmonton in the late 1960's, I
had dinner at the home of an old Regina buddy, Doug Hing-
ley. Doug was an executive with Imperial Oil, then a major
sponsor of the hockey telecasts. During the evening, he
showed me a letter the company had received from a hockey
fan who was returning his Imperial Oil credit card in protest over my work on the hockey telecasts. The fan wrote
that he couldn't patronize a company that would hire someone as pro-Montreal as Dick Irvin as one of its hockey broadcasters. He went on to cite examples of my bias during a
Canadiens game with Toronto, telecast the night before he
wrote the letter.

Another Regina buddy, Brian McDonald, was there and
recognized the writer as someone he knew who worked in
Calgary for Royalite Oil. Today, none of us can recall his
name, but I took it down at the time and, on a trip to Calgary about a month later, I called my non-fan. The conversation went something like this:

DICK: This is Dick Irvin of *Hockey Night in Canada*.
FAN: Uh, oh yes.
DICK: I understand you wrote a letter to Imperial Oil because
        you were upset with my work.
FAN: Yes, that's right.
DICK: I believe the letter was written after the game the Cana-
        diens won 7-2 against Toronto and Yvan Cournoyer
        scored three goals. Is that right?
FAN: Yes, that's right.
DICK: Obviously, I'm sorry you felt that way about my work

and I'm wondering if you could tell me exactly what it was that prompted you to return your credit card and write that kind of a letter.

Then came the magic words that confirmed my suspicions.

FAN: Well you see, I'm such a Maple Leafs' fan I couldn't stand to listen to you that night. You drove me up the wall.

DICK: I'm the colour commentator and you know my job is to describe the replays after each goal.

FAN: Yes, I know.

DICK: Let's see now. The Canadiens scored seven goals and each one was replayed at least once and probably twice. That means you had to watch the puck go into your team's net about twenty-one times. Was that my fault?

FAN: No.

DICK: And each time a replay came up you kept getting madder at me because I was the guy who had to describe what happened.

FAN: Probably.

DICK: Can you think of another way I could have done my job that night? The score was 7-2 you know.

FAN: I know. It's just that I'm such a Toronto fan.

DICK: I prefer not saying much about teams that play as poorly as yours did that night. Was there really anything positive I could have said about the Leafs?

FAN: Not much.

We talked a bit longer about the telecasts and I explained to him that I was learning how viewers seemed to hear what they wanted to hear. If the announcers were saying nice things about their team, they were happy. If the announcers were properly describing their team on a night when it was playing poorly, they took it out on the announcers, not their team.

I felt I had made a point or two and we parted on a friendly note. I told him I hoped my work wasn't going to turn him

into an ex-viewer of *Hockey Night in Canada*. I don't know
if it did. And I don't know if he ever renewed his Imperial
Oil credit card.

One of the reasons Danny and I ran the risk of being
tagged with the "homer" label was our home team. The
Montreal Canadiens have won a lot of games and a lot of
Stanley Cups since the arrival of the TV cameras. And the
Canadian trait of not enjoying the success of some of the
achievers in our country can be very evident in the sports
field. The more a team wins, the more some people want it to
lose. This happens right in Montreal too. We call them "Canadiens haters." They aren't in the majority, but they're out
there.

Fans are funny. Average players can ply their trade for
years and never draw much reaction, pro or con. But Super
Stars, like Gretzky, Lafleur, Orr, and Trottier, hear a lot of
boos in opposing rinks, especially if the home team is winning the game and their fans are in a good mood. It's a case
of being too good, and paying a bit of a price, even though
most of the people booing them would kill for a personalized
autograph after the game. Mario Lemieux is a marvel, and
so far has been treated that way by fans around the NHL.
But it won't be long before he hears it too, no matter how
many winning goals he might score against Team Soviet.

When a team goes through a string of successful seasons,
fans become jaded and quick to criticize when things go
awry. It never ceased to amaze me during the Canadiens'
great years in the late 1970's, when they were having seasons with only eight or ten losses, that someone in the office
would ask, "What's wrong with the Canadiens?" after they
had lost a game. I think what they were really doing was
jabbing a needle into me, the "home team broadcaster." My
mail contained a lot more negative letters during the Canadiens' winning years than it did when the team drifted into
the middle of the pack, and the Islanders and the Oilers
were dominating the Stanley Cup playoffs.

I received a lot more critical mail during my early years
on *HNIC* than I have in the past few years. During the 1986

playoffs, when the Canadiens went all the way, I didn't receive one letter, good or bad, and that was a first. Over the years, by far the most mail has arrived during the playoffs when emotions run much higher than during the regular season.

I never read a letter that is not signed. I have never been able to figure out how someone can sit down and spill out all kinds of abuse at the person being written to and send it off without the guts to sign his or her name. Some people sign their letters with phony names, another form of satisfaction that puzzles me. There is one guy in Montreal who keeps writing me, always signing "J.A. Taylor," but with a different home address on each letter. I answered the first two and my letters came back because of an incorrect address, so I gave up. But he keeps writing and blasting me, every time with a different home address.

A couple of years ago, I received a letter from Halifax. It started out with the line, "It's been two years since I wrote to you and you are an even bigger A.H. now than you were then."

I checked the last page and it wasn't signed. It ran for seven pages and was written entirely in longhand. I assume it got worse after that opening line, but I didn't bother to find out. It quickly went into File 13, where his first letter likely ended up two years earlier.

The American TV personality, Garry Moore, had a formula for answering "bad" letters. He would return the letter with a note enclosed that read, "Some moron is signing your name to hate mail and I'm sure you will want to advise the authorities immediately."

I must confess that I have answered a few as follows:

Dear So and So:

I wish to thank you for your recent letter. It is always a treat to hear from our viewers and I am very appreciative of your interest in my career.

Yours truly,

I like to imagine that my correspondent gets very excited when he, or she, sees that I have answered. Then I try to imagine how crushed they must be when they open the envelope and read my letter.

Likely, they couldn't care less.

Another mystifying group are those who preface remarks aimed at piercing broadcasters' egos with the line, "I never watch hockey anymore. I lost interest when they expanded the NHL." They then proceed to complain about the game and what they hear on the air. If they "never watch anymore," how is it that they know everything we say?

Some fans also like to catch media types making mistakes. "You said Mike Bossy was a left winger. He plays right wing you know." "Left" likely replaced "right" in the heat of a hectic play-by-play moment; the old slip-of-the-tongue routine. I often answer something like that by claiming, "I did it on purpose."

"Why?"

"Because unless we make mistakes, we never know if anyone is listening. Nobody ever calls when we don't make a mistake."

I doubt if the complainers really believe me, but it does seem to set them back just a bit. And I must admit that, so far, I've never purposely made a mistake just to see if there's anybody out there.

Another interesting source of complaints comes from the athletes themselves. Say nice things about a guy for years and chances are he won't ever acknowledge he knows what you do for a living. But say something he feels is critical of his play and chances are you'll hear from him, or he will hear from his wife.

Sometimes, on the road, a player will confront a writer or broadcaster to complain about something written or said about him in that day's paper or on last night's broadcast.

"How do you know that?" we'll ask.

"I was talking to my wife and she told me," is the usual reply.

The best story I know along these lines was when Jacques

Lemaire, then playing for the Canadiens, told Radio Canada announcer Richard Garneau his family was upset at something Garneau had said about him on a broadcast of a road game the night before. Garneau assured Lemaire he wouldn't say anything to upset his folks during the game to be played that night, in St. Louis, and he didn't. Richard simply didn't mention Lemaire's name during his call of the play by play, not once, even though Jacques took a regular turn on the ice. He got lucky because Lemaire didn't get a scoring point. Back home, Jacques' family must have been wondering why their man wasn't playing. It's something I've been tempted to do a few times on radio shows, but somehow I don't think I'm clever enough, or brave enough, to try it.

While there are listeners and viewers who tag broadcasters with the "homer" label, there are members of the print media who frequently hint that we are something else: incompetent.

Some of my favourite people are newspapermen. I have enjoyed good times and good conversation with Red Fisher, Ian MacDonald, Bert Raymond, and Glenn Cole in Montreal; John Robertson, Frank Orr, and Jim Proudfoot in Toronto; Bob Hughes in Regina; Leo Monohan in Boston; Bob Verdi in Chicago; and Bob Dunn in Vancouver, to name just a few. But sports broadcasters realize some writers don't care all that much for us, our cameras and our microphones. Many still harbour a long-standing feeling that their business came first and we are intruders on their turf.

A few years ago, a Philadelphia columnist, Bill Fleischman, wrote in the *Hockey News* that teams should stop radio and TV reporters from taping answers from players to questions asked by newspapermen. The inference was that we didn't know enough to ask the right questions, relying on newspaper types to do our thinking for us.

Just after the column appeared, I was in Philadelphia and Dan Kelly and I did a combined post-game radio interview with Larry Robinson. Three newspaper reporters were writing down everything Larry said in answer to our questions. They didn't say a word, and when we walked away from Larry, they did too. I wrote a letter to the *Hockey News* in reply to Fleischman's column. I certainly won't deny that what he said does take place. But that incident in Philly showed it can work the other way too, and I pointed this out in my letter. I wondered if they would print it. They did.

William Houston, a hockey reporter for the Toronto *Globe and Mail*, once wrote that "intelligence is not a criterion for working in the broadcast booth." Some American papers now employ full-time TV and radio critics writing exclusively about sports broadcasting and broadcasters, and much of what they pen isn't exactly in the form of rave reviews. Any broadcaster who says this sort of thing doesn't bother him is blowing a bit of smoke. But, as the cliché goes, it comes with the territory.

One of my first confrontations over the "homer" issue was with the Imlachs, Mr. & Mrs. Punch.

Punch Imlach was a good coach, and a good manipulator. Through the glory days of his Maple Leafs Stanley Cup winning teams in the 1960's, he had the newspapermen on the Toronto hockey beat wrapped around his little finger.

The Toronto-Montreal series in 1967 was the first Stanley Cup final I worked for *Hockey Night in Canada*. It opened in Montreal and, after the first game, I was told Mrs. Imlach had called the Forum, from Toronto, to complain that I was too pro-Montreal, and too anti-Maple Leafs.

Before the next game, Red Burnett of the *Toronto Star* told me Punch wanted to see me. I had a pretty good idea it was because of his wife's complaints about my work but, like a dummy, I went to see Punch anyway. Burnett was alongside and when we got there the rest of the Toronto writing fraternity was in a familiar spot – gathered around Imlach. He proceeded to blast and embarrass me pretty thoroughly and the reporters were duly impressed, which was the reason he picked on an unsuspecting greenhorn like me in the first place.

It takes a while, but one does get somewhat accustomed to the knocks from fans and other media types. So now, are we "homers"?

When you are a home-team broadcaster, there is an association between yourself and the club that can be difficult to handle. For many years, I have had the dual role of working both local radio broadcasts and national TV broadcasts of games involving the Montreal Canadiens. Dave Van Horne is in the same position with the Montreal Expos. In Dave's case, he is employed by the ball club. In my case, I am paid by CFCF for my radio games and by *Hockey Night in Canada* for my TV games. The Canadiens have the right to request that I be taken off the shows. They don't pay me, but they have the power to deprive me of my pay cheques. That's what I mean by a situation that can be difficult to handle.

American broadcasters often are out-and-out rooters for their team, especially in baseball. A couple of years ago, one of my colleagues at CFCF, Brian MacGorman, interviewed long-time St. Louis Cardinals broadcaster Jack Buck. Throughout the interview, Buck constantly referred to the Cardinals as "we" and "us." "We're very deep right now in the outfield. I don't think the Expos can catch us. We have more speed on the basepaths than any other team."

Always "we," never the "Cardinals." American broadcasters seem to be able to get away with this sort of thing. I don't think their Canadian counterparts are able to, certainly not to the same degree. I have no positive proof, just a feeling, that fans in this country are quicker to complain about "homer" announcers than fans in the United States. Believe me, there's a lot more cheering in announce booths south of the border.

When the Philadelphia Flyers were known as the Broad Street Bullies, they were a good and controversial hockey team. Their penchant for penalties was well known and if you listened to the broadcasts of their games, you would think that almost every penalty given to the Flyers was undeserved and that every dirty trick the other team pulled went unnoticed. In our business, the Flyers broadcasts were often discussed and many of us felt they were much too "homer" in nature.

The NHL Broadcasters Association holds a meeting each year during the League's summer Congress and, around that time at one of our meetings, some of the boys confronted the Philadelphia broadcasters with the "homer" charge. The Flyers announcers were Gene Hart and Don Earle, who happened to be the President of our Association.

Both men admitted they went overboard on occasion, but claimed they didn't do it on their own. They were employees of the hockey team, not the radio station, and they told us they were ordered to announce the games the way they did.

When I broadcast a Canadiens game on CFCF Radio, I take a somewhat different approach than I do when I am working a CBC telecast that is going to many parts of the country. On radio, I am more folksy and certainly more personal when it comes to the players on the home team. I won't hesitate to call Naslund "Mats," Roy "Patrick," or Smith "Bobby." After all, I travel with the players, know them all, eat the odd breakfast and play the odd golf game with some of them. First names come easy and I think the majority of home-broadcast listeners like to think the announcers are close to the players. And I don't hide the fact that I'm happy when they win. Objective, but happy.

It's different on the telecasts. I still have to come across as someone who is familiar with the home team and my employers expect me to come up with the odd "inside" story based on my close working association with the organization. But I am also aware that I am broadcasting to a national audience. Most of the listeners to the radio shows are Canadiens fans. That might not be the case on the TV side. So I try, on TV, to play it straight down the middle. I may not always succeed, but I try, knowing that people hear what they want to hear no matter how the announcer might say it.

One thing I don't believe in is getting close to players on my home team on a social basis. I know of cases where broadcasters, and writers, have not done a totally honest job of reporting because they let close personal ties get in the way of objectivity. In some cases, a few in my business have used these ties to impress their bosses, arrange it so they can rub shoulders with the stars, hoping it will further their own career. It works sometimes, but not too often.

When Frank Mahovlich played for the Canadiens, our family ended up at the same holiday spot in Jamaica as his family. The kids were about the same age and the ladies, Wilma and Marie, hit it off very nicely. The following season, we socialized a bit with the Big M's and were at their place for dinner during the 1973 Stanley Cup playoffs.

A couple of nights later, at the Forum, Frank overskated the puck in his own zone, in overtime. Rick MacLeish of the Flyers picked it up for a breakaway and scored the game-winning goal. So there I was having to point out that Frank had goofed on the first, second, and third replay of the goal. (The same Frank whose house I had been at for a lovely meal a couple of nights before.) It shouldn't have been a problem for me, but it was and it was a small lesson in the job-versus-socializing department.

"Root, root, root for the home team" is a line from the well-known song about baseball, and many home-team broadcasters in that sport do just that, openly and without apologies. *Hockey Night in Canada* announcers have been accused of the same thing on the theory that we say what our employers tell us to say; that the teams tell them if the announcers don't shape up, then ship them out and get someone else. Not true. At least in my case, not true.

In over twenty years of broadcasting NHL games, I have never been told by anyone, the Canadiens or the people who sign my pay cheque, what I can and cannot say on the air.

While I have been lucky in this regard, some of my fellow broadcasters haven't enjoyed the same freedom. The boys who worked for Jack Kent Cooke when he owned the Los Angeles Kings have some hilarious stories about how the bombastic Mr. Cooke interfered in the radio and TV broadcasts of his team's games. Cooke would be constantly phoning them while the game was going on to complain about things they were and were not saying.

He once wanted the announcers, Bob Miller and Dan Avey, to work sponsor mentions into their play by play. Cooke suggested phrases like, "Marcel Dionne is moving into high gear, just like a Toyota." His radio and TV employees had a tough time keeping straight faces when their boss got off on that kind of tangent.

When I began working for *Hockey Night in Canada*, I fully expected to be given strict rules about what to say on the air. I'm still waiting. Obviously, you have to use your head and not go off half-cocked, raving and ranting just to impress your audience. When it comes to what I've been saying on the air for over twenty years, I like to think the magic phrase is "common sense." In my business, those who have operated in this fashion have lasted the longest.

It isn't always fans who write letters who take shots at us. Brian McFarlane tells a story about when he was working as the colour commentator at Maple Leaf Gardens. One night, he was on his way downstairs from the gondola when he heard a fan come up with one of the great put-downs of all time.

"McFarlane," he yelled, "you're the reason I come to the games. It's better than staying home listening to you."

One of the best zingers fired at me came from a youngster who asked for an autograph outside the Forum after the Canadiens had been eliminated from the 1987 playoffs by the Philadelphia Flyers. It had been a long, emotional night that started with an ugly brawl during the pre-game warm-up. After ninety-six broadcasts, I had reached the end of another long season.

The autograph seeker was ten or eleven years old, cute as a button, with an Expos cap perched on the back of his head. When I returned his pencil and paper, he looked up at me with his big baby blues.

"You're a good announcer," he said. "But you're so biased."

Just what I needed after ninety-six games.

The Fans Provide Some Thrills

Jimmy Cannon was a highly respected sports writer in New York and had a great answer for anyone who wondered why he worked at his particular trade. He always replied, "Where else can you make your living at a place where everyone is having a good time?"

Cannon was talking about the paying customers at sports events, the fans. As one saying goes, without fans there wouldn't be any games.

During my travels, the athletes have provided the majority of my high moments, but I must say those same paying customers Jimmy Cannon had such respect for have provided a few as well. One night in Denver, Colorado, was one of the best.

In early February of 1980, the Canadiens played against the Colorado Rockies at the McNichols Arena. A few days earlier, members of the Canadian Embassy in Iran had been instrumental in the escape of some of the Americans being held hostage in the midst of that very serious international crisis. I was on the air with my pre-game show on CFCF Radio and the players were lining up across the blue line for the national anthems. There was an announcement being made over the public address system, and I barely caught a few words, when suddenly the fans erupted with a tremendous cheer and a standing ovation.

"Ladies and gentlemen," the announcer said, "the management of the Colorado Rockies would like to take this opportunity to thank our visitors from Canada. . . ."

That was when the standing ovation began. The fans knew what he was talking about and didn't wait for him to finish before reacting. They weren't cheering the Montreal Canadiens. They were cheering Canada – and what a cheer it was. I let it go over the air without trying to interrupt. It lasted for over a minute. I started to talk as the cheering was subsiding, but I was choked up, and needed a couple of deep breaths to get myself together. I was told by people who were listening that it was obvious I had been affected by what happened.

Two nights later, the Canadiens played the Kings in Los Angeles. As the players were lining up for the anthems, the PA announcer at the L.A. Forum started to make the same announcement and the reaction from the fans was exactly the same: as in Denver, a long, loud standing ovation for Canada. My reaction was the same too.

During one of the intermissions that night, I interviewed Canadian actor Larry D. Mann, who is well known as the "boss" in the telephone TV commercials, and who is a regular at Kings' home games. Larry and I get together every season and he makes his predictions about the next Academy Awards. Before I started asking him about the movie business, Larry summed things up for both of us with respect to the standing O.

"Let me just say that when this game began I was truly proud to be a Canadian," Larry said. I obviously seconded that motion.

The game of hockey hasn't become boffo at the box office in the area of Hollywood, California, nor was it in Oakland where the Seals had a rather short life. Jack Kent Cooke,

DICK IRWIN.

Dad's first hockey card, Regina Caps, 1922. Seems they had trouble with the spelling and the printing.

Dad and his father, Jimmy Irvin—then sixty-two years old—wearing Portland Rosebuds' sweaters, 1925.

The Allan Cup Champion Winnipeg Monarchs, 1915, with motorcycles given to them by the City of Winnipeg. Dad is fourth from the right, Uncle Alex, third from the left.

Dick Irvin, first captain of the Chicago Black Hawks, 1926. (*Hockey Hall of Fame*.)

The Ripley cartoon featuring Dad's nine goals in one game. They got his goal total right, but it wasn't a shut-out game. (© 1930 Ripley International Inc., a Registered Trademark.)

Dad's first year coaching in the NHL, with the 1930-31 Black Hawks and the eccentric owner of the team, Major Frederic McLaughlin.

The sartorially elegant 1930-31 Chicago Black Hawks at Windsor Station in Montreal, complete with Al Capone-style fedoras.

Conn Smythe greets Dad in the dressing room after having hired him to coach the Toronto Maple Leafs (November, 1931). (*Hockey Hall of Fame.*)

Mother, my sister Fay, and I at a game in Maple Leaf Gardens (January 2, 1943).

The Toronto Maple Leafs visit a pipe-making factory, circa 1933.

Dad's first season with the Canadiens and my first time on the ice at the Forum. The player is Jack Portland. It was Christmas, 1940.

The Canadiens sport their red "fire hats" after someone threatened to burn down the Forum if they didn't fire Dad. It was 1947-48, his first year out of the playoffs.

Gaston Bettez, the Canadien's trainer who replaced "Irvin's hatchet man," The Rocket, for a pre-game skate in Detroit. You certainly don't see pranks like this anymore.

In between seasons, back in Regina, Dad rarely strayed from his beloved racing pigeons, which he raised as a hobby (circa 1948).

Dad, Frank Selke Sr., and Elmer Lach. Lach was always one of Dad's favourite players.

Dad always said The Rocket played his best games when is hair stood on end. Judging by their smiles, and the hair, he must have had a good one. (*David Bier*.)

Dad coached the All-Star team in the first official All-Star game, Toronto, October 13, 1947. Fourteen men in this picture are now in the Hockey Hall of Fame. (*Hockey Hall of Fame.*)

An eighteen-year-old University of Saskatchewan student in awe of his hockey hero, Rocket Richard, who had just scored two goals against the Detroit Red Wing (December, 1950).

The Rocket, with the best punch in hockey, KO's Bill Juzda. The shocked referee is Bill Chadwick (October, 1951). (*David Bier.*)

Floyd Curry, Ken Mosdell, Tom Johnson, and Calum McKay of the Canadiens lift Dad on their shoulders after Elmer Lach's Stanley Cup winning goal at the Forum in 1953. (*Canada Wide*.)

Frank Selke Sr. and Dick Irvin Sr. share their last Stanley Cup, 1953. (*David Bier*.)

Dad in the Canadien's dressing room during the 1947-48 season with one of the Miniature Pinscher dogs he raised as a hobby. Leo Lameroux is in the background.

The Rocket, Frank Selke Sr., Dad, and Butch Bouchard in Detroit during the 1954 playoffs. (*Ray Glonka.*)

Fay and I, with Dad and Mother, looking over the old scrapbook after we have moved to Montreal during the early fifties.

Dad with what was left of the tear gas bomb that exploded the night of the Richard Riot, March 17, 1955. (*David Bier*.)

Maurice Richard presents Mother with a trophy in honour of his 500th career goal. He dedicated the goal to Dad, who had passed away a few months before (November, 1957).

Dad's last season coaching was in 1955-56 with the Chicago Black Hawks.

One of my biggest moments in hockey: celebrating with my Bantam team after they won the Provincial Championship in 1961.

I was as nervous as I looked for my first big-name golfer interview, Cary Player, at the 1962 Canadian Open. (*CFCF*.)

Brian McFarlane and I host Toe Blake on the fancy set of the *Sportsman's Club* when he was coaching the Canadiens in 1962. (*CFCF*.)

With Brian McFarlane and boxer Archie Moore in my early days at CFCF. This was the night I thought old Archie was going to break my arm. (*CFCF*.)

Presenting Jean Béliveau with the tape of my radio play by play of his 500th career goal (February, 1971). (*CFCF*.)

With Ralph Mellanby and Brian McFarlane on the set of *Hockey Night in Canada* at the Forum during my early days with the show.

The only time I had a serious case of sweaty palms on TV was when I interviewed Bob Hope at the Forum (April, 1976). (*Hockey Night in Canada*.)

Working the booth with Danny Gallivan.

The Danny and Dick Show at the Forum. (*Bellemare*.)

Doing the play by play with Scotty Bowman as my colour commentator. (*David Bier*.)

Interviewing the Firth Twins at the 1976 Winter Olympics in Austria. They thought I was Howie Meeker.

Scotty Bowman, the coach who broke Dad's record, joins the crew of *Hockey Night in Canada* (October, 1987). (*David Bier*.)

Don Cherry is "on," even at lunchtime at the Texan, a restaurant across the street from the Forum. Jean Béliveau is in the next booth. (*George Adamakos*.)

A formal moment with NHL President John Zeigler (centre), Lionel Duval of Radio Canada, and the Stanley Cup. Lionel and I MC'd the NHL Awards ceremony in Montreal.

Two chaps from Saskatchewan get together on CFCF's *Hockey Magazine*. The one on the right is a fellow called Gordie Howe. (*CFCF*.)

The two players who gave me the most hockey thrills: Rocket Richard and Guy Lafleur.

Maureen McTeer and I presented the "Coach of the Year" trophy at the NHL Awards show on CBC in 1984. (*Action Photographics Inc.*)

Mike Barnett of CorpSport International flanked by two of his clients. I think he does more business with the kid on the left than with the older guy on the right.

With Hall-of-Famers Bobby Orr, Jean Béliveau, Yvan Cournoyer, and one of Bobby's friends and admirers at the 1987 Skate-A-Thon in aid of Bobby's favourite cause: the Society for Disabled Children.

The *Hockey Night in Canada* crew before the Stanley Cup final game in Calgary in 1986. Left to right: Don Wittman, Dave Hodge, Producer John Shannon, John Davidson, and the announcer who got soaked with champagne after the game.

the ex-Canadian who was the original owner of the Kings, made a famous crack about lack of hockey interest in sunny California.

"There are 500,000 Canadians living in this area," Cooke said. "Now I know why they moved here. They wanted to get away from hockey." But those who do attend the games seem to have a good time. It's always fun to be at the L.A. Forum in mid-February and see people wearing Bermuda shorts at a hockey game.

When the Seals were in Oakland, a group of Hell's Angels attended games during the team's early years. They had seats right behind the glass, but when they tried scaling the glass when fights broke out on the ice, they were asked to move elsewhere in the Oakland Alameda Coliseum. The Angels didn't agree – and the Seals lost a faithful group of paying customers.

Oakland was where I actually saw the home-team goal-tender receive a standing ovation after letting in two goals late in a game as his team blew a lead. Gilles Meloche was the goaltender and the Canadiens were bombarding him from every angle. Meloche was acrobatically brilliant and halfway through the third period, despite being outshot 35-12, the Seals were still leading 2-0.

The Canadiens finally got on the board when Yvan Cournoyer scored. A couple of minutes later, the Seals defence collapsed and Cournoyer scored again, on a breakaway.

That's when the fans took over. Their appreciation for the beleaguered netminder slowly grew from polite applause to a standing ovation for his one-man stand. I was glad the game ended 2-2. Gilles deserved the ovation and at least a tie on the scoreboard.

Yvan Cournoyer was involved in another California story that didn't have a happy ending for one paying customer. One night in Los Angeles, Cournoyer had several good scoring chances but had drawn a blank. After one of his near misses, Jean Béliveau offered him some advice.

"You're shooting too low," Big Jean told him. "Shoot higher on this guy."

On his next shift, Yvan had a clear break in from the blue line and blasted a shot that was higher than his previous efforts. Too high. The puck sailed over the goal, over the glass, and struck a member of the U.S. Navy who was seated in the end zone. The poor sailor got it right on the noggin and had to be taken to the L.A. Forum clinic to get patched up. Cournoyer skated back to the Canadiens' bench.

"Was that high enough?" he asked Béliveau.

One of the best fan-related lines I've heard was delivered at the 1974 All-Star dinner in Chicago. For many years during the glory days of Bobby Hull, Stan Mikita, and company in Chicago, a big hockey joke was the Hawks' nightly announced attendance figure of 16,666. That was the limit allowed in the Stadium under the existing fire regulations, but everyone knew they were packing close to 20,000 fans into the old place anyway. Chicago was run in those days by "The Boss," Mayor Richard Daley, and he was at the head table at the All-Star dinner. The owner of the Black Hawks, Bill Wirtz, was one of the speakers.

"We welcome our visitors to a great city," he said. "We have a great team. We have a great Mayor. And we certainly have a great Fire Commissioner!"

On the other hand, when I saw my first game at the Montreal Forum on December 21, 1940 (Canadiens 3, Boston 1), there were a lot of empty seats – something that hasn't been the case in that building for well over forty years. Fans can be a big part of the show at a sporting event, and fans at the Forum through the years certainly fall into that category.

In polls taken of NHL players, the answer to the question "Where are the fans the most knowledgeable?" is almost always Montreal. But in recent years, I get the feeling that the atmosphere in the building isn't quite as serious as it once was. There seems to be a different ambiance, for whatever reason. Maybe the fans as a whole are younger. Maybe it's the organ (which no announcer in his right mind is a friend of) that gets them worked up, along with the fairly new computerized scoreboard that urges them to do the wave, or "MAKE NOISE."

The Canadiens have a lot going for them when it comes to tradition, with pictures of the team's past heroes on the dressing-room wall under the slogan, "TO YOU WE THROW THE TORCH," and a long line of Stanley Cup pennants hanging above their heads every time they practise or play at the Forum. But their fans, spoiled by success and demanding still more, play a part in it too. Former Canadien Réjean Houle told me the worst thing about not winning the Stanley Cup in Montreal is spending the summer constantly having to answer the question, "Why didn't you win the Stanley Cup?" The players are, after a fashion, frightened of fans, afraid of what their reaction might be should the wheels come off for a period exceeding two weeks. Forum fans help the Canadiens play good hockey, there's no doubt about that.

When he was coaching the Bruins, Don Cherry used to moan that the visiting team was down 1-0 before a game at the Forum even started. I like to kid him that, judging by his record there, he must have been right.

Among those of us who travel with the Montreal Canadiens, the most talked-about fans are in the West where some nights you would swear the Canadiens were the home team. There have been times when I have felt sorry for the Canucks in Vancouver and the Jets in Winnipeg, home teams that were actually being treated like visitors. The cheers for the Canadiens and chants of "Go Habs, Go" are long, loud, and continue almost from start to finish of the game, especially if the Canadiens are winning.

Canadiens' defenceman Petr Svoboda received a ten-minute misconduct penalty one night in Winnipeg. It happened with about five minutes to play in the second period, so Svoboda was sent to the dressing room. The game was tied 3-3 when he left the ice. A minute or so later, as he sat alone in the room, a big cheer went up inside the Arena.

"The Jets have scored," Petr said to himself.

Another minute went by and an even bigger cheer erupted. Now, Svoboda was really upset. There he was, banished, while his mates were falling behind.

"I wanted to hide in a corner when they came in the room," he told me. "But when they got there, I found out we had scored the two goals, not Winnipeg. I couldn't believe it."

Some individual fans have gained notoriety. One of the first was the chap at Maple Leaf Gardens whose cry "Come on Teeder" would boom through the building when Ted "Teeder" Kennedy was a star for the Leafs in the late forties and early fifties.

In Montreal, during the 1970's and the early 1980's, there was "Dutchy," who really was a Dutchman working for a company that imported cheese from Holland. Dutchy and his megaphone became well known at the Forum, and on *HNIC*, with his "Go Habs, Go" chant. In those days, he didn't have to battle an organist pounding on the keys the minute play stopped the way it is done now. (Some fans joke that Danny Gallivan actually retired as a form of surrender to the Forum organist.) Dutchy and his pals had a special standing-room area blocked off for their personal use and no one dared take it away from them. He used to say his dream was to be buried under the centre-ice face-off circle at the Forum.

A few years ago, Dutchy had a disagreement with the Forum's brass, and disappeared from the scene. But when they found themselves down 3-1 to the Boston Bruins in the 1988 Adams Division final series, the Canadiens figured they needed all the help they could get. So, on the night of the fifth game of the series, Dutchy was back in the Forum. It was like old times as he paraded around in his Canadiens sweater, megaphone at the ready, bellowing his familiar version of "Go Habs, Go." It didn't work. The Bruins won the game and the Canadiens were out of the playoffs.

Alongside Dutchy for many years was the guy with the

bugle, leading the way for the rest of the crowd to yell, "CHARGE." He was an RCMP officer who once refused a transfer to another city rather than give up the chance to blow his bugle at Canadien home games.

One of the stars of the show at the Spectrum, in Philadelphia, is the "sign man." He's the guy who sits behind the net defended by the visiting team in the first and third periods and holds up professionally printed signs to tie in with what is happening on the ice. "OUTTA SIGHT" is one of his familiar ones, used when the Flyers score or when their goalie makes a big save. Now, here's a secret: I've known him to be included in some of our HNIC pre-game meetings during the playoffs in Philly, so that he and the producers can get in sync about what signs he has ready for the game and when he plans to use them. If you wonder why the camera just happens to be pointing at the right sign at the right time, now you know.

Fans in all sports like to make signs to hang from the rafters or balconies and some of the best in hockey used to be in Buffalo. Pierre Larouche played his first game for the Canadiens there after he was traded to Montreal from Pittsburgh. There was a sign waiting for him at the Auditorium: "THE LAST TIME LAROUCHE BACKCHECKED HIS PEEWEE COACH FAINTED." Even Pierre was laughing as his new mates pointed it out to him during the warm-up.

My all-time favourite sign surfaced in Buffalo during the 1975 Stanley Cup final between the Sabres and Philadelphia. That was the series in which they played the "Fog Bowl" in Buffalo, on a night when hot, humid weather conditions produced foggy patches at ice level. That same night, a non-paying spectator, a bat, arrived on the scene and swooped about close to the ice. It put on quite a show until Jim Lorentz of the Sabres scored a direct hit with his hockey stick and the bat was no more. From then on Jim had the obvious nickname of "Bat Man."

During that era, the Flyers were making quite a show of singer Kate Smith and her stirring rendition of *God Bless America* before home games at the Philadelphia Spectrum.

The hype involved when Kate appeared in person was incredible. So the sign makers in Buffalo grabbed the opportunity to combine that with the Lorentz bat incident. When the teams skated out for their next game in Buffalo, my all-time favourite sign was there.

"THE FLYERS HAVE KATE SMITH AND WE HAVE AN OLD BAT TOO."

That one is tough to top.

There are times when it's obvious fans don't pay too much attention to what the media are saying, or writing. For example, the Toronto Maple Leafs had a wretched 1987-88 season. But even though they won just twenty times in their first seventy-nine games, the Leafs still had a chance to make the playoffs as they played Detroit in their final game of the season, in Toronto. The Leafs fell behind early, 3-0, then came back with what likely was their best forty minutes of hockey all year, and won the game 5-3. The capacity crowd in the Gardens went wild. The team had been battered from pillar to post by newshounds in Toronto, and elsewhere, and with good reason. Yet in that one last night of victory, the paying customers couldn't have cared less about the shortcomings of the team and the Leafs organization that had been laid bare to the public for weeks on end.

People who were there told me, "You'd swear they had just won the Stanley Cup." Which goes to prove that in hockey, as in all sports, the game is the thing.

I have attended two hockey games when the fans caused an early end to the proceedings. The most famous of course was the Richard Riot at the Forum, in Montreal. But I had gone through a similar experience eight years before in Regina.

In 1947, the Memorial Cup Final was played in the West between the Toronto St. Mike's and the Moose Jaw Canucks. Toronto had a powerful team and several of its players, including Red Kelly, Fleming Mackell, and Ed Sandford, were playing in the NHL the following season.

Toronto easily won the first two games. Game Three was played on a Saturday night before a capacity crowd at Queen City Gardens in Regina. The underdog Canucks started well, but a series of penalties led to goals by Toronto and the fans were in an ugly mood.

Late in the second period, another Moose Jaw penalty was the last straw. Somebody threw a bottle on the ice. That was quickly followed by another and another, and soon a bottle barrage was on.

Joe Primeau was coaching St. Mike's. Primeau had played for Dad in Toronto and had gotten front row tickets for Mother and me. As the bottles kept coming, I quickly began to feel we were far too close to the action.

"Let's get out of here," I said to Mother.

"Sit still," she sharply admonished her trembling fifteen-year-old son. "I'm not moving!"

Al Pickard, who had been the principal of Davin School when I was in kindergarten, was president of the C.A.H.A. He tried to calm the crowd over the PA system.

"If there are any more objects thrown onto the ice, the game will be forfeited to the Eastern team," he proclaimed.

By this time, some of the players, including Fleming Mackell, had taken refuge inside the goal nets. Pickard's warning had no effect.

Zingo! Down came another bottle. Game over and everyone went home. I was glad, but I think Mother was sorry to see it end. She had been having a great time.

My greatest moment as far as fans are concerned was the All-Star game in Detroit, February 5, 1980. The game marked the opening of the Joe Louis Arena, and drew a record NHL crowd of 21,002.

That season, Gordie Howe had come back to the National League to play for the Hartford Whalers at the age of fifty-one. From the standpoint of nostalgia and memories, it had been a triumphant return, and of course no city had memories of Gordie to match those he had left behind in Detroit. There was unanimous agreement amongst hockey officials and fans when he was named to the Wales Conference team for the All-Star game.

They played his appearance to the hilt. All the players skated out to polite applause, but you knew the record crowd was waiting for the legendary Number 9. He was the last player to be introduced and was greeted by what will surely stand as the loudest, longest ovation in hockey history. Everyone was on their feet, including all of us in the media section, as the cheers kept cascading down in an emotional outpouring of respect and love for a man who had done so much for his game. The ovation lasted almost five minutes.

I worked on the *Hockey Night in Canada* telecast that night. When the game was over, Joe Falls, a fine sports columnist in Detroit and a good buddy, spoke to me in the press room.

"What did you guys say?" he asked. I knew he meant when Gordie's salute was going on.

"Nothing," I replied.

"Good," said Joe. "There wasn't anything you could say."

Moments like that one, and many others, prove Jimmy Cannon was right. We are lucky to be making a living this way.

· · · · · · · · · · · · · · · · · · · ·
Jocks in the Booth

"*W*hat do you think of ex-athletes in the broadcast booth?" My answer to that often-asked question is that I have no quarrel with the idea. The only thing I ask of former players and coaches who join the broadcasting fraternity is that they do their homework. I have seen some succeed because they were willing to work hard and learn the business. I have seen others fall by the wayside because they felt their name was all they needed.

When jocks go on the air, they should be able to tell the listeners and viewers more about their sport than announcers who have never played the game. Some do, and some don't.

In Canada, we have been pretty well served. I thought Leo Cahill and Russ Jackson did excellent work as colour commentators on CBC football shows, telling me things I otherwise would not have known or spotted. That's the main job of ex-athletes on air and if they work at it, and are informative, then more to the good.

Jocks can talk. I get upset when I hear the CBC Radio *Air Farce* routine with Dave Broadfoot and the interview with the dumb hockey player, Bobby Clobber. They paint every player with the same brush, and it's way off the mark considering today's athletes.

Certainly not all athletes give good interviews. Neither do a lot of doctors, lawyers, politicians, and even radio comedians. But most hockey players handle themselves very well in front of a camera or microphone. Denis Potvin, Bob Gainey, Doug Risebrough, Mike Gartner, and Chico Resch are just a few of the players who have come straight off the ice and into the intermission studio to give thoughtful, intelligent answers to my questions. I'd like to see some of the people who make fun of player interviews come out of a pressure cooker like an NHL game played in front of 18,000 screaming people and be as calm, collected, and intelligent with a coast-to-coast TV audience watching.

I am amazed at how cool some players are in tough situations. In 1980, the Minnesota North Stars eliminated the Montreal Canadiens from the playoffs in a bitterly fought seven-game series. The clincher was played at the Forum where the outstanding player was Minnesota goalie Gilles Meloche. Meloche was brilliant in the final hectic moments as he preserved a one-goal win for his team. Then he came directly off the ice into our studio. There was a delay before we went on the air, so we sat and chatted. I couldn't believe how composed he was. You'd think he had just dropped in after a leisurely walk to the corner store.

The opposite also happens. During the 1967 playoffs, my first year on HNIC, John Ferguson scored the series-winning goal, in overtime, against the Rangers, in New York. I interviewed Fergy when he came off the ice. When he sat down, he was so hyper he had trouble getting his breath. I tried talking with him before we went on the air, but all I got in return was a lot of deep breathing and stares from a wild-looking pair of eyes.

Finally we got the standby to get ready and, frankly, I wasn't too thrilled with the idea.

"You OK?" I asked him.

In return I got a grunt, a nod of his head, and more gasping for air. We got the cue and I asked the first question, terrified Fergy would answer with more of the same. But he managed to croak out some noise and the words started to come. The viewers got a good look at John Ferguson, tough competitor. But not before *HNIC*'s rookie interviewer got one of the big frights of his broadcasting career.

Several of the biggest names in hockey have worn *HNIC* blue jackets and the biggest provided me with one of my most amusing moments in the booth. Unfortunately, it was one I couldn't share with the viewers. It concerned one of the most courageous plays I've ever seen in hockey, one that happened in an All-Star game, where the intensity level normally ranges from ho to hum.

The 1972 All-Star game was played at the Sports Center in Bloomington, Minnesota, home of the North Stars. At that time, it was the East against the West. Late in the third period, with the East leading 3-2, Bobby Hull, playing for the West, unleashed a slap shot from the East blue line.

Now remember, this was an All-Star game and nobody would have thought anything of it had the members of the East team all moved to one side and let their goaltender worry about a booming Bobby Hull slap shot. But that didn't happen because the shot was blocked by a defenceman who threw his body at the puck. Chap by the name of Bobby Orr.

I was working the telecast with Bill Hewitt. The way I saw it when it happened, and again on the replay, the puck struck Orr smack in the middle of one of his much-talked-about knees that even then were starting to hinder the career of the player many call the greatest of all time.

Orr crawled on his hands and knees to the bench, and you can imagine how the Boston Bruins brass was feeling.

So Orr was through for the few minutes that remained in the game, right? Wrong.

With the seconds ticking down, and the West goaltender pulled, there was Orr, back on the ice, helping preserve a victory that nobody cared about in the first place.

Six years later, Bobby, retired as a player, was in the television booth with me and Danny Gallivan working the

1978 All-Star game in Buffalo. The game was held up because of an injury, so I started to tell the story of Bobby's big play in Bloomington.

"Bobby, I know you'll be embarrassed by what I'm about to say," I began, "but . . ." and then launched into a description of his gallantry in shaking off what looked like a serious blow to a tender knee and all that.

When I finished, Bobby mumbled, "Thanks, Dick," and at that moment I was told to give the commercial cue, "This All-Star game is coming to you from Buffalo."

While the commercial was rolling, Bobby took off his microphone, leaned over to me, and whispered, "Wasn't the knee. Puck hit me right in the crown jewels."

When you're the best hockey player of your time, you should be able to talk knowledgeably about your sport and, despite his own opinion that he wasn't able to do that, Bobby Orr was a great TV analyst.

Had he been able to work only in the booth, I think Bobby would have lasted a lot longer than he did with *Hockey Night in Canada*. What he didn't like was appearing on camera. After all his years in the spotlight, he was still painfully shy. As a player, he was famous for avoiding the media. He wasn't a good interview. At trophy-award functions, he would struggle through a brief speech to the effect "I want to thank my teammates for making this possible," and not much else.

Perhaps he was too protected by the people managing his affairs. While he was with *Hockey Night in Canada*, I arranged for Orr to appear at the annual Montreal Sports Celebrity Dinner. I had to go through Alan Eagleson's office. At that time Orr and the Eagle were in business. I was assured Bobby would attend the dinner, but under no circumstances would he speak. Leaning on my recently acquired friendship with him through HNIC, I asked him to help us make a presentation to former NHL President Clarence Campbell, also a Head-Table guest. Bobby readily agreed, and he said all the right things.

During his short time on *Hockey Night in Canada*, Bobby Orr was, understandably, the Number One celebrity on the show. His name was magic, his presence rather awesome.

The night after his appearance at the Celebrity Dinner, we opened the telecast at ice level, near the "Zamboni entrance" as it's called. It's never my favourite spot to go on camera. The fact that a couple of million people are watching the show doesn't bother me. But I am never comfortable in an arena with the TV lights turned on, a camera pointing, and a few thousand people in the building looking at me, live, with the morbid fascination the public seems to have when someone is doing something on TV.

I have opened shows there dozens of times with some very well-known personalities. But I have never experienced the scene that developed that night. Suddenly, every photographer and his camera in the Forum were clicking and whirring away. It also seemed that every fan who had come to the game with a Nikon or an Instamatic was there too. And believe me folks, they weren't there to take my picture. Every other time I've stood there, I've never heard a camera click or seen a flashbulb pop.

That night was a different story. Bobby Orr was there.

Another time when Orr worked a TV game at the Forum, we had to be in the studio in the middle of the afternoon for some taping. When we were finished, we went out for a pre-game meal with Red Fisher. We were headed for the Texan Restaurant, a walk of about two minutes under normal conditions. Red and I have walked there many times, always in two minutes. That afternoon it took closer to fifteen by the time Bobby had satisfied all the autograph seekers.

Earlier in the day, Bobby had phoned me at home to go over pronunciations of certain names. He was especially concerned with Jocelyn Guevremont who was playing that night. Good as he was as an analyst, pronunciations were a hang-up with him. When we worked the three-game NHL-

Soviet Challenge Cup Series in New York in 1979, where he did a brilliant job as the analyst, Bobby would call my hotel room two or three times a day to go over the hard-to-pronounce Soviet line-up.

Jocelyn Guevremont's appearance at the Forum that particular Saturday night coincided with Bobby Orr's last game as a TV analyst. They asked him to go downstairs to the studio during the first intermission. So there he was again, on camera, just where he didn't want to be. But when you are Bobby Orr, your TV bosses want you to be more than just a voice. Despite Bobby's obvious desire to be just a voice, you can understand why the brass felt differently.

That night we paid tribute to his election to the Hockey Hall of Fame the previous summer. They ran a film clip of his acceptance speech at the Hall of Fame Dinner. Looking at it, you saw a young man who seemed happy and relaxed at the podium, making a joke or two and, again, saying all the right things. Maybe that's the way you and I saw it, but that's not how Orr saw it. "I hate doing that, just hate it," Bobby said as we watched the studio monitor.

It certainly didn't look that way, but that's how he felt. As it turned out, a few days later, he wrote *Hockey Night in Canada* to thank them for the association. Thanks, but no thanks. It was a letter of resignation.

If Bobby Orr had difficulty relating to announcers and cameras in the TV business, he certainly doesn't have the same problem with disabled children.

He now does a lot of work in this important field and it is heartwarming to watch him at skating parties and other functions designed to raise money for the kids. He is marvellous with the youngsters. He seems to know every one by name, how to talk and deal with them, and they love him in return. In their hearts he is still Bobby Orr, Number 4 – the greatest of them all.

Bobby Orr may have been shy in front of the *HNIC* cameras, but that certainly hasn't been the case with the show's two most colourful and controversial performers, Howie Meeker and Don Cherry.

I was the first *Hockey Night in Canada* announcer to introduce Howie Meeker as our game analyst, something an unsuspecting nation wasn't quite ready for. It was during the mid-70's, when the between-period analyzing in Montreal was done in the broadcast booth. A TV monitor was built into a wall behind the booth and that's where we saw the replays during the intermission interviews.

Howie and Bob Goldham were the first to handle the job on a regular basis. During my early years on the show, a variety of former players and media men did the analyzing. A few like Donnie Marshall, Dickie Moore, and Red Fisher performed well on a semi-regular basis. Then Toronto discovered Goldie, who had a laid-back, folksy style, while in Montreal Ralph Mellanby discovered Howie, whose style was anything but folksy and laid back.

Right from the start Howie was Howie, which meant he was different. In the first intermission of the first game he worked, he pointed out a mistake by a defenceman that led to a goal.

"You don't do that!" Howie screeched. "You just don't do that!" Viewers weren't accustomed to analysts, or colour men, saying that kind of thing in that tone of voice. And they certainly weren't accustomed to seeing them bounce up and down on a stool at the same time.

Howie wasn't using his famous phrase, "Stop it right there," on that first night. But he laid into the players with some criticism, something the show's knockers had long claimed wasn't being done often enough. Along with it, Howie peppered his comments with "Meeker-isms" such as "Gee Whillickers" and "Gollie Gee," sayings that were soon being mimicked.

HNIC quickly learned there was no middle ground when it came to public acceptance of Howie. Viewers either liked him or didn't like him. His fans appreciated his freshness and enthusiasm. His detractors called him "corny" and an "actor."

Among those who felt uneasy about his work were the people managing the Montreal Canadiens. They, like other hockey types, weren't ready to totally accept his up-front style of pointing out mistakes their players were making. But they tolerated his presence on Montreal telecasts, until one fateful night when Howie came up with a familiar problem in broadcasting – a slip of the tongue.

The Canadiens felt that Howie, with his background as a player and coach with the Toronto Maple Leafs, had blue and white closer to his heart than red, white, and blue. During a Canadiens-Leafs game at the Forum, Howie referred to the Leafs as "we." I cringed. I knew there would be trouble.

At the Canadiens' practice the next morning, Scotty Bowman called to me from the ice.

"Did you hear Howie Meeker last night?" he asked, knowing full well I had because I was the guy who had interviewed him. The phone was hot between the Forum and the HNIC offices in Toronto that same day. Howie rarely worked games in Montreal after that.

There was a time when Howie Meeker seemed like a hockey industry in this country, with schools, toys, equipment, and sundry other items carrying his name. I always felt it was a just reward for someone who loves hockey the way he does.

When Howie raves about a great play, he is truly enthused. When he laments about a bad one, he is truly dismayed. He wants to see hockey played at its best as much as possible, because that makes him as happy as possible.

Howie has had an interesting life. He played and coached in the NHL, was a member of Parliament, moved from Newfoundland to Vancouver Island, and at one time raised pigeons as a hobby.

"Wish I'd thought of that when I was coaching," he said to me when I told him how Dad would compare his hockey players to his racing pigeons. In both sports there were some who performed best when the conditions were toughest, with a strong team or a stiff wind against them. Others were at their best only when the other team was weak, or the wind was at their backs. That was one of Dad's theories, and Howie wholeheartedly agreed.

During an interview for CFCF's *Hockey Magazine* program, I asked Howie which part of his career he had enjoyed the most.

"Playing," was his emphatic reply. "When you have played a good game, and your team has won, it's the greatest feeling in the world."

Normally, that would sound corny. Coming from Howie Meeker, it was sincere.

Don Cherry has never met a television camera he didn't like, but the first time I interviewed him on *HNIC*, I was surprised he showed up in the studio. He was coaching the Boston Bruins and was booked for the second intermission. When Don coached the Bruins, they rarely won in Montreal, and that night his team was in another deep Forum freeze, trailing 6-0 at the end of the second period.

Hockey Night in Canada employs a man who brings intermission guests into the studio, and I was sure Don was going to tell him what to do with the interview. We have had "no shows" for lesser reasons than a coach refusing to come on with his team trailing by six goals.

But in he came and down he sat, nostrils flaring slightly and obviously in much distress. I knew the questions I had prepared were of no use, especially the first one, which I had noted on a piece of paper: "Get opinion of first two periods."

So I set aside my trusty clipboard and started from scratch.

"I know the fans out there would like to hear your opinions of some players in the NHL" was my opener. I then named some names – Bryan Trottier, Denis Potvin, Mike Bossy, Guy Lafleur, and about a half dozen more. Don had something to say about each one, but he wasn't the fiery, bouncy Don Cherry viewers see today, and he certainly wasn't a barrel of laughs with his team down by six.

Don's daughter, Cindy, was in the studio and sat behind the camera during the interview. When we were off the air, I thanked the beleaguered Bruin coach for honouring his commitment, considering the situation on the scoreboard.

"I promised her she could come and watch," Don replied, nodding toward Cindy. "Otherwise you wouldn't have seen me in here."

Not too many NHL coaches have gone out of their way to help entertain the fans. Morrie Kalin, who has had season tickets just behind the visitors' bench at the Forum since the 1940's, told me he can recall only three, Dad, Punch Imlach, and Don Cherry, who tried to put some fun into some games. The rest, says Morrie, "act like robots."

My favourite Punch Imlach story in this regard was provided by the goaltending Dryden brothers, Ken and Dave. Punch was a good showman and did his best to give the paying customers a show one night at the Forum when he was coaching the Buffalo Sabres in their first season, 1970–71.

Ken had just been called up by the Canadiens from their American League farm team. Ken's older brother, Dave, was a goaltender with the Sabres. When Buffalo came to Montreal for a game on March 20, Imlach told everyone it was going to be a historic night in the NHL because, for the first time, brothers would be the opposing starting goaltenders.

Imlach had the right idea. However, in those days the Montreal Canadiens didn't lead the League when it came to providing their fans with something out of the ordinary to help them get their money's worth. When the game began, much to Imlach's chagrin and the fans' disappointment, the Canadiens had Roggie Vachon in goal and Ken Dryden on the bench as his back-up. Imlach started Dave Dryden, but removed him during the first stoppage in play and replaced him with Joe Daley. The fans were being cheated, until fate intervened. (Or was it the Unseen Hand?)

At 13:07 of the second period, Vachon fell down to make a save and didn't get up. He had suffered a groin injury. So while the Canadiens were helping him limp off the ice, their coach, Al MacNeil, had no choice but to send the younger Dryden brother into the net. At the same time, Imlach was also changing goaltenders. Punch had a feel for some hockey history – not to mention a bit of show business. So Ken got to play against Dave (the younger Dryden defeated the older Dryden 5-3), and the fans loved it.

Don Cherry also liked to entertain the fans. The TV shot of "Grapes" Cherry which opens the "Coach's Corner" segment on *Hockey Night in Canada* is lifted from a game at the Forum during the 1979 playoffs when he pretended he was leading the fans in a cheer after his Bruins had received a penalty he felt they didn't deserve. After he left the Bruins, one of Cherry's best moves came in Boston, the first time he coached there with the Colorado Rockies. With his team ahead in the final minute, a gloating Grapes called a time out. He spent the thirty seconds signing autographs while his former boss and nemesis, Harry Sinden, and the rest of the Bruins brass, smouldered at the sight.

Coaches who go out of their way to let the fans in on some fun are usually well liked, and Cherry certainly was in Boston. In 1983, Don was working on the telecasts of a Bruins-Quebec Nordiques playoff series. After a game in Boston, he went out with some friends and the next morning couldn't wait to tell everybody what had happened to him on the way back to the hotel.

"I know it's dangerous to walk in that area, but I did. Sure enough, as I got near the underpass close to the Garden there seemed to be trouble ahead." The way Don was telling it we knew he had triumphed again, in the face of overwhelming odds.

"These guys are sittin' in a car, it's pitch dark, and there's no one else around. I keep walkin' and I see one of the guys get out. He looked tough and I figured it was my wallet or my life. He was leanin' against the car, cigarette hangin' out of his mouth, and as I walked by him he says, 'Hi Grapes. How's Blue?' Honest. Anybody else and his wallet's gone."

Chalk one up for a coach and his beloved bull terrier who were liked by the fans, if not the management.

Don Cherry joined *HNIC* for the 1980 playoffs, just after he was fired by the Rockies. He was uneasy at first, trying too hard to prove "I don't care if they did fire me" and it wasn't working. After a couple of appearances, Ralph Mellanby took Don out for a "few pops," as Grapes says.

"Relax," Ralph told him. "It'll work. Just be yourself, and promise me you'll never turn into a professional broadcaster." Cherry likes to say that anyone who has seen him on TV knows he kept the promise.

I wasn't impressed by his first few appearances until he worked with me in Montreal during the Canadiens-Minnesota series, in 1980. One of the games ended early. To help us out during the "fill" situation, they brought in the Minnesota coach, Glen Sonmor. Like Cherry, Glen can be a non-stop talker and I let the two of them take over. Actually, I had no choice. They got rolling and Cherry seemed to relax. He was in his element rapping with another talkative coach, whose team had just won a hockey game. It was good TV, and an omen of things to come for Don.

Grapes is a staunch advocate of violence in hockey. Maybe he truly feels this way, although sometimes I wonder if he goes overboard a bit with the on-camera theatrics, clenched fists, and fighting words to rile those of us who think otherwise.

He worked with me as the colour commentator on the last telecast of the 1987-88 season. I mentioned that referees were going to call playoff games much more closely than they had in past years.

"That should make you happy," he snarled.

Earlier in the season, Grapes was in the production studio at the Forum when a big fight broke out. He went to the phone and called my wife, who he knows hates hockey fights.

"You should be here tonight, Wilma," he chortled. "You're missing a dandy."

Great players like Bobby Orr, Phil Esposito, Jean Ratelle, and Lanny McDonald played for Don when he coached in the NHL. And yet, on TV, he has mentioned John Wensink,

Stan Jonathon, Bobby Schmautz, and Ron Delorme more often than any of the Hall of Famers he coached. They were the guys who did the fighting for him and if he had his way they would be in the Hall of Fame. Certainly he's tried to make them into legends, after their time.

For someone who watches hockey fights on his VCR, Don certainly has had the knack of being in the right place at the right time when things happen that turn him on. He was the analyst at the Forum on the night of Good Friday, 1984, when the Canadiens and the Quebec Nordiques had two big brawls. The first took place at the end of the second period, and they went at each other again when they came out to start the third period. I was with Don in the studio and he had a ball. I don't like hockey fights, but that time he got me into it too.

Then there was the infamous Canada-Soviet brawl at the 1987 World Junior Championships. Again there was Cherry, in a studio in Toronto with Brian Williams, working as the analyst on the CBC's coverage of the Tournament.

During the 1987 playoffs, the Canadiens and the Philadelphia Flyers really did a number with a full-scale brawl *before* the game even started. Guess who just happened to be in the Forum that night waiting to go on with Ron McLean to open the show? You're right.

If ever there was a chance for the guy in the "Coach's Corner" to have a field day about fighting, that one was it. But instead of coming on all fired up, Don fooled a lot of people, me included, with a low-key, insightful analysis of one of the ugliest incidents he, or any of us, had ever seen. But that time he wasn't championing the cause of the players who were doing the dirty deeds. He made it plain he was opposed to that brand of hockey thuggery, and he stated his case very well.

When the game was over, I told Don I thought his assessment of a very difficult situation was the best thing I had ever seen him do on the show. He seemed grateful for the compliment, and a little taken aback.

There was one announcer in the Forum that night who

didn't react nearly as calmly when the pre-game brawl broke out. Me. I was hosting a talk show on CFCF Radio from the broadcast booth, so I described the scene, live, on the radio. Listening to it on tape afterward gave me quite a jolt. There I was, a guy who is supposed to be turned off by that sort of thing, screaming and shrieking like a wild man. They should have hired Cherry.

Gary Dornhoefer and Mickey Redmond are former NHLers who were colour commentators on *Hockey Night in Canada* for several seasons. I enjoyed working with both and wasn't surprised when they arrived in the booth. Both had been excellent sources of post-game news interviews during their playing days.

Dorny played for the Philadelphia Flyers' championship teams when Fred Shero was the coach. Shero left the Flyers to join the New York Rangers, and was with them one night in Montreal when Gary was working on our show. Ex-players have an edge when it comes to talking to coaches and players before a game. They seem to open up more to someone who was once one of them. But Shero, known as "Freddie the Fog" for his strange work habits and hockey theories, didn't do his former player Dorny any favours that night.

"Hi Fred," Dorny greeted him. "What can you tell me about your team? I notice the power play has been good lately. How come?"

Shero thought for a moment, then said, "You know, the Islanders played us all wrong that year when we beat them in the seventh game."

Gary waited, but that was all he got.

"See you Freddie," he said, and walked away shaking his head. I kidded Dorny that, when he was a player, he and his Flyer teammates likely had a few good laughs because of Shero's weird and not-so-wonderful way of dealing with the media.

"Welcome to the club," I told him.

Mickey Redmond started in the NHL with Montreal, but became a star in Detroit. Mickey was one of the players involved in the deal that brought Frank Mahovlich to the Canadiens, one of the few times the Canadiens traded for an established star. Mickey was the first Red Wing to score fifty goals in one season, a bit of trivia that often fools Gordie Howe fans.

In March of 1986, Mickey and I worked a game in St. Louis, and visited the coffee machine at the back of the media section during the first intermission. I returned to my seat before Mickey and when he got back, the play was just about to start.

"I'm in trouble here Dick," I heard him say just as the puck was dropped and the second period began. Then a whistle was blown to stop play. I looked over and saw that he was indeed in trouble. He had his pants pulled down around his knees and there was blood dripping from a deep cut in his right thigh.

The broadcast booth is normally a much safer place than the ice during a game. But that night Mickey had been bodychecked by a garbage can. On his way back from the coffee machine, he had brushed against the can which had a piece of metal sticking out of one side. It was sharp enough to cut a neat slice through his right pant leg and into his right thigh. Mickey bravely put on his microphone, but I waved at him to forget it. The Blues scored and I did the commentary over the replay. I heard the director ask, "Where's Redmond?"

At the first commercial break, I yelled for help to Suzie Mathieu, the very efficient PR Director of the Blues. Suzie hurried back to our broadcast location to be met by the unusual sight of a hockey broadcaster with his pants off and blood oozing out of his leg.

Once her initial shock passed, Suzie swung into action. I couldn't believe how quickly a doctor arrived. It was the first, and I hope the last time I had to call a game while the colour commentator next to me was getting a tetanus shot.

The most recent trend on *HNIC* has coaches working in the

booth rather than ex-players. During the 1987–88 season, there were occasions when three games were being telecast on a Saturday night and three ex-coaches, Don Cherry, Scotty Bowman, and Harry Neale, were doing the colour.

Bowman was never in love with the media when he was coaching, so a lot of us got a kick out of him wearing a blue *HNIC* jacket. Scotty's mind operates at a machine-gun-like pace. I'm sure that when he started in the booth he would see three or four things he wanted to talk about as the play was going on. This posed a problem for him when the play stopped and he had to make his comments. But he soon got the knack of things, and learned to concentrate on one aspect of what had just happened, rather than try to talk about three or four things in the few seconds available. I found Scotty easy to work with, and he provided our viewers with a lot of good information.

Harry Neale, ex-coach of the Vancouver Canucks and the Detroit Red Wings, ranks with former goaltender John Davidson as the best when it comes to having notes and ad libs ready for each telecast.

When Harry was coaching, he was the king of the one-liners, and the media loved it. He was told the Canucks didn't like his practices.

"That makes us even," Harry replied, "because I don't like their games."

We were working a Montreal-Boston playoff series when the camera took a shot of a Boston sub, Kraig Nienhaus, standing near the Bruins bench in civvies. He was sporting a punk-style hairdo, with much of it standing straight up.

"There's Kraig Nienhaus," Harry said. "Looks like he combs his hair with a hand grenade."

Another time, he wanted me to ask him, on the air, how many goals he thought Rocket Richard would score if he were playing today. So I did.

"I'd say about twenty-five or thirty."

"Only twenty-five or thirty?" replied his straight man.

"That's right, Dick. But don't forget, he's sixty-four years old."

Harry Neale has a million of 'em, but he came up with by far his best, and most quoted, when he was running the lowly Canucks and his team was in the throes of another terrible slump.

"We're losing at home, and we're losing on the road. My failure as a coach is that I can't think of anywhere else to play."

Scotty Bowman – One of a Kind

Scotty Bowman is my second favourite hockey coach of all time. (For information on Number One, check Hockey Hall of Fame under Irvin, James Dickinson.)

One of the toughest tasks for a coach is to keep a good team good over a long period of time. In Bowman's case in Montreal, he was able to keep a great team great over a long period of time.

Scotty coached the Montreal Canadiens for eight years, winning the Stanley Cup five times. All of us who were around during his era have Scotty stories to tell.

My favourite is one I'm sure he has forgotten, but I certainly haven't. In his second year with the team, 1972–73, the Canadiens lost only ten games and Scotty won his first Stanley Cup.

Late in the season, the Canadiens played a game in Detroit that was televised back to Montreal. The teams were lined up along the blue lines for the national anthems, but there was a delay before the music began. *Hockey Night in Canada* was in a commercial break and the producer wouldn't give the cue to begin the anthems until it was over. (Who says TV controls sports?) The fans became impatient and began whistling and booing and I guess Scotty was fuming a little bit.

The Canadiens won the game. The trip on the charter flight home was routine, until the plane came to a "complete and final stop in front of the terminal building." On Canadiens' trips, the players sit in the front and the media in the back on buses. On planes, the coaches and team officials sit in the front few rows, media in the middle section, players in the rear.

After that particular landing, Scotty was putting on his coat when he began talking very loudly, addressing no one in particular, but obviously directing his comments at me and Neil Leger, a *Hockey Night in Canada* V.P., who was sitting beside me.

"Whose idea was it to hold up the game at the start?" he said loud enough for us to hear. "Television. It's always television. *Hockey Night in Canada*. What a disgrace."

"Disgrace" is one of Scotty's favourite words of disgust, and he said it again as his monologue continued.

I don't like to get involved in such things, but that time I did. I piped up, "It must be nice to have a team that's lost only eight or nine games. Then you can go around sticking your nose in other people's business."

He snapped, "At least we know how to run our team," and I came back with, "Take your team and shove it." Leger was still in his seat turning a pale shade of grey. The plane door opened at that moment and Bowman was far ahead of us down the corridor by the time we got into the terminal.

Scotty and I both lived in the West Island area of Montreal and often shared a cab after a late-night arrival. I said to Leger, "There goes my cab ride."

When I walked outside the airport, I expected Scotty to be long gone. Instead, I heard him hollering, "Dick, over here. I've got a taxi."

On the ride home, the first thing he said was, "Did you see Lafleur's line tonight? One of the worst games they've played all year. Can't understand it."

Our situation was back to normal. Not a mention of the little blow-up we had had on the plane. That's Scotty.

I've often thought about another of our shared cab rides. Again, we were home from a game in Detroit that had ended in a 3-3 tie. Marcel Dionne had scored all three goals for the Red Wings. Because Dionne would become a free agent at the end of that season (he eventually signed with Los Angeles), the Wings were trying to make a deal for him, and had approached the Canadiens while the team was in Detroit.

"Would you trade Ken Dryden for Marcel Dionne?" Scotty asked me. That was what the Wings had proposed.

"I don't know, but I don't think so," I waffled. "Would you?"

"I don't think it will happen," he replied and changed the subject. But I got the feeling he was somewhat intrigued by the idea.

It didn't happen. But think about it, all you Montreal and Detroit fans.

Scotty Bowman grew up in Montreal and was a promising junior hockey player when his career was ended by a serious head injury during the early 1950's. He went to work, coaching minor hockey as a sideline, and used to spend some of his lunch hours at the Forum watching my dad coach the Canadiens in practice. Thirty years later, the kid who tried to learn from my dad broke his record for most career coaching victories.

Scotty scouted, and then coached, in the Canadiens' minor system. When St. Louis joined the NHL in the 1967 expansion, Lynn Patrick was their General Manager and Coach, and he hired Scotty to be his assistant. A month into the season, Patrick gave up the coaching job and Scotty took over, a move that raised a few eyebrows. A lot of people thought he wasn't ready, that expansion hockey was breeding expansion coaching. But Bowman grew into the job very quickly, and the greatest years enjoyed by the Blues in St. Louis were when he was coaching the team.

In their first season, the Blues won the expansion division
championship. Although not really in the same class as the
Canadiens, they gave Montreal four good games in the Stanley Cup finals. That was the year Scotty had Glenn Hall in
goal and had resurrected several veterans at a time when
they were thought to be finished as players. Dickie Moore
and Doug Harvey were two of them, and defenceman Jean
Guy Talbot was another. Talbot's presence in a Blues uniform said a lot about Scotty Bowman. Scotty's playing career had ended when he was slashed over the head and
seriously injured. The player who had slashed him was Talbot, who went on to play twelve seasons with the Canadiens.
Talbot's career was in decline when Scotty brought him to
St. Louis, where he added valuable experience to the fledgling club for about three years.

The Blues, after a slow beginning, became a very hot
ticket in St. Louis, so much so that the National Basketball
Association team based there, the Hawks, moved to Atlanta.
St. Louis became a great hockey city and the St. Louis
Arena was, for a few years, a tremendously exciting place in
which to do a broadcast.

Hockey interest in St. Louis reached its peak during the
Bowman era of the late 1960's and early 1970's. The Arena
organist, Norm Kramer, was the cheer leader and became
as well known as the players. Visible to the crowd as he sat
on a shelf dressed in a sequined jacket, Kramer would
pump out *When the Saints Go Marching In* when the Blues
came on the ice to start a game and the fans would sing
along, substituting "Blues" for "Saints." Visiting coaches
began complaining about Kramer – and the way he pumped
the organ and pumped up the crowd while the games were
being played.

The Canadiens played a Saturday night game there that
was one of the wildest I have ever broadcast. Kramer was in
top form and the crowd of close to 20,000 was too. The Canadiens, as they so often have over the years, silenced the home
crowd by dominating the first period and taking a 2-0 lead.
After some fiery words of wisdom from their young coach,

the Blues came out with bodychecks blazing to start the second period, led by the Plager brothers, Barclay and Bob.

Bodies were flying. The Plagers goaded John Ferguson into a rage that finally got him thrown out of the game. Fergy smashed his stick to bits as he left the ice, the Blues scored a couple to tie the game, and bedlam reigned supreme. I can't recall a game in which I kept wondering whether my voice was being heard by the folks out in Radioland – it was that noisy in the Arena.

Jean Béliveau scored to put the Canadiens ahead in the third period, but the Blues bounced back again and, with the organ music blasting and the crowd bellowing, they tied the game in the final few moments – and that's how it ended. It had been a terrific evening of hockey entertainment, typical of what was happening in St. Louis at that time.

It's too bad that kind of scene didn't last in the St. Louis Arena. One reason it didn't was Syd Solomon the Third, son of the team's original owner, who became involved in the management of the club and began to think he knew more about hockey than the capable men his father had hired to build the franchise. Scotty always speaks highly of Solomon the father, but not of "The Third." As the son moved deeper into the operation of the team, Scotty moved closer to the door, and finally went through it at the end of the 1970–71 season. Cliff Fletcher, who like Bowman had joined the Blues out of the Canadiens organization, was another victim of The Third's management style.

After solid hockey men like Bowman and Fletcher left, the Blues went through a dizzying succession of managers and coaches, and soon the good things that had been done began to unravel. The Solomon era is long gone in St. Louis, and so is the kind of fan enthusiasm that made it such a great hockey city when the Blues were Scotty's team.

Why was Scotty Bowman able to become the all-time winning coach in the NHL? Good teams of course, but there's a bit more to it than that. Two key factors stand out in my mind after watching him coach the Canadiens for eight seasons: the way he changed lines during a game, and the way he kept a great team playing great hockey, night after night, with carefully thought-out game plans.

Scotty Bowman was likely the best coach hockey has ever known once a game began. In Montreal, he had "the horses," as they say, and his ability to manipulate those horses was at times incredible.

Fred Shero was a fine Stanley Cup winning coach in Philadelphia. Yet every time the Canadiens played the Flyers in a big game, especially in the playoffs, Scotty would do a number on Shero in the coaching department. He would drive Shero, and other coaches, crazy with his line switches and match-ups. There were times, when his Canadiens of the late 1970's were at the peak of their championship form, that I considered Scotty's game tactics the highlight of the evening.

The first time Harry Neale coached against Bowman was in Vancouver – and he joined the club. Harry spent most of the game looking totally confused as Bowman poured fast line changes and different line combinations over the boards at the Canucks. At one point, he used three different lines between whistles while the Canucks stayed with one. Scotty could orchestrate games in that fashion and it was a delight to watch.

My dad is credited with being the first coach to change lines while the play is going on. Write-ups of that particular Irvin strategy refer to "three-minute shifts." Today, coaches often change lines two or three times in less than one minute. Most of today's players like it that way but, as usual, Wayne Gretzky is an exception. Glen Sather told me that Wayne often plays four-minute shifts.

"I don't know how he does it," sighed Slats, "but he does."

Some nights Bowman would go overboard in using different line combinations on the ice. Media types would sit in the press box and count the different threesomes he employed. I seem to recall nineteen in one period as the recorded high.

Coaches usually call out the next line they want on the ice using the name of the centreman. During a game when he was doing one of his all-time numbers in the line-changing department, Scotty hollered, "Lemaire's line next!!"

Steve Shutt hollered back, "Who's on it?"

The other key factor of Scotty's coaching that impressed me was how he came up with a different game plan every night. It didn't matter who the Canadiens were playing, a strong team or a weak team, Scotty had a scheme to make his players think about that particular game in some particular way.

I was able to get this insight mainly because of *The Scotty Bowman Show* on CFCF Radio. Before every Canadiens game, I would interview Scotty for about five minutes. We did the show during the most successful of his years in Montreal, when the Canadiens weren't losing very many games. As the team was merrily rolling along, it was difficult for me to come up with a decent variety of questions for him to answer. But Scotty always bailed me out. He would talk refreshingly about the game to be played that night, and how he wanted his team to approach it.

I used to wonder how many other coaches in the NHL could think the same way. Scotty not only provided our listeners with some very interesting comments, he was also giving his players something new to think about before every game.

There were times when the coach crossed up listeners to *The Scotty Bowman Show*. One time in Minnesota, we sat down to tape the program late in the afternoon on game day.

"What's new?" I asked, in my usual imaginative fashion.

"New lines," Scotty replied. "Want to talk about it?"

We did, and for five minutes Scotty gave a detailed description of his new line combinations and why he was making the changes.

The show ran on air, and a couple of minutes later the game began. Not once during the entire game, not once, did the line combinations Scotty had so painstakingly described show up on the ice.

"What happened to your new lines?" I asked after the game.

"Changed my mind," was his terse answer.

That's Scotty.

A successful coach isn't always a popular coach, and Scotty Bowman is a prime example. In his relationships with players, the media, and autograph-seeking fans he could be pleasant and caring, or he could be abrupt and curt. When it came to hearing them out concerning their personal life and possible problems, the players used to say he sometimes had an attention span of about twenty seconds.

A typical, and for some a favourite, photo of Scotty shows him behind the bench with a stern look, jaw jutting out like Mussolini, obviously the boss.

Some coaches may blend into the woodwork a bit, but never Bowman. When the team bus would go from airport to hotel, or from the arena back to an airport, Scotty always sat in the back row. And he almost always made sure he was the last person to get on the bus, slowly striding down the aisle, always very much in charge.

During his last season in Montreal, on a western road trip in November, he promised the players they could have a post-game party in Vancouver, their last stop, if they won all their games, which they did. But along the way, in Denver, Scotty caught two of them out after curfew. Following a convincing win over the Canucks, with visions of the party dancing through their sweaty heads, the players heard their not-so-kindly coach announce that, because of the curfew-breaking episode in Denver, the party was off. The boys were told that they had to go back to the hotel and pack their bags. They were going home to Montreal on the red-eye flight leaving at 1:00 a.m. There was a near-mutiny. The players threatened to ignore his orders and stay in Vancouver. But they didn't, and the next morning a bleary-eyed group of Stanley Cup champions deplaned in Montreal.

A few of the players on those great Canadiens teams might tell you today that Scotty is their all-time non-favourite coach. In turn, he had some non-favourite players. Pete Mahovlich was one. Scotty always felt Pete took his role as the team's resident clown a lot more seriously than he did the games. And Pete didn't do much to make his coach, or a lot of others, think otherwise.

But, like Doug Harvey before him, Pete Mahovlich wasn't quite as casual about his work as some may have thought. The Canadiens traded him to Pittsburgh in December, 1977. The first time the Penguins played in Montreal following the deal, Pete was told during the morning skate that his Stanley Cup ring from the previous spring's championship was ready in the Canadiens' dressing room.

People who were at the Forum that morning saw Pete skating across the ice, back to the Pittsburgh dressing room, the ring proudly on his finger, and tears streaming down his cheeks.

Pierre Bouchard was another who was in and out of the Bowman doghouse on a regular basis. Unlike Mahovlich, who was a first-string player, Pierre was a fringe defenceman. He is the son of "Butch" Bouchard, who played for my father. Big Butch had a dry sense of humour, and Pierre does too. Unlike most of his teammates, Bouchard was able to deflect his coach's carping with a good sense of humour.

For example, during a change of planes in the Chicago airport, Pierre was asking, "Why did Scotty tell me to go to Gate D4, when he told everybody else to go to Gate G12?"

I once talked with Jean Béliveau about Bowman, and the players' feelings toward him.

"You know Dick," he replied, "some things never change. I can remember how we used to get mad at your father, and at Toe Blake, for the things they did. But then, in the summer, we'd get our playoff cheques, and it didn't seem so bad after all."

The playoff cheques were a lot richer for Bowman's players than they were for Irvin's or Blake's. And there has never been a time in sports history when a player didn't cash a cheque because he didn't like his coach.

The Canadiens of the 1970's may not have liked Scotty Bowman, but they certainly played hockey for him. Great hockey. One big reason was because they were playing for the man who was, simply, the best coach of his time.

Scotty Bowman's seven and a half years with the Buffalo Sabres weren't happy ones. His talents as a coach and his knowledge of the game of hockey were far superior to his ability to deal with people as the overall boss of a hockey operation.

That was the job he wanted in Montreal. Specifically, Sam Pollock's job. Pollock retired prior to the 1978-79 season, just after Molson Breweries bought the Canadiens from Edward and Peter Bronfman.

The new owners asked Sam to name his successor. Sam nominated Irving Grundman, not Scotty Bowman.

Scotty and Irving had an uneasy relationship. The Canadiens finished second in the overall standings behind the Islanders, who were then upset by the Rangers in the playoffs.

Scotty wasn't Scotty during that 1978-79 season or in the playoffs. He was very subdued, very much within himself, although there was one moment when he let loose a bit. That was the night the Canadiens came from behind late in the game to tie the Bruins and then won in overtime on Yvon Lambert's goal in Game Seven of their semi-final round. Scotty jumped onto the ice to join in the celebrations after that one.

The Canadiens defeated the Rangers in the final. I interviewed Scotty every time his team won the Cup, but that night (the one I almost got together with Pierre Trudeau), he was far from the excited, joyous man he had been on TV following his previous four Cup wins. It had been a very unhappy season for him, Stanley Cup and all.

A few weeks later, he joined the Buffalo Sabres, getting the kind of job he had wanted in Montreal. Just before that happened, I was playing golf with Steve Shutt.

"What do you hear about Scotty?" I asked.

"Not much," replied Steve. "I don't care what happens to him as long as he leaves and goes somewhere else."

Shutt's feelings pretty well summed up how most of the Canadiens felt at the time. The following season started poorly for the team. Bernie Geoffrion, Grundman's choice to replace Scotty as coach, was a disaster and quit just before Christmas.

Shortly after that, Shutt and I were again talking about Bowman. Steve's attitude had totally changed. He told me, "I never knew how much he meant to us until now."

Scotty Bowman broke my dad's record for most wins by a coach and I can honestly say I was pulling for him to do it. He kept trying to quit his coaching duties while in Buffalo. Roger Neilson handled the team for one complete season and Jim Schoenfeld and Jimmy Roberts had brief careers coaching the Sabres. But Scotty would always come back. I used to kid him that he was staying on the job only because he wanted the record, which of course he did. When he reached it, I wanted to help him celebrate, but he seemed determined, somehow, to stop me.

Dad finished his career with 690 regular-season coaching victories. It was obvious at the start of the 1984–85 season that Scotty would pass that figure fairly early in the campaign. As he was nearing the record, Dad was getting a lot of publicity because stories about Scotty always referred to "Dick Irvin's record." I won't embarrass the player involved, but around that time one of the younger members of the Canadiens mentioned to one of the veteran players, "I didn't know Dick Irvin was a coach before he became a broadcaster."

So much for hockey history books.

The Sabres won a Saturday afternoon game in Boston in early December. It was Scotty's 690th win and he had tied the record, or so everyone thought.

I decided I would go to Buffalo for a Sabres-Quebec Nordiques game the next night. It would give me a chance to personally congratulate him and be there for the record breaker, if Buffalo won.

I took a late morning flight and before leaving called the Sabres office to ask for a media pass. Gerry Helper, the PR Director, wasn't there so his secretary took the information.

In Toronto between planes something told me to call again. (Was it the "Unseen Hand"?) This time Gerry answered.

"I'm awfully glad you called," were his first words. "Scotty has just thrown us for a loop. He says he hasn't tied the record yet. Claims there were games he wasn't at that he got credit for. We were planning a ceremony and now he's called the whole thing off."

So I cancelled my ticket to Buffalo, and flew back to Montreal.

Several weeks went by with Scotty still claiming the record book was wrong. The large anti-Bowman media group in Buffalo kept wondering, "Why did he wait until everyone thought he had tied the record? Why didn't he say something at the start of the season?" There were people in the NHL office feeling the same way.

To many of us it seemed like another Bowman ploy to keep everyone, especially the press, off balance. He was a master at that.

Finally, in February, Scotty conceded that somewhere along the way he had passed Dad's record. The Sabres were at last able to hold a big celebration at centre ice before a home game.

The night before it was to take place, I received a call around midnight from Paul Weiland, the Sabres Director of Communications.

"I'm embarrassed by the timing of this," Paul began, "but Scotty just called me. He says he wants you here for the ceremonies tomorrow night."

I had to decline because of a long-standing commitment for a charity sports dinner in Montreal the next night. I truly wanted to go to Buffalo to represent Dad, so the call left me flattered, and frustrated.

But that was Scotty.

Flower Power

"**W**ho's the best hockey player you've ever seen?" People in my business are often asked that question.

A few years ago, my travelling buddy, Red Fisher, and I were having dinner in a restaurant in Vancouver. The male member of the nice young couple seated at the table next to ours asked us that question.

"Bobby Orr," was Red's quick reply.

"Guy Lafleur," was mine.

"Wrong!" Red barked at me.

"What do you mean wrong?" I barked back. "There's no right or wrong to that question. It's a matter of opinion."

We continued our mini-spat for a while longer. By the time we were finished, the nice young couple next to us was concentrating on their soup, no doubt sorry they had asked the two strange hockey reporters from Montreal that question.

I don't claim to have the definitive answer to the "Who's the best?" question. Who can? Who out there can prove Howie Morenz was the best, or Rocket Richard? How about Bobby Hull, Jean Béliveau, or Doug Harvey? Let's hear it for Gordie Howe, Bobby Orr, and the Great One Gretzky. The list is long. Maybe it's a cop-out, but there have been so many players who have been so great at what they did through the years that it's too tough for me to make a definite call.

But I do say this. For a period of six seasons, when he was at the peak of his career, Guy Lafleur of the Montreal Canadiens was the best hockey player in the world.

"Best in the world?" you ask. Again, as I tried to explain to Red, that's my opinion.

His nickname was "The Flower." I called the play by play on radio of his first NHL goal October 23, 1971 when he scored in Los Angeles on Kings' goalie Gary Edwards. I called the play by play on radio when he scored his 518th, his last goal, October 25, 1984 against Buffalo Sabres' goaltender Bob Sauvé at the Montreal Forum. During that period of thirteen years and two days I saw almost all of the great goals he scored, and the great plays he made.

Sam Pollock, the Canadiens' General Manager at the time Guy Lafleur became available in the draft, gained fame as the builder of great hockey teams. He was a fine hockey man, but certainly was never known for his humour, one reason he was nicknamed "Sad Sam." But when it came time for the Canadiens to draft first in 1971, a position they were in thanks to Sam's wheeling and dealing in the hockey flesh market, he brought the house down. When NHL President Clarence Campbell called on the Canadiens to make their pick, Sam replied, "Time, Mr. Campbell," as though he needed a few more minutes to decide on his Number One pick.

Lafleur had been the dominant player in Canadian junior hockey, the most publicized junior in the Province of Quebec since Jean Béliveau. Had Sam not selected Lafleur, it would have meant his bags were packed, and he would perhaps have left the province forever.

The day before the draft, Jean Béliveau had retired. The Canadiens had a history of stars succeeding stars. Not that long after Howie Morenz, there had been Maurice Richard. When The Rocket retired, Béliveau was firmly in place. Now Big Jean was gone, but no matter, Lafleur was next in

line and all was still right in the hectic hockey world of
Quebec. Three years later, they weren't so sure. The flashy
youngster who had scored 233 goals in his final two years as
a junior looked like he was about to become a big-league
bust.

Lafleur scored twenty-nine goals in his first season,
twenty-eight in his second, and had a very disappointing
total of twenty-one goals and thirty-five assists in seventy-
three games in his third season. The Canadiens were thinking that maybe they should make a deal for the once-promis-
ing right winger.

Scotty Bowman related the story during an intermission
on *Hockey Night in Canada*, the night the Canadiens honoured Lafleur following his retirement. Scotty's Buffalo Sabres happened to be the visiting team at the Forum.

"Sam Pollock called me and my assistant coach, Claude
Ruel, into his office and grilled us about Lafleur," Scotty
told our coast-to-coast audience. He asked us, "Should we
keep him or should we trade him? We decided to keep him.
Sam signed him to a ten-year contract shortly afterward. In
hindsight, I guess you could say we made the right decision."

Scotty made that last statement with a very satisfied
smile on his face. Players like Guy Lafleur make coaches
like Scotty Bowman look like geniuses, and no one knows
that better than the coaches.

Frank Mahovlich was Lafleur's roommate on the road during part of The Flower's disappointing first three seasons.

"Never saw a kid as nervous as him," the Big M told me
one day. "All he does is smoke one cigarette after another.
Must be the pressure. Sometimes I feel sorry for him."

Maybe it was the pressure of trying to be all things to all
hockey fans and the hockey media in the province of Quebec.
Maybe one day between season number three and season
number four, Guy Lafleur made some kind of a decision
about how he would play hockey. Whatever, when the 1974–
75 season began, there was a new flower in bloom wearing
Number 10 for the Montreal Canadiens.

The Canadiens opened on home ice against the New York Islanders. Two things were obvious about Guy Lafleur that night. The first was that he wasn't wearing a helmet. After wearing the protective headgear, starting at the pee wee level, Lafleur skated out without one, and never wore one again in the NHL.

The second obvious thing about Lafleur was the way he played the game. It prompted Canadien watchers to wonder "Who's that wearing Number 10?" He was a different player. It was that sudden. He wasn't only different, he was great, and the greatness would continue for a full six more seasons before his career started to decline.

Lafleur finished 1974–75 with fifty-three goals, four more than he had scored in the previous two seasons. He added sixty-six assists and finished fifth in the scoring race, something he would win each of the next three years.

I keep referring to Lafleur's greatness over a six-season period. Some statistics show what I mean. Starting with that 1974–75 campaign through the 1979–80 season, he scored 327 goals and 439 assists for 766 points. In the playoffs during those six years, he registered 106 points in sixty-nine games. The Canadiens won the Stanley Cup four straight times beginning in 1976. During those four Cup-winning years, The Flower had eighty-seven points in fifty-eight playoff games.

Perhaps all of the above isn't too impressive to Wayne Gretzky fans. All I can say is that while your man is the greatest of his era, my man was the greatest of his. Let's leave it that way, and still be friends.

For Lafleur watchers there are many highlights from his great career. I particularly recall one game against the North Stars in Minnesota when he scored three goals in an eight-minute span in the first period. Each one was a classic, a great play, Lafleur at his best.

"What's it like being on the ice with him when he plays like that?" I asked his linemate Steve Shutt after the game.

"It's easy," Shutt replied. "All you do is stand along the boards, and watch him fly by."

Teammates and opponents had been watching The Flower fly by since he was a seedling, playing pee wee hockey. Former NHL referee Red Storey often officiated games at the annual Quebec Winter Carnival Pee Wee Tournament. Red raved about Lafleur when he saw him at that tender age, calling him, "The best eleven-year-old player I've ever seen."

When Guy became a star in the NHL, the plaudits came from everywhere. Bobby Orr said, "He does things with the puck that are incredible." Ken Dryden marvelled at his unselfishness and dedication, pointing out, "He's the best player in the League, yet he's still the first on the ice at practice."

Harry Sinden, working with me as an analyst on *HNIC*, said Lafleur was the best forward he had seen "without the puck." That meant The Flower had the amazing ability to be at the right place at the right time. He not only knew where the action was, he knew where it was going to be.

Howie Meeker never spares the superlatives when he feels they are deserved. During the height of Lafleur's stardom, Howie told me, "He has great hockey sense. He knows exactly when to give a pass, and where to go to get one. He's like The Rocket, because when he's on the ice, things happen. He sells tickets!"

Lafleur was the last All-Star forward to play without a helmet. His fans still love to recall the sight of the flying Flower, hair flowing in his skating breeze, wheeling up and down right wing, scoring goals, and selling tickets.

Lafleur's career was often compared to the career of Marcel Dionne. They were chosen one-two in the draft in 1971, and Dionne got off to a much better start in the NHL, scoring forty goals in his second season. People watched them closely when their teams would meet. One night in Los Angeles, Lafleur clearly had a better game.

"Not much of a contest between Lafleur and Dionne last night," I mentioned to Ken Dryden the next morning, as we were waiting for the bus to take us from the hotel to the airport.

"It's never much of a contest when Lafleur plays against Dionne," replied Kenny, ever the deep thinker.

When Guy retired, there was a lot of mention made that while he was a burned-out, fallen superstar, Dionne was still enjoying one-hundred-point seasons with the Kings. I thought Marcel was very fair in his assessment of that particular comparison.

"Don't forget," he said, "Guy has played a lot more hockey than I have. Check the playoff records."

Anyone who bothered to check discovered that while Lafleur had played in 124 Stanley Cup games, Dionne, who came into the League at the same time, had appeared in just thirty. Not the whole story of course, but an interesting observation just the same. And to those ninety-four extra games on a stats sheet, you can add the intense pressure that went with them.

I am tempted to write that Guy Lafleur was the most exciting hockey player I ever saw. More correctly perhaps, would be ". . . ever broadcast." Memories of Maurice Richard are still very vivid, even though I saw much more of The Flower in his prime than I did The Rocket in his. But for someone who had a lot of thrills watching both, comparisons are inevitable.

Both scored a goal many claim was their "greatest." I've already described Richard's, which came in the seventh game of a Stanley Cup semi-final series against Boston, late in the third period, and into the net at the south end of the Forum.

Lafleur's also came in the seventh game of a Stanley Cup semi-final against Boston, late in the third period, and into the net at the south end of the Forum. The Canadiens' "tradition" had struck again.

Lafleur's "greatest" goal happened during the great semi-final series Montreal and Boston played in 1979, maybe the best series I've seen. It went into a seventh game, at the Forum. Rick Middleton scored at 16:01 of the third period to put the Bruins ahead 4-3. The Canadiens were the defending Cup champions (having won it three straight years, and beating Boston in the finals in '77 and '78). Now Don Cherry and his Bruins were that close to gaining some revenge by knocking the champions out of the playoffs.

They played through another minute, the Canadiens that much closer to elimination. Then came the penalty that Cherry has made famous, the one that nailed the Bruins for having too many men on the ice. He has never questioned linesman John D'Amico's call. The Bruins did have too many men on the ice. The penalty came at 17:26.

The Bruins killed off the first minute of the Canadiens' power play. Suddenly, Montreal was less than two minutes away from relinquishing the Cup.

The Canadiens moved the puck out of their zone, down the right side. Jacques Lemaire was coming off the bench just as the puck got to him. He shoved it ahead, to an onrushing Lafleur. The Flower was in full flight as he picked up the puck, took a couple of strides to move inside the Boston blue line, drew back his stick, and blasted. Ken Dryden always said the most underrated part of Lafleur's game was his shot. At that moment, Bruins' goaltender Gilles Gilbert must have agreed. The puck streaked past Gilbert before he could react, bulging the net inside the far post, stick side. The Canadiens then won in overtime on Yvon Lambert's goal, and went on to defeat the Rangers in five games to win their fourth straight Stanley Cup, a couple of weeks later.

Guy Lafleur scored over 500 goals in the NHL, but that's the one that is best remembered. When he retired, it was played over and over on television sportscasts recapping his career.

Great hockey players are consistent and Lafleur was all of that. His seasonal goal totals during the peak of his career read 53, 56, 56, 60, 52, and 50. His overall play was just as consistent. Night after night, on home ice or on the road, he would give the paying customers their money's worth, and then some. Night after night the same brilliance, and what impressed me most of all, the same maximum effort. There are highs and lows in the performance level of even the best, but in Guy's case he ran on high almost every night.

I feel the same way about Wayne Gretzky. I marvel at the way he does what he does game after game, season after season.

I broadcast The Flower's 400th career goal, in Winnipeg, and his 500th, in New Jersey. On the night he reached 500, his long-time linemate, Steve Shutt, scored his 400th. It reminded me of the night in 1952 when Elmer Lach scored his 200th goal and his long-time linemate Rocket Richard scored his 325th, to become the highest scorer in hockey history.

When Maurice Richard's career ended, it happened suddenly. He had captained the Canadiens to a fifth straight Stanley Cup in 1960. He started training camp the next fall and, in a morning scrimmage, scored four goals. The Canadiens then called a news conference, and The Rocket retired, just like that. In Lafleur's case, the end to his career dragged on for a long time.

The date April 11, 1980 should rate at least an asterisk in the NHL record book. On that night in Hartford, the third game of a Montreal playoff series against the Whalers, two of the game's all-time greatest players, Gordie Howe and Bobby Hull, played their last game. It was also the night one of their Whaler teammates, Pat Boutette, threw a check that was the beginning of the end of the career of Guy Lafleur. Lafleur had scored three goals in the series, but when he went down after being hit by Boutette, his knee was injured and he was through for the balance of the playoffs. The Canadiens lost the chance to win a record-tying fifth straight Cup when, without The Flower, they lost in a seven-game series to Minnesota in the next round.

Lafleur was never the same after that. He had been one of the NHL's most durable players. Then, like Richard in his final few seasons, he began spending lengthy periods out of the line-up. In his final four seasons, he played in all games just once. He had three straight twenty-seven-goal years, then a thirty. In twenty-three playoff games in those four years, he scored only twice.

His last goal was scored October 25, 1984, a good shot into the far corner on Buffalo goaltender Bob Sauvé.

He played twelve more games with just one assist. He had lost his confidence. He kept looking for someone to pass to on scoring opportunities he would have turned into a goal in a flash when he was in his prime. He scored only twice in his last fifty-two games in a Canadiens uniform.

Guy played his last game on Saturday, November 24, 1984, at the Forum, against the Detroit Red Wings. In the first period, he had a great scoring chance with the Detroit net wide open. Again, he hesitated to shoot and when he finally did it was a pitifully weak effort that went over the net. Sid Abel, a Hall of Famer who had been a star with the Wings for many years as centre on the Production Line with Gordie Howe and Ted Lindsay, was working as the colour commentator on the Red Wings' broadcast back to Detroit.

"If I hadn't seen it I wouldn't have believed it," Sid said to me as we talked about the play during the intermission. "It's really sad to see something like that."

The Canadiens left after the game for Boston. As the charter flight was about to take off, we were told Lafleur wasn't making the trip. The party line was that he had a sore ankle. What really happened was that Guy had asked the coach, Jacques Lemaire, if he could be excused from the trip so he could think things over.

Two days later, at a late afternoon news conference, Guy Lafleur announced his retirement. The room was filled with media and many of his teammates, past and present. He spoke far too long trying to explain his decision to a subdued group of friends, who were obviously feeling very sad.

Guy was still talking when our CFCF cameraman had to leave to take the tape back to the station in time for the six o'clock newscast. I walked him to the door of the Forum and was going to go back to listen to the balance of what Lafleur was saying. But I decided I had heard enough. For the first time in my sportscasting career, the retirement of one of my favourite players had got to me emotionally. I wasn't the only one.

As I walked out onto the street, Larry Robinson was right behind me. I held the door for him and caught myself before I said anything. After all, what was there to say? Besides, Larry had a tear or two in his eyes. So did I.

The original manuscript for this book referred to Guy Lafleur's 518th goal as "his last goal". Shortly after the first printing, that phrase no longer applied.

The Flower went through four winters of discontent, steadily convincing himself he had retired too soon. In the summer of 1988 he contacted several NHL teams, asking for a tryout. The New York Rangers gave him one. They liked what they saw at training camp, and when the 1988-89 season began, thirty-seven-year-old Guy Lafleur was in a Rangers' uniform. A lot of people, including me, said it couldn't be done. But he did it, playing the entire season and adding 18 goals to his lifetime total.

One of his two games against the Canadiens was in Montreal. I have been in the Forum on many an electrifying evening, none more so than that one. The fans began cheering Guy every time he took a shot during the pre-game warmup. When he scored two goals on Patrick Roy, in typically dramatic Lafleur fashion, he received the loudest ovations any visiting player has ever been given in Montreal.

Flower Power, indeed.

The Best Team

*A*sk me about the best player of all time and I'll hedge. Ask me about the best team and, without hesitation, I'll give you my opinion: the Montreal Canadiens who won four straight Stanley Cups, beginning in 1976.

On October 24, 1987, I was riding in a taxi in Washington, D.C., and guess who was with me? That's right, Scotty Bowman. The late night taxi-twosome was together again, but now we were both wearing blue *Hockey Night in Canada* jackets. Scotty had become a colour commentator on the show, and we were heading to the Capital Center for a Saturday night telecast. I was reminiscing.

"I remember one night here when you were coaching," I said, "when the teams shook hands after the last game of the season. Your guys congratulated the Caps because they gave them a real battle. I'd never seen that before."

"That was an important game for us," Scotty snapped back.

"Important?"

In those days, the Canadiens were far ahead of everyone else in first place and the Caps were behind almost everyone else, close to last place.

"We were going for our sixtieth win," Scotty said. "We really wanted it."

The final score in that final game of the 1976–77 season was 2-1. All goals came in the first period, Guy Lafleur and Steve Shutt scoring for Montreal, Mike Riley for Washington. For the rest of the game, the Canadiens held on to edge a gritty team of Capitals, the same team they had thrashed 11-0 the night before, in Montreal. So the Canadiens had their sixty wins, a record that will stand all the tests of time, one that will always remind me of the best hockey team I have ever seen.

When the Canadiens defeated the defending champion Philadelphia Flyers in four straight games in the 1976 Stanley Cup Final, it was said they had done for hockey what Babe Ruth and the New York Yankees had done for baseball following the "Black Sox Scandal" of 1919. That was the year several members of the American League Champion team from Chicago conspired to throw the World Series. The Babe and the Yankees gave fans great baseball rather than skullduggery. In 1976, many people said the Canadiens proved that pure hockey was better than thuggery.

When the Flyers won the Cup in 1974 and 1975, there was no shortage of skilled players on the team; far from it. Bill Barber, Rick MacLeish, and Reg Leach were good players who left the rough stuff to their teammates. Bobby Clarke, the Flyers' leader, could play it both ways. Bernie Parent's goaltending was superb, especially in the playoffs. But there was much hand-wringing over the more publicised part of the Flyers' game, the one that made the Broad Street Bullies the terror of their opponents and the darlings of box-office managers around the NHL. The exploits and penalty records of their designated hitters like Dave Schultz, Don Saleski, Moose Dupont, and Hound Dog Kelly received more media attention than did the play of those Flyers who were skilfully putting the puck into the other team's net or keeping it out of theirs. The team's reputation led to frequent outbreaks of the "Philadelphia Flu." That was the term used when players, apparently in good health, were suddenly hit with mysterious ailments making it impossible for them to play against the Flyers, especially in Philadelphia. They would then make a miraculous recovery and suit up for the next game, somewhere else.

In the late 1970's, the Canadiens reversed the trend, intimidating the opposition with speed and talent rather than with fist and high stick. In the process, they compiled a record, particularly through the first three seasons of a four-year reign at the top, that will never be matched. They too brought joy to the hearts of the box-office managers around the NHL. Not everyone goes to a hockey game hoping to see a fight break out.

My mother used to caution me about statistics on my hockey broadcasts. "Don't use all those figures. People will get bored if you talk about them too much."

As usual Mother was right, but I think she would excuse me in this case as I try to make a point. In the three seasons starting with 1975–76, the figures in the Canadiens' loss column were eleven, eight, and ten, only twenty-nine defeats in 240 games. Add in the playoffs and you have 213 wins, thirty-four ties, and just thirty-four losses in 281 games, a three-year reign of excellence I'm sure will never be equalled. When they were beaten seventeen times in eighty games in 1979–80, the cry went up in the streets of Montreal, "What's wrong with the Canadiens?" They survived that terrible slump to win a fourth straight Stanley Cup.

The team that won sixty, tied twelve, and lost only eight in the 1976–77 season was a perfect blend of offence, defence, muscle, and finesse. Orchestrating the operation of my best team from a spot just behind his jutted-out jaw was the coach, Scotty Bowman, whom I have described in an earlier chapter as being "one of a kind."

Guy Lafleur and Steve Shutt were constant linemates, with Pete Mahovlich or Jacques Lemaire as their centremen. This prompted the gag that Guy and Steve played on the "Doughnut Line" – no centre. Lemaire, stronger defensively, took over as the season went on.

Yvan Cournoyer played a lot on right wing alongside Doug Risebrough and Yvon Lambert. Mario Tremblay, Réjean Houle, and Murray Wilson were spotted, as per the coach's whims, a situation that didn't sit too well with Tremblay. He had been a regular alongside Risebrough and Lambert the previous two seasons. Following a pre-game warm-up at the Nassau Coliseum, Bowman told Tremblay he wouldn't be playing. Mario replied with a major temper tantrum, throwing his equipment around the room as he angrily undressed for an early shower. Bowman was silently impressed, the way my Dad had been when young Maurice Richard slammed a door in his face when given the same news some thirty-five years before.

The Canadiens didn't lack gunners up front, but the great team of that era won more because of defence than offence. The checking line had Doug Jarvis centering Jimmy Roberts and Bob Gainey, a threesome that handled the other teams' top snipers and shared most of the penalty killing. Jarvis was the best face-off man in hockey, Gainey the game's top defensive forward. And behind them was the main reason for the dynasty of the late 1970's: the "Big Three" – and Ken Dryden.

There is no need to identify "The Big Three" to staunch Montreal fans. For the rest of you, their names were Guy Lapointe, Larry Robinson, and Serge Savard. All great teams have had great defencemen. But I don't think any ever had as talented a threesome playing at the same time.

As was the case with Doug Harvey on previous Montreal teams, Guy Lapointe might have been its best all-around player on those nights when he was at the top of his game. In the 1970's, only Bobby Orr was a more complete defenceman.

Larry Robinson, an awkward, gangly kid out of the Ottawa Valley when he joined the team in 1973, was now a towering physical presence on the Montreal defence. I still get calls from people wanting another look at the replay of a bodycheck he threw at Gary Dornhoefer during the Canadiens-Flyers Cup Final in 1976. They say the boards were bent at point of impact, a story that may have grown in the telling.

Another time, Robinson levelled the Bruins' Terry O'Reilly with a thunderous thump. O'Reilly was my intermission guest on TV a few minutes later, so I had an obvious first question.

"How does it feel to be hit like that by Larry Robinson?"

"Like running into a Redwood tree," was O'Reilly's reply.

Robinson's talents weren't confined to defence and body-checking. In 1976-77, he set a team record for defencemen with eighty-five points on nineteen goals and sixty-six assists, and he won the first of his two Norris Trophies as the NHL's best defenceman. Larry's popularity grew to match his on-ice talents. In my years covering the team, Robinson and Jean Béliveau have been the Canadiens most respected by players around the League, and fans from coast to coast.

While Lapointe gave the defence mobility and Robinson provided muscle and offence, Serge Savard directed the traffic. Savard played the Doug Harvey role, setting the pace of the game with brains rather than brawn. Danny Gallivan had great fun describing a "Savardian Spinne-rama" every time Serge baffled an opposing checker with a pirouette and a quick pass to a speeding Lafleur or Cournoyer.

Bill Nyrop was the main man as fourth defenceman, with Bowman using Rick Chartraw and Pierre Bouchard when he felt the occasion called for their rugged services, which was usually against teams like the Flyers and the Bruins. Neither one was among the coach's favourite people, but he never let personal feelings get in the way of throwing extra muscle at a physical opponent.

And then there was Ken Dryden, the goaltender who succeeded Bernie Parent as the best in the business. Dryden often heard the comment, "Who wouldn't look good playing goal for that team?" - as have other great goaltenders with other great teams. It comes with the territory. He was able to distance himself from that kind of talk and from the fun-loving members of the team whose personalities were far different from that of the scholarly, book-reading goal-tender. Kenny quietly got a kick out of many of their antics. For example, Guy Lapointe would rush to be the first on an escalator or moving sidewalk at an airport and push the switch to shut it off so the rest of us had to climb or walk.

Lapointe was also fearless in some of his practical jokes. On one of his rare appearances at the Forum, Pierre Trudeau paid his customary visit to the Canadiens' dressing room after the game. In politics it's known as a photo opportunity. The PM shook hands with all the players, and no doubt was somewhat taken aback when he reached Lapointe who had, in honour of the occasion, plastered the palm of his right hand with vaseline.

Perhaps Dryden looked askance at that one, but Kenny could join in on the fun too, like the time Jimmy Roberts got fooled. Roberts broke into the NHL with the Canadiens in the mid-60's. He went to the St. Louis Blues in the expansion draft in 1967 and became a valuable, and popular member of the team. Shortly after Bowman joined the Canadiens, they made a deal with the Blues that returned Roberts to Montreal.

His first appearance as a Canadien back in St. Louis had drawn a lot of media coverage. Jimmy was obviously in a bit of a spotlight, and when the Canadiens came on the ice to start the game he was really in it.

The players shuffled around in the dressing room so that Roberts was right behind Dryden when they headed for the ice. In St. Louis, the visiting team defends the end of the rink opposite to where it comes out for the first period, and the Canadiens made sure they came out before the Blues. Dryden drifted casually to one side of the ice as Roberts, head down, charged out of the gate and skated at a pretty good clip toward the other end of the rink. In the meantime, everyone else on the team had stopped in the corridor. Jimmy received a nice hand from the fans and it wasn't until he reached the far end of the rink that he realized he was the only skater on the ice. . . . His buddies had made sure his return to the St. Louis Arena would be a memora-

ble one. In the weeks ahead Roberts gained a fair measure
of revenge with shaving cream.

Jimmy was a terror with a can of shaving cream when
anyone fell asleep on a plane. He always got a laugh from his
victims, except for Dryden, who became genuinely angry
during a long ride home from Atlanta when he awoke to
find his shoes overflowing with Gillette Foamy.

Dryden could be witty in his own, dry manner. After an
easy shutout against the mighty Colorado Rockies, I kidded
him about being overworked in the third period when the
Rockies were credited with three shots on goal.

"Three?" Kenny mused. "That's strange. I remember only
one."

During his final season, Dryden roomed on the road with
Guy Lapointe. Guy began noticing pieces of paper on which
Dryden had written down thoughts and ideas pertaining to
the team and the season.

"Be careful what you say to Kenny these days," Lapointe
warned the boys. "I think he's going to write a book." And
that's exactly what happened, a book that became Number
One on the national best seller lists a few years later.

We have a piece of video tape in our CFCF library, recorded in the Canadiens' dressing room the night they won
the Stanley Cup in 1979, showing Ken Dryden peeling off
his Number 29 sweater and chest protector for the last time.
He had played his final game. To my knowledge, he has
never put on a pair of goal pads since. When they organized
a "Relive the Dream" oldtimers' series in 1987 to bring together the players who had taken part in the Canada-Soviet
series of 1972, Kenny said he would play, but only as a
forward or on defence. There was no way he was going back
into the nets, even just to fool around with the boys from the
office. It's called pride.

In 1976–77, the Canadiens were coming off a Stanley Cup
winning year in which they had lost only eleven regular
season games. They picked up where they had left off with
an opening night 10-1 win over Pittsburgh. The Philadelphia Flyers were still considered their top opponent and

had spent the off-season vowing revenge for the four straight losses they had suffered in the '76 final series. One week into the season, the Canadiens were in Philadelphia and won the game 7-1. The Flyers didn't defeat them all season.

To prove their opening night outburst against the Penguins was not a fluke, in late October they played them in Pittsburgh and won 9-1.

The beat went on all season. In their last forty-eight regular-season games, the Canadiens lost only three times. When the playoffs were over, they had been beaten only five times in their last sixty-two games.

The Bruins handed them three of their eight regular-season losses, and I'm sure Don Cherry remembers every one. Buffalo defeated them twice, the Rangers, Blues, and Maple Leafs each once. Only one of the eight losses came at the Forum, 4-3 to the Bruins on October 30. They didn't lose another game on home ice until the playoffs, when the New York Islanders defeated them 4-3, in overtime, on May 3.

It was truly a team effort. For example, they scored four goals in 2:23 against the Washington Capitals in their last home game. There were two assists on each goal yet Bob Gainey was the only one to earn two points. Eleven different players shared in the scoring stats on those four quick ones. And there were only four hat tricks that year. Shutt, who scored sixty that season, did it twice, Lafleur and Risebrough each once.

In the playoffs, they swept the Blues in four straight in the opening round, were extended to six games by the Islanders, and then defeated the Bruins in four straight in the Stanley Cup Finals.

The end of hockey's most remarkable season came in Boston, in overtime. Early in the extra session, there was a scrum in a corner in the Boston zone. The puck was trapped under skates and referee Bob Myers hollered at the players to "keep it moving." Al Sims, a Bruins defenceman who had been brought up by his parents to obey the voice of authority, did just that. Sims kicked the puck right onto the stick of Guy Lafleur. The Flower quickly whipped it to the front of the Boston net where an unguarded Jacques Lemaire just as quickly fired it past goalie Gerry Cheevers – and their amazing season was complete. The Canadiens had played ninety-four games, winning seventy-two, tying twelve, and losing only ten.

After the game, I joined the media throng in the dressing room to get some interviews for CFCF Radio. I talked with Serge Savard, who told me, "A big reason we won is the kind of players we have. There are no bad apples on this team."

The following season was almost a repeat of 1976-77. The Canadiens lost ten times, which of course prompted some wise guys to crack that "a team can have a bad year." Lafleur scored sixty goals, and again they clinched the Stanley Cup in Boston, although that time Grapes and his Bruins extended the series to six games.

When it was over, I was back in their dressing room getting interviews for CFCF, and again I sat down beside Serge Savard.

"Like I told you last year Dick," he began, "there are no bad apples on this team."

Right out of the blue, with no prompting, he had picked up right where he had left off the year before. With a memory like that no wonder Serge has become a good General Manager.

During those four straight Cup seasons, on the rare occasion the Canadiens happened to lose, it was interesting to watch the reaction of the other team when the game ended. The celebration on the ice would always be wild, but lacking one thing: the Stanley Cup. The players and coaches of those teams would react as though they had just won it and, if it happened on their home ice, which it usually did, the fans would too.

Like any coach of a dominant team, Scotty didn't mind

the odd defeat because it gave him a rare chance to point out a few mistakes and maybe get mad at somebody. After all, what can a guy say to a team that loses only thirty-four times in 281 games?

His team was just as impressive off the ice as on. Their big years coincided with the Parti Québécois' rise to power and there was a lot of pressure on the French-speaking players to publicly support the separatist cause. Before the 1976 Canada Cup Tournament, some Québec Nationalists started a campaign for a Team Québec. If only a couple of the Canadiens had agreed, a circus would have been underway. But the players quickly defused the idea at a news conference. Yvan Cournoyer, Serge Savard, and others said they were only interested in playing for their country.

The Canadiens were the best example at that critical time that French and English can work together. I always said it would mean trouble if I ever got onto a team bus or charter plane and found the French players sitting on one side and the English on the other. That never happened. Some of the French players had political views that differed from many of their teammates, but they never let that interfere with the operation of the hockey club and the togetherness a team needs if it is going to be successful. That tells you something about why the Montreal Canadiens of the late 1970's did what they did.

The players on that team loved to play hockey, which is a lot more fun when you're winning than when you're losing. There would often be an "optional" practice at the Forum on a Sunday morning. It was up to the players whether or not they showed up, and in those days everybody did. Scotty was seldom around, so the boys had a ball, picking up sides and playing a practice game with accompanying whoops and hollers like a bunch of kids let loose on a neighbourhood rink. Some of those games were actually better than some of their League games.

The fourth straight Stanley Cup was won in 1979 following a season in which the Canadiens lost seventeen games, one fewer than the two previous seasons combined. The team was not quite as sharp while certain other teams, notably the Islanders and the Bruins, were better.

Yvan Cournoyer was forced to retire because of a recurring back injury. The Road Runner played his last game in Vancouver in November and was the best man on the ice. Two days later, he was in hospital for treatment of the injury and never played again.

Bowman had problems working for Irving Grundman and was thinking of leaving the team. Dryden was contemplating retirement. When the season ended, Bowman left and Dryden retired.

The Islanders finished 1978–79 in first place overall, one point ahead of Montreal. But they were upset by the Rangers in the playoffs, while the Canadiens made it to the finals thanks to Lafleur's great goal after the Bruins' famous penalty for too many men on the ice.

A somewhat forgotten man was back-up goaltender Bunny Larocque, who replaced Dryden twenty-five or thirty times during the season. Larocque had never started a playoff game, but after the Rangers won the opener of the 1979 final series, with Dryden looking shaky, Bowman decided to make a change. Larocque was named to start the next game. Near the end of the pre-game warm-up, Doug Risebrough fired a shot that struck Larocque on the mask. Down he went, stunned. He was carried off the ice suffering from a slight concussion. So Dryden was back in the nets, and poor Bunny had to wait until Kenny retired before getting his first start in the playoffs.

The Canadiens won that game, and the three after that for a fourth straight Stanley Cup championship. They didn't win again until 1986, with Larry Robinson, Bob Gainey, and Mario Tremblay the only players from the '79 winners still with the team. Nostalgic types like me were happy to see three good guys win another one.

Five players from the four-straight era, Lafleur, Dryden, Savard, Lemaire, and Cournoyer are in the Hockey Hall of Fame. Bowman should be; Robinson and Gainey will be.

Could Scotty's great teams have won in a best-of-seven series against Gordie Howe and the Red Wings of the early 1950's, or Toe's Canadiens of the late 1950's? Were they better than Punch's Leafs of the early 1960's, or Bobby and the Bruins of the early 1970's?

More to the modern-day point, who would win the series if Glen Sather's Edmonton Oilers played Scotty Bowman's Montreal Canadiens?

Now here's the "dream match-up" of this or any other era. Picture it. Ken Dryden and Grant Fuhr standing in the goal creases. The free-wheeling Oilers up against the Canadiens' Big Three on defence. Mark Messier and Yvan Cournoyer streaking up and down the ice, Steve Shutt and Glenn Anderson doing the sniping. And, of course, the best part of the dream, Guy Lafleur in his prime going against Wayne Gretzky in his.

I think my "Best Team" would have beaten them all, but it's only my opinion. Would Joe Louis have KO'd Ali? How about Bobby Jones against Jack Nicklaus, or Rod Laver playing Ivan Lendl?

We'll never know, but it's fun thinking about it.

The Best Games

I attended a National Hockey League game for the first time on April 7, 1938, when I was six years old. Dad was coaching the Maple Leafs and his Regina-based family had travelled to Toronto to join him for the playoffs and the drive back home in his new 1938 Buick.

The Leafs were playing the Chicago Black Hawks in the Stanley Cup finals and, while I don't remember anything about the game, I faintly recall what happened afterward. Toronto won 5-1 and the teams then left on a midnight train to Chicago. Several players went to Murray's Restaurant across from the Toronto station before boarding the train and that's the part I remember because Busher Jackson, one of my early hockey heroes, sat me on his knee. Years later, when I was doing some reminiscing, Mother confirmed my memory of that moment.

The second NHL game I saw was also played in Toronto when the Leafs defeated the New York Americans 5-1 on January 20, 1940. That was just after Dad had moved us from Regina to be with him for the balance of what would be his final season as the Maple Leafs' coach. Don't worry, I'm not about to list the rest of the 2,000 plus games I have seen, but I'd like to mention a few that stand out as the best.

The first time I felt real emotion in an arena was at a senior game in Regina on a rainy night in the spring of 1941 when the Regina Rangers defeated the Sydney Millionaires to win the Allan Cup. The Millionaires had won the first two games of the best-of-five series and the third game ended in a tie. That meant Sydney needed only a tie for the championship.

The Rangers had several local players in the line-up, including a forward line of Grant Warwick, Frank Mario, and Scotty Cameron who were young enough to have still played junior hockey. They battled back to win two games and even the series and I was with Dad at Queen City Gardens when they took the sixth game 3-0. Dad became very wrapped up in the series and it was the only time I saw him cheer at a hockey game. There was a wild storm raging that night and the next day in the *Regina Leader Post* sports writer Steppy Fairman began his account of the game with:

> The lightning flashed, the thunder roared,
> The crowd went nuts when Kunkel scored.

Hockey fans become very emotional at playoff time and broadcasters can too. I guess that's why the games that stand out in my memory are almost exclusively from the playoffs. The goal Bryan Hextall scored to win the Stanley Cup for the New York Rangers in 1940, and the one Elmer Lach scored to win it for the Canadiens in 1953 are so vivid they could have happened yesterday.

The Hextall goal was scored in Toronto, April 13, 1940. Mother and I were sitting in a seat in the reds at Maple Leaf Gardens in what was, in those days, Box 4, and the goal was scored at our end of the building. It was the sixth game of the final series and the goal came early in overtime, at 2:07. Hextall shot and scored from what we call today "the slot," a position directly in front of Leaf goalie Turk Broda. I recall that the teams didn't line up to shake hands as is the custom now. Instead, they stood in a circle, like people at a cocktail party, and I remember that that spot on the ice had the most snow when it was all over. As the eight-year-old son of the losing coach watched the handshakes, he was, as I mentioned earlier, in tears.

Elmer Lach's winning goal came at the Forum on April 16, 1953, and again was scored early in overtime, at 1:22. I don't believe the play stopped between the opening face-off and the goal (that same opening face-off during which Lach and Milt Schmidt held up the game briefly while they discussed plans for their summer holiday). Eddie Mazur, a gangling left winger out of Winnipeg, was alongside Lach and Maurice Richard. The Cup-winning play was started by Mazur when he lugged the puck into the Boston zone. He was checked behind the net. Schmidt picked up the puck and when he saw Richard swooping toward him to forecheck, passed it to his left, toward the boards. Lach intercepted in the face-off circle, turned, and let a shot go. Elmer's shot didn't strike fear into the heart of the goaltender, but it was accurate and cleanly beat the Bruins' goalie Jim Henry. The scoring play was "Lach, from Richard." I've seen the film of the goal many times, and Richard didn't touch the puck. But nobody complained when it was recorded as a combination of The Rocket and Elmer on the official scoresheet. It was their last big year together, and their last big goal.

A regular-season game I remember vividly was played in Montreal on December 30, 1950. Again, Mother, Fay, and I were in Montreal on a Christmas holiday visit. Two nights earlier, the Canadiens had lost 8-1 in Detroit and Dad felt his players had quit on him as the Red Wings were running up the score. Before the December 30 game, he said he would retire if the Canadiens lost that night to the Chicago Black Hawks. Dad told this to the players at their morning meeting after which several of them, including Elmer Lach and Glen Harmon, spent a lot of time with him trying to calm him down. Whether it was for effect or whether he was serious I don't know, but for the rest of the day he was in a deep depression. By the time the game began, the rest of the Irvin family were nervous wrecks.

Chicago had a weak team in those days, but they gave the Canadiens a real battle. The game was tied 3-3 in the third period, when Dad's old pal, the Unseen Hand, came to his rescue. Chicago's Roy Conacher unleashed a terrific shot from the blue line that had Canadiens' goalie Gerry McNeil beaten, but it hit the goal post.

The Chicago goalie was Harry Lumley who, as an eighteen-year-old rookie, had been in goal for Detroit when Maurice Richard had had his five-goal and three-assist game six years and two days earlier. A couple of minutes after Conacher hit the goal post, the Rocket scored a typical Richardian goal. He cut in from the right wing and when he was in front of the goal crease jammed on the brakes. Lumley, moving with him, was thrown out of position. Richard wheeled around and whipped a backhand shot into the unguarded corner of the net for the winning goal. That game is not mentioned in any of the history books of hockey, but it was a big one for the Irvins.

The earliest game that I would classify among "the best" in my broadcasting career was played in St. Louis on May 3, 1968, the seventh game of a playoff series between the Blues and the Minnesota North Stars. The Blues line-up contained several old pros Scotty Bowman had recruited, including Doug Harvey and Dickie Moore. When the North Stars scored to take a 1-0 lead in the third period, Harvey and Moore were on the ice. I remember thinking, "That's it, the last time for those two." Obviously, I underestimated their pride because a couple of minutes later the Blues tied the game, goal by Moore, assist Harvey.

The game went into overtime tied at 1-1, and the extra twenty-two minutes and fifty seconds the teams played were sensational. The Blues' Red Berenson had the best backhand shot of his era and he unleashed one that hit the post behind Cesare Maniago. A minute or so later, Gary Sabourin was in alone on Maniago, who stopped him with a great

glove grab. At the other end of the ice, the veteran Glenn
Hall was working similar miracles for St. Louis. Hall
robbed Bill Goldsworthy, Bill Collins, and Elmer Vasko
with tremendous saves.

Late in the first overtime, Blues defenceman Barclay
Plager tackled Wayne Connelly when he was on a breakaway. It should have been a penalty shot, never mind two
minutes, but the referee Art Skov didn't call anything. In
the third minute of the second overtime period, the Blues'
Ron Shock, scoreless until then in the playoffs, got behind
the Minnesota defence and, on assists from Bill McCreary
and Gerry Melnyk, fired the puck past Maniago to end a
terrific hockey game.

That night, my *Hockey Night in Canada* job was as a
"roving reporter." I watched the game from behind the
glass at one end of the building, at ice level. A camera was in
place there for a couple of post-game interviews with the
victorious Blues, including Glenn Hall. He had gone to the
dressing room at the other end of the rink. Glenn never
enjoyed being interviewed, so I was surprised when he
came on the ice and started to slowly skate toward our interview area. Hardly anyone had left the building and when
Hall appeared he was greeted by a tremendous roar from
the crowd. The ovation continued for Glenn as he made his
solitary skate toward me. By the time he arrived, we had
the undivided attention of 18,000 Blues fans in the Arena, as
well as the folks watching across the network. The ovation
and the atmosphere had me all shook up. Hall, who said he
didn't enjoy being interviewed, was great on the air. His
nerves were back to normal while mine were still full of
electricity.

The following year, the Canadiens and the Bruins played
a game, in Boston, that was one of the best I've seen. On
April 24, 1969, Montreal needed a win to clinch a playoff
series in Game Six. Again the goaltenders put on a great
show, in this case Roggie Vachon of Montreal and Boston's
Gerry Cheevers. Vachon was particularly sharp against
Phil Esposito. In those days, there were bumper stickers

around the Boston area reading, "Jesus Saves, and Espo Scores on the Rebound." Vachon's best save that night came early in overtime, off Espo, on a rebound. After Roggie made the first stop, Phil pounced on the rebound and fired a quick wrist shot. Vachon kicked out his left foot and deflected the puck into the corner, with Danny Gallivan describing it as a "scintillating save." As the play headed up the ice, Esposito stood in front of Vachon and rapped himself across his forehead with his stick, no doubt muttering, "You dummy. How could you let that little mutt do it to you again?"

I came close to looking like a genius that night. The game was tied 1-1 after regulation time, and it was still that way after the first twenty minutes of overtime. During the next intermission, I interviewed Detroit Red Wing star Alex Delvecchio. We were down to the "Who do you think will score the winning goal?" question when Ralph Mellanby yelled into my earpiece that we were out of time and I had to wrap up the interview. I was going to follow up Delvecchio's answer with my guess that Jean Béliveau would score the goal, but I didn't get the chance. I was sort of glad, at the time, because I'm chicken when it comes to predictions.

The teams were nearing the twelve-minute mark of the second overtime period when Béliveau took a pass from Claude Provost on the left wing inside the Boston blue line. Bruins defenceman Ted Green sprawled to block the shot, a bit too late, and Béliveau fired the puck over Cheever's left arm and into the net. The goal ended one of the best games I've seen and was a milestone for Béliveau. It was the only overtime goal he scored during his brilliant career.

A little over a year later, it was 'déjà vu' time for Danny and me as we broadcast another dramatic overtime goal at the Boston Garden. The Bruins were playing the St. Louis Blues in the 1970 Stanley Cup Final. Boston had easily won the first three games, but the Blues put up a surprisingly stiff fight in Game Four and it was tied 3-3 at the end of regulation time. The Bruins had not won the Stanley Cup in twenty-nine years and the pressure was on them to do it on home ice. Unlike the year before, this overtime was a quick one, with the ending similar in one respect. The winning goal was scored by a superstar wearing Number 4.

In the first minute of overtime, Derek Sanderson passed the puck to Bobby Orr. Orr cut in from the right wing, headed straight for the net, and fired the puck past Glenn Hall just as Blues defenceman Noel Picard yanked his feet out from under him. I suspect only Orr could shoot, be tripped, score, and fly through the air in joy, all at the same time. It was a memorable moment caught on camera, one of hockey's all-time best photographs. The instant the photographer snapped that picture, Danny and I were showered with beer thrown down from the gallery above us by some long-suffering, but now jubilant, Bruins' fans.

I have done most of my hockey watching and broadcasting in the Montreal Forum. But that game in Boston and the one in Philadelphia four years later, when the Flyers defeated the Bruins 1-0 to win their first Stanley Cup, produced the largest outpouring of fan emotion I have ever seen – and I've seen more than a few emotional finishes, including twenty-two Stanley Cup winning games, of which I've broadcast sixteen. (Come to think of it, do I hold a record in there somewhere?)

The Stanley Cup playoffs of 1971 are still my most memorable. The Bruins were the NHL's best team that season, finishing with a record 121 points. Phil Esposito shocked everyone, including himself, by scoring seventy-six goals and seventy-six assists in seventy-eight games. Orr, John Bucyk, and Ken Hodge all finished with over a hundred scoring points. Their second straight Stanley Cup seemed only a formality.

Boston played Montreal in the first round. The Canadiens had finished in third place, twenty-four points behind the Bruins. They had changed coaches during the season, Al MacNeil replacing Claude Ruel. Ken Dryden, a law student at McGill, was playing goal for their American League farm team based in Montreal, the Voyageurs. Early in March, I joined Floyd "Busher" Curry for lunch at the

Texan Restaurant across the street from the Forum. (Floyd played with the Canadiens for nine seasons, did some coaching after retiring as a player in 1958, and has been working in the team's front office for the past several years.)

"They called up Ken Dryden today," Busher told me.

"So what?"

"If they use him, they'll win the Stanley Cup," he replied. That one tops my hit parade of the all-time greatest predictions.

Dryden played six regular-season games in fairly impressive fashion, but it was still a surprise when MacNeil started him in the first playoff game in Boston. The Bruins didn't overpower the rookie goaltender, but they did control the game, winning 3-1. MacNeil wouldn't say who his goalie would be for Game Two and a lot of media types felt he should come back with Roggie Vachon. I happened to walk into the Garden just as Dryden was arriving at the same door.

"Are you in the barrel?" I asked him, borrowing a phrase I often heard Dad use when talking about his starting goaltender.

"I'm led to believe that is the case," replied the scholarly rookie, who likely had spent most of his day reading law textbooks.

By the time the second period was over, the Montreal media people who thought Vachon should have played were in full cry. The Bruins built a 5-1 lead on the shaky rookie and his equally shaky teammates. A goal late in the second period by Henri Richard made the score 5-2, but nobody thought the Canadiens had a chance, especially the Bruins.

Little things can sometimes mean a lot in a hockey game. In the final minute of the second period, Boston defenceman Don Awrey was hit with a terrific check by Phil Roberto. I thought Roberto should have drawn a charging penalty, but he didn't, and when the Bruins came out to start the third period Awrey was obviously in some pain as he kept twisting his neck and working his shoulders in a circular motion. He was indeed playing hurt as events proved.

There was another thing happening as the teams had their warm-up skate. Our TV cameras caught Bobby Orr and Derek Sanderson sharing some kind of a joke and having a good old time laughing it up. Ralph Mellanby, directing from the CBC mobile, called through on the headset.

"I wonder if these guys will be laughing when it's over tonight. They might not be you know."

I didn't believe Ralph at the time and didn't mention the incident on the air, but I should have. What followed still rates as the best comeback I have ever seen the Canadiens muster in all the years I've been watching them play. And it was a comeback that to me was the definitive Last Hurrah for the great Jean Béliveau.

Early in the period, Big Jean pinned a Bruin on the boards behind the Boston net, took the puck from him and passed it out to John Ferguson whose quick shot beat Eddie Johnston, and it was 5-3. A couple of minutes later, it was Béliveau with the puck again, this time directly in front of E.J. Béliveau stickhandled to the right, to the left, and, with Johnston now out of position, went to the right again and tucked home a beautiful backhander. The Canadiens were to within one.

Midway through the period, Orr misplayed a pass at the Canadiens' blue line, allowing Jacques Lemaire to break away. Lemaire caught Johnston by surprise when he unloaded a big slap shot from just inside the blue line. Tie game.

Bobby, Espo, and the rest of the Bruins were floundering. Béliveau was winning face-offs and making passes the way he did during his greatest years. He was turning back the hockey calendar, and it was something to behold.

With just under five minutes left in the period, Béliveau again stripped the puck from a Bruin behind the Boston net and fed a perfect pass to Ferguson who scored to put the Canadiens ahead 6-5. Frank Mahovlich added the clincher a minute later. The final score of 7-5 is indelibly etched in the minds of Canadiens' fans from that era.

Gerry Cheevers, replaced by Johnston for the second

game, was back in the nets for the third game. It would be Cheevers, the old pro, against the rookie Dryden the rest of the way. The teams split the next two games at the Forum, 3-2 Canadiens, 5-2 Bruins. Boston was one win away from clinching the series after an easy 7-3 win on home ice in Game Five. MacNeil's choice of goaltender for this series now wasn't looking very good. But back in Montreal, the Canadiens won big, 8-3. Dryden played very well in Game Six that night, especially in the first period, when he had stopped a big shot from Orr with a brilliant glove grab. The save was made early in the period and seemed to give the Canadiens, and the Forum crowd, the lift they needed. When Dryden's name was announced for an assist on a goal late in the game, with the Canadiens well on their way to victory, the fans gave the rookie goaltender a standing ovation.

The seventh game of that 1971 Canadiens-Bruins series was played at the Boston Garden on a Sunday afternoon. The Bruins took a 1-0 lead on a first-period goal by Ken Hodge. They were dominating the game early, but Dryden was brilliant against the team that had set several scoring records during the regular season.

One save in particular has been replayed many times on *Hockey Night in Canada* as part of a "playoff flashback" montage. Esposito is in close, but Dryden, down on one knee, makes the save as Espo careens past him and into the cross bar. To show his frustration that time, Espo smashed his stick against the bar as he skated away. At least that way he didn't end up with a sore forehead as he had when robbed in a similar fashion by Roggie Vachon two years before.

The Canadiens won the game 4-2, Frank Mahovlich setting up Jacques Lemaire on a perfectly executed two-on-one break for the winning goal. As I was leaving the broadcast booth, I ran into Punch Imlach.

"I'm not surprised," said Punch who had just completed his first year as boss of the Buffalo Sabres. "Any time there's a seventh game, I want it on the road. All the pressure is on the home team." Imlach's theory certainly worked for the Canadiens that year.

Montreal played Minnesota in the next round, winning in six games in a series that ended on a bizarre note. The North Stars scored a goal that would have tied the game, but the green light signalling the end of the third period flashed on a fraction of a second before the goal judge tried to put on the red light. No goal, and the series was over. Half the Minnesota team stormed around the referee and the goal judge, violently claiming the goal should have been allowed. At the same time, the rest of the North Stars were lined up at centre ice shaking hands with the Canadiens. It made for a very strange scene.

The Canadiens defeated the Chicago Black Hawks in the final series that was strictly a home-ice affair until Game Seven at the Chicago Stadium, May 18, 1971. That was the day John Robertson of the *Montreal Star* scooped everyone with the story that Jean Béliveau would retire after the game. It didn't happen quite that quickly, but the big guy did announce it a few weeks later.

The Black Hawks had a 2-0 lead in the second period and should have made it 3-0 when, with Dryden out of position, Bobby Hull let loose one of his patented slap shots. Dad's old phrase, "The Unseen Hand" flashed through my mind as I watched the puck hit the post and rebound all the way out to the blue line.

Had Hull scored, the Hawks would have won the Cup. A few minutes later, Jacques Lemaire drilled the puck past an unprepared Tony Esposito from outside the Chicago blue line and, before the second period ended, the Canadiens tied the score on a goal by Henri Richard.

When The Pocket Rocket scored again in the third period, swooping around defenceman Keith Magnuson and deking Esposito to give the Canadiens a 3-2 lead, I described the replay with mixed emotions. Henri wasn't my favourite player at that moment because he had blasted Al MacNeil during the series, calling him the worst coach he ever played for. It is no surprise that I usually take the coach's side at a time like that, and I did then. Fans and media in Montreal seemed split on language grounds over the controversy, the French supporting Richard and the English supporting MacNeil. The courage Al MacNeil showed by hanging in and staying cool was one of the most memorable aspects of the 1971 Stanley Cup Finals. However, it wasn't enough to earn him another shot at the job. By the time the next season began, Al had been replaced by Scotty Bowman.

Richard's third-period goal held up and the Canadiens were Cup winners. I flew home with the team on their charter flight after the game. Walking toward the gate in the Chicago airport, I fell into step with the goaltenders, Dryden and Roggie Vachon.

"I didn't have a very good view of the last goal," said Dryden. "What happened?"

Roggie and I explained how Magnuson had fallen to the ice totally eliminated from the play as he slid helplessly into the corner of the rink; how Richard, a right-hand shot, had cut in on goal from the left wing, waited until Esposito dropped to his knees, and then lifted the puck over the goalie's shoulder into the top corner of the net.

"Incredible, just incredible," was Kenny's response. He wondered how far out from the net Lemaire had been when he blasted home the long shot that had started the Canadiens' comeback. Yes, Kenny, Esposito was on his knees before that shot too. Yes, Béliveau was outplaying Stan Mikita as much as it looked to you. Dryden kept asking and we kept answering.

"Incredible, just incredible," said the Canadiens' new hero, over and over again.

We didn't have to describe the greatest save of the series to him, the one he made off Jim Pappin. The Chicago forward seemed to have a wide-open net to shoot at, but was foiled as Dryden stretched leg, arm, and goalstick to make an incredible stop. That one has been replayed on TV more than any other of his career. It was a big reason he was awarded the Smythe Trophy as the Most Valuable Player of the playoffs after playing in only his twenty-sixth game in the NHL.

The Canadiens, mentally and physically exhausted, were fairly quiet on the flight home. Bobby Sheehan, a seldom-used fringe player, tried to liven things up by mooning the boys, but nobody paid any attention.

I was touched when Jean Béliveau came down the aisle, shook my hand, and said, "A lot of memories tonight, eh Dick? For both of us."

Ralph Mellanby and the big boss at *HNIC*, Ted Hough, were on the plane and told me the CBC was predicting the largest audience in Canadian television history for the game. (I think it worked out that way with around eight million viewers.) So I was feeling very much like a big-shot TV star when I arrived home to find a note from my sleeping wife. It read, "Don't forget, tonight is garbage night."

As always, Wilma knew just when to remind me to come back down to earth.

In retrospect, the Canadiens' well-remembered Stanley Cup victory in 1971 wasn't as big an upset as it seemed at the time. They had been overshadowed all season by the exploits of Orr, Espo, and the rest of the Bruins, but the Montreal roster wasn't exactly a collection of stray pieces of chopped liver. Seven players on the plane ride home from Chicago that night, Béliveau, Dryden, Jacques Laperrière, Yvan Cournoyer, Jacques Lemaire, Henri Richard, and Frank Mahovlich have since been voted into the Hockey Hall of Fame. By contrast, the Bruins of that season had four Hall of Famers: Orr, Esposito, John Bucyk, and Gerry Cheevers. The Montreal team was full of stars. It just took them a while to get their act together – and for a young goaltender to leave his McGill classroom in time for Floyd Curry's amazing prediction to come true.

The best playoff series I've worked was the Montreal-Boston semi-final in 1979. Most fans remember the seventh game when the Bruins had the lead late in the third period, then drew a penalty for having too many men on the ice. Guy Lafleur tied the game on the Canadiens' power play and Montreal won it in overtime on a goal by Yvon Lambert.

That seventh game was memorable, but so was the entire series. The level of intensity was high when the puck was dropped to start Game One and it stayed high until Lambert's goal went into the net.

Home ice was the main advantage. Montreal won the first two games, at the Forum, 4-2 and 5-2. Back in Boston, the Bruins won two close games, 2-1, with Brad Park scoring the winner, and 4-3 on an overtime goal by Jean Ratelle. Park and Ratelle had long and distinguished careers, but were fated to end their playing days without ever being on a Stanley Cup winning team.

The Canadiens won the fifth game in Montreal, 5-1. The Bruins took the sixth, in Boston, 5-2.

I always prepare notes on the teams and the players to help fill time during hockey broadcasts (and you thought it was all ad lib, didn't you?). Normally during the playoffs, I update the notes game by game. In that series I didn't have to do that, the games were that good. There was very little time to "fill." The action took care of everything.

That was during my upstairs-downstairs period on HNIC and, with a few minutes to play in the seventh game, I headed downstairs to the studio. The Bruins were leading 4-3 and I had been told Wayne Cashman would be a post-game guest and likely Bruins coach Don Cherry too. Leo Monohan, a Boston newspaperman and a good friend of mine, happened to be heading down at the same time. As we got to the bottom of the stairs and were cutting through the Forum garage, I caught the end of a PA announcement.

"I think the Bruins just got a penalty," I said to Leo. Sure enough, that was the famous too-many-men-on-the-ice call against Cherry and his team.

Grapes has made a good part of his living since then talking about that penalty and everyone remembers it as the big mistake that cost his team the series. I think he made an even bigger one by starting Gerry Cheevers for the first two games at the Forum, games Boston might have won with better goaltending. Gilles Gilbert took over after that and, even though he was never one of Cherry's favourites, Don had to admit Gilbert almost won it for the Bruins.

That memorable 1979 game was played at the Montreal Forum. However, most of the games I recall as being among "the best" were played in other NHL buildings, mainly at either the Boston Garden or the Chicago Stadium. Another is Madison Square Garden in New York, where the most recent Stanley Cup Championship Pennant hanging from the rafters is dated 1940. It was there, in the 1979 Stanley Cup Finals between the Canadiens and the Rangers, that Larry Robinson scored what should have been an overtime, game-winning goal. But the puck went clean through the netting and the play continued. The Canadiens were furious and Scotty Bowman was frantically trying to calm down his players on the bench. Luckily the referee was spared a rough time when, before the play stopped, Serge Savard shot the puck past Ranger goalie John Davidson. That time it stayed in the net.

The Rangers were on home ice again for another of my best games, this time in 1984 in the deciding game of a best-of-five series with the Islanders. Bob Cole and I worked the telecast. The teams were tied 2-2 at the end of regulation time and when overtime began, the word "defence" was forgotten. It was end-to-end action in the purest sense of the phrase. Glen Hanlon was in goal for the Rangers, Billy Smith for the Islanders. They were spectacular, and then some. Hanlon had to contend with two wild scrambles in his goal crease but, somehow, managed to keep the puck out of his net. The Rangers had a couple of breakaways on Smith and he was the winner both times in that classic hockey confrontation. After Smith stopped Bob Brooke on the second one, the Islanders carried the puck up the ice, and Ken Morrow scored the series-winning goal. Morrow was one of those defensive defencemen who managed to score overtime goals in the playoffs. That was his third, a lame-duck type of shot from a sharp angle along the right-wing boards that eluded the unfortunate Hanlon who had been brilliant on much tougher chances all night.

The hair-raising overtime had lasted 8:56. After Morrow was pummelled by his happy mates, and the teams had completed their hand-shaking ritual, we threw the cue for a commercial. Our mikes were on the air long enough for my voice to be heard across the network saying, "That's the best overtime I've ever seen. . . ."

The team of Cole and Irvin was in the booth at Madison Square Garden again during the 1986 playoffs when the Canadiens' rookie goaltender, Patrick Roy, made thirteen saves in the first nine minutes of overtime. Montreal then won the game on a shot by Claude Lemieux, only their second of the period. We cranked out the phrase, "Can you believe it?" a few times during those hectic nine minutes. Jean Béliveau called Roy's performance "Maybe the best stretch of playoff goaltending I've ever seen." That's good enough for me too.

I've been fortunate to have been involved in the broadcasts of several playoff "firsts." I was in Philadelphia the first time the Flyers won the Stanley Cup and at the Nassau Coliseum when the Islanders won the first of their four straight championships. I got a big charge out of being in the Olympic Saddledome for the first Stanley Cup final series played in Calgary, and I was in the Northlands Coliseum when Wayne the Wonder Kid and the Edmonton Oilers won their first Cup in 1984. Great firsts. Great memories.

I've been ensconced in front of my TV set for a few memorable moments as well. The Islanders-Washington marathon in the 1987 playoffs was a classic, lasting through two complete games and into the first period of a third. There's not too much wrong with hockey when you see it played that way.

There are two hockey games that will live forever in Canadian sports history, games that have spawned the questions, "Where were you when Paul Henderson scored his winning goal, in Moscow, in 1972?" and "Where were you when Mario Lemieux scored the Canada Cup winning goal in 1987?"

In 1972, when Henderson's goal gave Canada victory in the historic eight-game series against the Soviets, I was in my basement, leaping off a chair and cheering just like everyone else who was watching CTV and listening to Foster Hewitt.

In 1987, I was at the Canyon Meadows Golf Club, in Calgary, when Lemieux's goal was scored. I had just finished MC-ing the Calgary Flames Charity Golf Classic, which is held annually in aid of Special Olympics. When Lemieux scored, the room full of hockey players and fans erupted with a big cheer. But when the game was over, nobody cheered. Instead, they applauded. I thought it was a fine salute to both teams, thanking them for what might have been the greatest three-game series ever played.

I was asked on a talk show on CFCF Radio what I liked best about my job. I told the caller it was the moment the referee dropped the puck to start a hockey game and I was in the booth starting my broadcast. You never know when a game begins what is going to happen and, after all the years and all the games, I still look forward to that opening face-off. It just might be a game I will remember as one of "the best."

No Shortage
of Stories

Hockey has never suffered from a lack of story tellers. Listening to them, and hanging around long enough to have a few of your own to tell, can be a lot of fun.

One of the best is "The Old Redhead," Red Storey, who has been the source of much laughter at dinners and charity functions, from coast to coast, for years. Red once told me he tried to figure how much money had been collected at the many fund raisers he'd been at. He said he stopped counting when he reached ten million dollars.

Red was a good all-around athlete, a Grey Cup hero, a fine lacrosse player, and a referee in both the CFL and the NHL. His days wearing a black and white sweater, and blowing a referee's whistle, provide him with most of his banquet material.

He often tells of the night at the Forum when my dad, upset with his work, sent his captain, Butch Bouchard, onto the ice to question him.

"Butch didn't have a clue what Irvin was mad about, but he had to put on a show just the same. The fans saw him waving his arms and yelling at me, and thought he was giving me the business. What he really was saying was, 'I wouldn't have your job for all the money in the Forum. You have to be nuts to do this.' I waved back at him and told him our time was up, and he went back to the bench and told Irvin I wouldn't listen to him, and that was that."

Red has a similar story involving King Clancy, when King was coaching the Maple Leafs. Clancy sent Harry Watson out to question Red's competence. When he got back to the bench King was yelling, "What did he say? What did he say?"

"What he said," Watson replied, "was that you can go and stuff yourself."

My favourite from Red's repertoire goes like this: "I was working a Detroit-Boston game, there was a power play, and I was standing where I was supposed to stand, along the goal line beside the net. Johnny Bucyk let a slap shot go from the blue line. It was comin' right at me, so I opened my legs to let the puck go through. But it was a rising shot, and it kept rising, and it drilled me right in a place where it hurt a lot.

"I went down like a stone. Marcel Pronovost skated over to me and said, 'For God's sake Red, don't grab them. We're on national TV!'"

I've been with Red at many dinners and often use the line, "My father always said the excitement of a hockey game was in direct proportion to the incompetence of the referee. He told me Red Storey refereed more exciting games than anyone in hockey history."

One of my dad's favourite stories concerned another colourful redhead, Red Dutton, the man who checked him when he fractured his skull when he was playing in Chicago.

Dutton was President of the NHL during the mid-1940's. Phil Watson played for the Canadiens in the 1943–44 season and was involved in a scrap during a game in Toronto. Watson was thrown out of the game after he took a poke at a linesman. A couple of days later, he was called on the carpet in Dutton's office in Montreal, and Dad went with him.

"Well, Mr. Dutton, it was like this," began the colourful

little character whose nickname was Fiery Phil. "The lines-man had my arms pinned behind me and the other guy was pounding hell out of me. It got so I wasn't mad at him, I was mad at the linesman. So when I got free, I let him have one."

Dutton, a tough character himself in his playing and coaching days, thought for a moment.

"You know, gentlemen," he finally said. "I would have done the same thing myself. Case dismissed." Rocket Richard should have been so lucky.

During the 1940's, Dutton was the manager and coach of the New York Americans, a team short on talent but long on characters to match Dutton's flamboyant personality. On one occasion, during a game between his team and the Canadiens, in New York, Dutton almost did what a lot of coaches have wanted to do in the heat of the battle.

It was in the early 1940's, when neither team was what you could term a powerhouse. They were having a shoot-out, the kind of a game Dad used to describe as "last shot wins." Late in the third period, the Americans were leading by a goal. A Montreal rookie, Tony Demers, had one of the hardest shots in the game. He fired one from outside the American blue line. The New York goalie was, as we say, "caught napping," and the puck flew past him into the net.

Dutton went wild, ranted and raved for a few seconds behind the bench, then suddenly charged out of the gate and onto the ice, headed for his goaltender. The word "kill" likely crossed his mind. Dutton's players grabbed him and hauled him back to the bench before he went too far.

Many times a coach has wished he could throttle one of his players, on the spot, and to heck with the game. Dutton tried to do it, and no doubt would have had the sympathy of many a man who has stood behind a bench had he succeeded.

The same thought may have crossed Dad's mind one night in Chicago during his first season as coach of the Canadiens. His goalie that game was Wilf Cude, a bouncy little guy who had been in and out of the Canadiens' nets for a few years. Cude played three games for Dad that season. The game in Chicago was a wide-open affair. With less than a minute to play, Elmer Lach scored to give Montreal a 6-5 lead. As the referee was dropping the puck to resume play following the goal, Dad glanced toward the Canadien net. It was empty. . . .

"Where the hell is Cude?" he bellowed. Then he saw him. Cude, an excitable type, had skated to the end of the Canadiens' bench and was hugging Lach and congratulating him for scoring the goal.

"The game's on!" Dad hollered, and everyone else on the bench picked up the refrain. Cude, realizing the error of his ways, frantically raced back to his goal crease, arriving just in time to stop a shot that would have tied the game. The Canadiens held on to win. Dad loved to tell that story, but at the time it was no laughing matter.

One of hockey's greatest raconteurs was King Clancy, the lovable little Irishman who had the Toronto Maple Leaf logo tattooed on his heart.

I might have been the last person to interview King Clancy for TV. I had wanted to get together with him for a reminiscing session to use on our CFCF show *Hockey Magazine*. We finally arranged it in early October of 1986 and did the interview in his office at the Gardens.

King was, as usual, in rare form. He began by saying he was going to tell me a story about my dad that he was sure I had never heard.

"We were having trouble with Sylvio Mantha of the Canadiens," King began. "Your father took me aside before a game one night and told me I had to look after Mantha. I asked him if that meant doing something that wasn't allowed in the rule book. He just told me to use my own judgement, but I knew what he meant.

"It happened at this end of the ice," King continued, pointing in a direction I assumed was the scene of what had transpired that night many years ago. Like most of the oldtimers from that era, he seemed to have total recall.

"Mantha had the puck and was coming out of his own end. I saw my chance. I jumped at him and pushed my stick right in his face. Down we went and you should have seen the mess. He was cut and there was blood all over the place. And you know what?"

King paused for dramatic effect.

"I didn't even get a penalty. Imagine."

He had many more tales for me that day, including his first experience at trying to check Howie Morenz, then considered the greatest player in the game.

"I was a rookie with the Ottawa Senators and was on defence with George Boucher. Morenz came down the ice skating right at me, gave me a nice 'howdy doo' with a shake of his head and the next thing I know he's behind both of us and the puck is in the net."

King was laughing at the recollection.

"I said to Boucher, how did he get through us? Did he go through the middle? Boucher said he didn't know, but he was sure Morenz hadn't gone between us. But we weren't sure because it had happened so quickly.

"As Morenz skated past us after he scored, I told him 'Try that again and I'll knock your block off!' He said, 'Don't go away. I'm comin' right back.'"

King was a great admirer of Morenz and unhesitatingly called him the best player he had faced in his career.

"Morenz was the greatest on and off the ice. He was a wonderful fellow," King told me.

King Clancy wasn't one of those old-timers who constantly knocks today's game and today's players. On the contrary.

"People now are so lucky they can watch a player like Gretzky," he said during our interview. "We've had Howe, and Orr, and Hull. And now this Gretzky comes along. He's some player. Would have been a star in my day too. That's for sure."

We edited the interview and it ran on the show in early November. The weekend it was aired, King entered hospital in Toronto and passed away a few days later. He was one you could truthfully say they broke the mould for so he could pass our way. Anyone who knew King Clancy knew someone very special.

King had a lifetime contract with the Maple Leafs,

thanks to his best friend in the final years of his life, Harold Ballard. There's no doubt King loved the controversial owner of his favourite hockey team and, quite frankly, I haven't found him to be too bad a guy myself.

One night at Maple Leaf Gardens, I was showing the Toronto HNIC gang my dad's lifetime pass to the building. In the days when the Leafs were winning Stanley Cups, each member of the championship team received one. Dad's was from the Leafs Cup win in 1932, the team's first. Harold passed by and the boys called him over to take a look at it.

"You can use that here any time you want to," he said to me.

"Thanks Mr. Ballard, but this belongs to my father, not to me. I didn't earn it."

"Don't worry about that kid," he replied. "As far as I'm concerned it's yours now."

Now, I'm not what is known in my business as a "knocker." I prefer leaving the washing of dirty linen to those who feel more comfortable in that role. Over the years on *Hockey Night in Canada*, I have said a lot of nice things about a lot of hockey executives. Yet only one has ever gone out of his way to say "thank you." Harold Ballard. So, despite what some say, Uncle Harold isn't all bad.

I don't say nice things just to get a compliment in return either. But it's nice when it happens, whether it comes from the owner of a team, or a player.

In the 1986 playoffs, Edmonton Oilers defenceman Steve Smith became a household name overnight, for all the wrong reasons. In the third period of the seventh game between the Oilers and their big rivals, the Calgary Flames, Smith passed the puck out from behind his own net. The puck hit goalie Grant Fuhr on the back of the leg and caromed into the Oilers' net. It turned out to be the winning goal in Calgary's big upset of the defending Stanley Cup champions.

Smith's miscue was the main post-game story. A couple of nights later, I was working on the telecast of a Canadiens playoff game that I knew was being seen in Edmonton. I decided to send a message to Steve Smith.

"I don't know if Steve Smith is looking in out in Edmonton," I began, "but Steve, if you are, I just want to let you know that a lot of players who have gone before you can sympathise with you tonight. A lot of great ones. In 1954, Doug Harvey tried to knock the puck out of the air with his hand, and instead knocked it into his own net for the Stanley Cup winning goal, in overtime. So you see, it has happened to the best and, believe me, in his day Doug Harvey was the best. So hang in Steve, and good luck in the future."

I had never met Steve Smith. In fact, right then I wouldn't have recognised him if he had walked into the broadcast booth. The following season, when the Oilers were in Montreal, I was coming out of the *Hockey Night in Canada* studios a couple of hours before game time. The studios are across the hall from the visitors' dressing room and a member of the Oilers, dressed in his hockey underwear, was standing in the hallway.

"Mr. Irvin," he said, "I'm Steve Smith. I just want to thank you for what you said about me on television. I really appreciated it."

The feeling was mutual.

Speaking of "Mr. Irvin," that's what one of Steve Smith's former teammates always calls me. Here I'm referring to someone I would certainly recognise if he walked into the broadcast booth: Wayne Gretzky.

A couple of years ago, we taped an interview before a game. Wayne always calls me "Mr. Irvin," so I warned him that if he called me that during the interview I'd stop, and we'd start over again. It's tough enough dealing with the generation gap when players tell me, "I've been watching you all my life." It may be true, but why do they have to rub it in?

We did the interview, with Wayne patiently answering

questions he'd likely been asked many times before. He didn't call me "Mr. Irvin." He didn't call me by any name. When the interview ended, he unhooked his microphone and started to leave the studio.

"Thanks very much," he said. "See you when you're in Edmonton next month, Mr. Irvin."

I'm sure that a few fuzzy-cheeked rookies feel like calling many of the established NHL stars "Mister" when they first arrive. When the Canadiens had their great teams in the 1970's, I used to see youngsters on the other teams sneaking glances toward the Canadiens when the teams were warming up. I used to imagine what was going through their minds.

"There's Dryden. There's Lafleur. Oh my God, Cournoyer and Robinson, and Savard."

These kids had watched the Canadiens' powerhouse win a few Stanley Cups, and now there they were about to play against them.

I'm sure today's rookies steal the same kind of glances at Gretzky, Messier, Lemieux, Bourque, and Hawerchuk.

I remember one time in this regard when Bobby Orr was in his prime. The Bruins were playing the Washington Capitals, when a Washington centreman held up a face-off to tell a rookie teammate playing in his first game where to stand before the puck was dropped. The Washington rookie moved over, and at the same time shot a quick glance at Boston's Bobby Orr. Bobby figured the kid had been given bad advice, so, despite the fact they were on opposite teams, he motioned to him to move to another spot on the ice – where Orr thought he would be better positioned. The rookie, obviously a bundle of nerves, nodded to Bobby, "OK," and moved. . . .

It's called hero worship.

In the summer of 1987, I attended the Rick Wamsley Charity Golf Tournament, in Port Dover, Ontario. Alan Bester, the Toronto Maple Leafs' goalie, was there and wanted to talk to me about his hero, Ken Dryden.

He showed me a picture of Dryden that he carries in his

wallet. I asked him if he had ever met Kenny. He said he hadn't.

"I was in the same room with him once," said Bester. "But I was too nervous to speak to him."

The dumbest question you can ask a hockey player is, "Do you remember your first goal in the NHL?" I have, dumbly, asked it many times. A guy can score a million, but the one he's likely to remember best of all is Number One.

During the 1988 playoffs, in Boston, Phil Esposito overheard me talking with writer Leo Monohan about Terry Sawchuk.

"Got my first goal against him," said Phil. "I broke in all alone from the blue line. I'd seen him on TV and remembered he often went down on one knee on breakaways. I waited for him to go down, and when he did I threw it into the top corner. I thought, hey, this is easy. I hadn't played much until then. After that, they didn't play me again for seven games. I was crushed."

Goaltenders are the same when it comes to their first game or shutout. One of the best answers I have received to "the dumbest question" came from Wayne Thomas, who played goal for the Canadiens in the early 1970's. Wayne made his NHL debut, in Vancouver, on a Sunday afternoon during the 1972-73 season, a day he well remembers because he turned in a shutout against the Canucks.

I lugged my trusty CFCF tape recorder into the dressing room after the game and asked Wayne the obvious question.

"How did you feel when the game started and you were playing in the NHL for the first time?" I expected the usual routine about how he was nervous, how his teammates helped him relax and played well in front of him. Instead, I got an answer I've never forgotten.

"Quite honestly," Wayne said, "I thought I was going to throw up."

Gordie Howe, who has scored more goals than anyone else, had a great comment about one he didn't score. His son, Mark, had scored a winning goal for the Philadelphia Flyers with one second to play in the third period. A cou-

ple of days later, I saw Gordie at the All-Star game in New
Jersey.

"Did you ever do what Mark did?" I asked him. "Ever
score a winner at 19:59 of the third period?"

"Nope," said Gordie. "But once I was at the blue line on
the point and had the puck with five seconds to play. Somebody yelled at me to shoot, but I told him it wouldn't get
there in time."

During an interview on *Hockey Magazine*, Gordie was
talking about the stick work that is so prevalent in the game
today.

"In our time," he explained, "you'd hook a guy just enough
to throw him off stride. Give him a good nudge. Today, they
put the stick under the arm pit, hang on, and go for a sleigh
ride."

I don't know if hockey in the Soviet Union has its versions
of The Old Redhead, King, or Harry Neale. Watching the
Soviet hockey robots, it's hard to imagine the comrades sitting around and laughing it up with tall tales about the old
days. But they certainly have made a lasting impression on
hockey in our part of the world. My dad was never involved
with them, but he wanted to be, and it's one of my favourite
stories about him.

It took eighteen years and the invention of Alan Eagleson
before the Lords of Hockey followed some advice Dad tried
to give them in 1954.

That was the year the Soviet Union arrived on the world
hockey scene and our concept of the game has never been
quite the same since. Until then, Canada had little trouble
winning Olympic and World Championship tournaments.
In 1954, we were represented by a Senior B team, the Toronto Lyndhursts. It seems unreal today that a Senior B
team would actually be dispatched to play the best in Europe, but in 1954 nobody paid too much attention. Another
ho-hum win for Canada, or so it was thought. Then on Sun-

day, March 7 in the deciding game for the Championship in Stockholm, Canadians found out about hockey in the Soviet Union. The final score was Soviets 7, Canada 2. The uproar that followed on the home front was predictable.

The Montreal Canadiens were playing in Detroit on that same March 7. I don't imagine Dad had paid any more attention to the World Hockey scene than most people, but on the train back to Montreal he was full of ideas about what had happened in Stockholm.

Sports writer Andy O'Brien sat up with Dad into the wee small hours discussing the events of the day in Sweden. That's when Dad had his idea.

"We have to show them right away we have the best players, before they start their propaganda," he told Andy. "We've got to send over our best and play them, now. Every NHL team (there were six at the time) should send three players and play them a best of three. Right in Moscow."

"What kind of players?" Andy asked.

"The best," snapped Dad, who was warming to his idea. "We'll give up The Rocket, Elmer Lach, and Doug Harvey." The Red Wings and the Maple Leafs were his main targets for a needle in those days, so he threw out a challenge. "Let the Wings send Gordie Howe, Red Kelly, and Terry Sawchuk. Let the Leafs give up Ted Kennedy, Tod Sloan, and Tim Horton. Everybody else give up their three best players. We can play a couple of weeks without them. It's worth it. But let's do it now." There wasn't any question he would have picked himself to do the coaching.

Dad's theory gave Andy a good column and drew a few comments from some hockey people, but not much more. His main antagonist, Jack Adams of the Red Wings, was quoted as saying, "Irvin's gone off the deep end as usual. We don't need an NHL team to beat them, just a better organized amateur set-up."

A year later, Adams seemed to be on the right track when the rambunctious Warwick brothers from Regina, Grant, Bill, and Dick, led the Penticton Vees overseas and recaptured the championship for Canada in the World Tournament at Krefeld, Germany. They clobbered the Soviets 5-0 in the final game. But through most of the 1960's, the Soviets always defeated Canada until a meeting at the hockey summit took place in 1972. That's when a team of Canadian-born NHL players won the greatest international series ever played.

A team like the one Dad had wanted to take to Moscow eighteen years before.

I don't have a good feeling for international competition and I don't do a very good job broadcasting that type of hockey. The best Canadian for that assignment is Ron Reusch, who has worked with me at CFCF for almost twenty years. Ron worked in Europe in the 1960's and keeps very close tabs on European hockey players and how their names should be pronounced.

A few years ago, Canada's team at the World Tournament was doing a lot better than anyone thought it would. The hastily put-together collection of players whose teams didn't make the NHL playoffs was in a position to win the Gold Medal and suddenly people were jumping on their bandwagon.

No one was televising the tournament in Canada, so CTV made a last minute arrangement to show a game between Canada and Czechoslovakia. Ron went to Toronto, joined Johnny Esaw and Darryl Sittler in a studio, and called the play by play off the TV monitor. He did a great job under very difficult conditions.

I worked the 1979 Challenge Cup Series for *Hockey Night in Canada*, a three-game set between an NHL All-Star team and the Soviet National squad, played in New York. *HNIC* also produced the games for Soviet TV and their representatives attended our production meetings. But they never seemed to get involved in discussions relating to the intermissions. Ralph Mellanby of *HNIC* was in charge. After one of the meetings, I asked him, "What do they do in Russia during intermissions?"

"Nothing," Ralph replied. "They just shut off the picture,

the screen goes blank, and they wait until the game starts again."

Ralph was the one who brought Don Cherry and Howie Meeker into the TV business. The fans in Moscow and Minsk don't know what they're missing.

This is now the jet age for travel in the NHL. Old-timers claim hockey lost something when teams began taking to the air instead of hitting the rails. They claim train travel promoted a form of camaraderie that players of today don't get to enjoy.

Almost everyone who travelled the rails during that particular era of hockey has a story to tell. One of the best was related to me by Emile Francis.

"The Cat" made his rookie debut as an NHL goaltender with the Chicago Black Hawks in 1946. Team rules called for players to have the use of lower berths according to seniority, which meant rookies always slept in the uppers. But that didn't apply to goaltenders. They apparently needed extra sleep, so were always assigned to a lower berth, at least with the Black Hawks.

When the season ended, Emile looked for the cheapest way to return home to North Battleford, Saskatchewan, and found it was by train on an upper-berth ticket. He awoke the first morning of the trip to one of the biggest shocks of his young travelling life.

"I swung my feet through the curtain and jumped out," he told me. "But the floor wasn't where I thought it was. I had completely forgotten I was in an upper berth, not a lower. Almost broke both my legs when I hit the floor."

In those days of train travel, Dad, who like his boss Frank Selke was quite a chicken and pigeon fancier, used to bring the odd bird across the border. These would be high-priced purchases from a fancier in one of the cities the team had visited in the United States. He used all kinds of methods to hide them from the customs inspector checking the train at the border crossing. Sometimes he would stay in his berth, holding a chicken under the covers, hoping the valuable bit of feathered property wouldn't crow or cackle at the wrong time.

Dad once had a basket of birds with him and left them in the smoker part of the train car. That was a mistake. Some of the "boys," no doubt egged on by a mischievous type like Doug Harvey, opened the cage and let the birds out for a late-night stroll. They managed to corral them and somehow get them back into the cage, but when Dad arrived on the scene in the morning there were just as many feathers floating around the train car as there were on the birds themselves.

One of the best hockey travel stories I've heard concerns the legendary Eddie Shore, one of the greatest players and toughest characters in the history of the game.

In the late 1920's, Shore, then an outstanding defenceman with the Boston Bruins, missed the train for a trip to Montreal. So he immediately hired a taxi to drive him there. Normally, there would have been plenty of time to complete the trip before the game began the next night, but a winter storm met them halfway. From then on, the cab slipped and slid, got stuck and unstuck, and the trip became a nightmare. It lasted all night and most of the next day.

He finally made it to Montreal, arriving at the Forum about an hour before the game began. Shore took a twenty-minute nap on the trainer's table, then went out and played his usual fifty or fifty-five minutes.

The Bruins won the game 1-0. And guess what? Eddie Shore scored the goal on an end-to-end rush through the entire Montreal team.

So the story goes.

On the Air

I have only two regrets about my broadcasting career, one sentimental and one commercial. I am sorry my dad didn't live to see me in the business. Hockey was his life and it would have pleased him to know that, eventually, it would become a major part of mine. He would have been an excellent critic and I would have become a better announcer because of it.

I am also sorry I have not been able to earn a living solely as a hockey announcer, but that's something very few have been able to do in Canada. Our American counterparts seem to be in a different world when it comes to the financial side. Most of them spend the summer golfing, fishing, and lolling around their swimming pools. No such luck for those of us in Canada who are back on the late TV news or morning radio shows as soon as the hockey season is over. Many of us also do things like that during the season as well, between games.

Sport Magazine annually publishes a story listing how much money the highest-paid people in sports make. Their 1988 story had a picture of CBS sportscaster Brent Musberger who, the story claimed, made $1,950,000 in 1987. My daughter Nancy spotted it and asked, "Dad, couldn't you get a job as Brent Musberger's assistant?" Not a bad thought.

People often ask me what I do in the summer. Most viewers outside of Montreal assume *Hockey Night in Canada* is all I do. I'm not bothered by this, although I do wonder once in a while when someone from Montreal asks me the same question.

For the past quarter of a century at CFCF, I have done all the jobs sportscasters do at local stations. I have read newscasts on radio and TV numbering in the thousands. I've hosted quiz shows, magazine shows, and shows from the race track. I've announced bowling programs where the contestants were kids and others where they were housewives. I worked with two different Montreal Alouette coaches on football shows early in my career and currently produce and host a weekly program called *Hockey Magazine* that has been on the air since 1981.

My first sportscasting hero was Bill Stern whom I heard broadcasting American College football during the 1940's via Station KFYR, in Bismark, North Dakota. Stern was a master at dramatizing almost every play and he was at the microphone for many games involving the powerful Army team that starred Glenn Davis and Doc Blanchard in the backfield. Army's best lineman was Tex Coulter who later played professionally for the New York Giants and the Montreal Alouettes. Tex settled in Montreal and worked alongside me for eight years when I did radio play by play of Alouette games starting in 1965.

Tex was a gentle giant who took great pride in being named in a poll of old-time NFL players as the meanest man ever to play the game. He said there were two things he had never seen, a bad football game or a bad western movie. That was stretching it a bit as far as football was concerned, especially during a three-year period in the late 1960's when the Alouettes won just seven times. I figured that was meant to keep me humble because of the success of the other team I covered – the one winning the Stanley Cup almost every year at that time.

Tex Coulter and I parted company when it came to my home town, Regina. He didn't like it.

"You know Dick," he drawled once during a cab ride to Taylor Field on our way to a game, "maybe this city of yours isn't so bad after all. It kind of reminds me of San Antonio, Texas."

There was a pause, then Tex added, "At the turn of the century."

Anyone who grew up in Regina has to have a soft spot for the Saskatchewan Roughriders and I am no exception. It was a thrill to be in Vancouver reporting on the 1966 Grey Cup game for CFCF Radio when the Riders won it for the first time. Twenty-one years later, I helped host a "Rider Pride" telethon, selling tickets to help keep the franchise alive.

During the 1966 season, the Alouettes were as bad as the Riders were good. The teams played in Regina on Labour Day and Tex and I did the radio broadcast back to Montreal. When I returned to the office the next day, one of my bosses took me to task for letting my western roots show through.

"Heard you yesterday boosting your old city's football team. You're a Montrealer now and our team is the Alouettes."

I had a hard time believing what I was hearing as I hastened to remind him the final score had been 44-0 for the Riders.

Johnny Esaw, the head of CTV Sports, is a former Reginian who can also relate to Rider pride. Johnny has been very good to me over the years with CTV assignments. I was the pre-game and half-time host on CTV's Grey Cup telecast in 1968, and the anchorman for the network's coverage of the sports events at Expo '67 when our major show was a World Class International Track and Field meet. I did the play by play alongside Lloyd Percival, who gained fame as Canada's first physical-fitness guru. I had never met Percival and felt rather uncomfortable at the thought of working with him because I had taken a dislike to the man many years before.

In the 1940's and 50's, Lloyd Percival hosted a network radio show called *Sports College*. One show included the results of a survey he claimed proved that when the top twenty talents of a hockey player were used to compare Gordie Howe and Rocket Richard, Howe was better in nineteen. This enraged Richard fans like me. It also enraged my dad, who was Richard's coach at the time. Dad went on a CBC Radio program shortly after and blasted Percival from stem to stern, so much so that someone in the CBC hierarchy sent down an order that Dick Irvin was never again to be allowed on the network.

I took the easy way out with Percival and never mentioned Dad during the three days we worked together at Expo. At the same time I learned that Canada's top fitness expert, who had designed all kinds of exercises, wasn't all that sharp himself in some physical activities. We opened every show from the roof of our TV booth, which provided a great background shot of the Montreal skyline and Mount Royal. Percival was scared stiff of heights and I had to push him up the ladder onto the roof. I'm not exactly fond of climbing ladders myself, but I was able to handle that one because it had only six steps.

Each time I boosted Percival up by the backside, I was thinking, "I'll bet The Rocket can climb ladders better than Gordie Howe."

In 1962, a year after I joined CFCF, Ralph Mellanby and I came up with the idea of *Montreal Minor Hockey* and turned it into a series that ran four seasons. We would tape three games a day at the Town of Mount Royal Arena with teams made up of bantam-age players. The station re-ran the games in the summer and I could always tell if the game on the air had been the third one of the day because my voice would be getting pretty weak by the end of the show.

The teams played three fifteen-minute periods straight time, except in the final minute of the game – a format that fit right into a sixty-minute show. Some former NHLers, including Rocket Richard, worked as referees and a few of the kids eventually made it to the NHL, including Gilles Gratton, Richard Leduc, and Bobby Lalonde, who had the best career of them all.

For Ralph and me, it was our first experience at telecasting hockey. Years later, when we were in the same positions, but at places like the Forum and Madison Square Garden instead of the TMR Arena, we liked to remind each other that we were "a long way from *Montreal Minor Hockey*."

At the same time *Montreal Minor Hockey* started, we also began doing a weekly quiz show called *Know Your Sports*. Ralph and I would make up the questions and a panel of three sports fans would try to answer them with the appropriate number of bells ringing and scoreboards flashing. The first series ran four years, followed by a hiatus of six years. Then the show came back on the air for another four-year run. It was a very popular program and was syndicated to several other stations.

In its final season, the show was called *Celebrity Know Your Sports*. By that time, Ralph had moved on to *Hockey Night in Canada* and the production was handled by other talented producers such as Lawrence Kimber and Lucien Albert. Marv Moss, a *Montreal Gazette* sports reporter, worked as our talent scout and came up with a great array of big names for the show. These included Pete Rose, Johnny Bench, Rusty Staub, Angelo Mosca, George Chuvalo, and Ken Dryden. Former Heavyweight Champion Jack Sharkey was on the show and so was basketball superstar Bob Cousy, who captained a team of fans against one headed by Jean Béliveau. I think their show gave me the biggest thrill of all of our celebrity match-ups.

One of the best-remembered moments in Canadian football was the Jackie Parker-Chuck Hunsinger play in the 1954 Grey Cup game. With his Montreal Alouettes leading late in the game and marching in for what would have been the clinching touchdown against the Edmonton Eskimos, Hunsinger fumbled the ball. Parker scooped it up and ran ninety yards for a touchdown. Bob Dean kicked the extra point and the Eskimos won 26-25. Hunsinger and the Alouettes insisted he had thrown the ball and the play should have been ruled an incompleted pass. The controversy continued for many years.

Early in December of 1974, twenty years after the play, both men were head table guests at the Montreal Sports Dinner. They had taped *Celebrity Know Your Sports* earlier that same day. We had arranged to pick them up at the hotel and told them to be in the lobby at two o'clock. I had no idea that they had never met and, when they got to the station, they had quite a story to tell.

"I saw this guy standing by the door and wondered, is that Chuck?" Parker said.

Hunsinger had the same line. "I thought he was Jackie, but I wasn't sure." It was hard to believe the two men hadn't been together, somewhere, in the preceding twenty years, considering the legend that had grown around their controversial play. We didn't let them look at the re-run of the play until we were taping the program. Their reactions were marvellous. Hunsinger got right into it and insisted he hadn't fumbled.

"Watch my arm. Look, see that, I tried to throw it. No way I fumbled, no way." And he meant it. Jackie was laughing and kidding his more serious quiz-show opponent.

"Come on Chuck, you fumbled. Cool down." It was quite a moment.

The first time I broadcast a play by play of a hockey game where the players were older than fourteen was in March of 1966 when CFCF televised a Canadiens-Detroit Red Wings Old-Timers Game at the Forum. It was billed as a revival of the 1950's rivalry between the teams and it drew a standing-room only crowd. Gordie Howe was still playing for the real Red Wings, but they let him suit up for the first period. When the game began, the Detroit Production Line of Howe, Sid Abel, and Ted Lindsay was lined up against the

Canadiens' famed Punch Line of Elmer Lach, Toe Blake, and Maurice Richard.

It was a great night for nostalgia. Ken Reardon, one of about ten Hall of Famers in the game, scored a great goal on an end-to-end rush and The Rocket proved he still had a flair for the dramatic with a goal to break a tie in the third period. The crowd at the Forum went crazy, and you'd swear he had never been away.

They tried to make it into an annual home-and-home series between the teams, but it didn't last because the boys found it tough to break old habits. Reardon, Lindsay, and a few others played just a bit too rough and it was decided to call a halt to what were supposed to be fun occasions before someone got hurt.

Speaking of nostalgia, the White House in Washington once held the All-Star luncheon in 1982. It was presided over by a former sportscaster, Dutch Reagan, who later changed his name to Ronald and ended up as President of the United States.

Mr. Reagan was relaxed and in good form as he spoke to the room full of hockey players and personalities. Gordie Howe was there and the President got off his best line when he said, "Gordie, I remember when Mother used to take me by the hand and we'd go to the rink to watch you play." Reagan was seventy-one at the time.

In 1967, CFCF televised a series of junior games on Saturday afternoons. The Montreal Junior Canadiens were playing in the OHA and future NHLers like Brad Park, Gary Unger, Pierre Bouchard, and Walt Tkaczuk were among the top players in the League.

Jacques Plante was out of hockey that year, having retired for a little while. (He was back with the St. Louis Blues a couple of years later.) I hired Jacques as the colour man, which bothered my boss at CFCF, Bud Hayward. Bud wasn't sure Jacques' English would be good enough, not realizing Plante was perfectly bilingual. We had a meeting shortly before our first telecast. I had warned Jacques about

Bud's fears over his English pronunciations. Jacques didn't say a word at the meeting. Then Bud gave us a pep talk about the kind of show he wanted and how important it was for junior hockey to receive exposure of this kind for the first time in the Montreal market.

"You OK, Jacques?" asked Bud when the meeting was coming to an end. "Think you can handle it?"

With a straight face, Plante replied, "Don't worry you. I try to do de best I are."

The colour drained from Bud's face for a few seconds, until we started to laugh and let him in on the joke.

I had a fair amount of contact with Plante over the years and often thought of his first game in the NHL. Jacques had been playing for the Montreal Royals in the Quebec Senior League and was famous throughout the province for wearing a toque during games. To make the story even better, he knitted the toques himself.

Gerry McNeil was the Canadiens' goaltender and, when he suffered an injury, Plante replaced him for three games. The first one was played November 1, 1952, at the Forum against the New York Rangers. The day before, the Canadiens' coach, Dick Irvin, told him he couldn't wear his toque. So here was Plante, about to play his first NHL game, without the familiar toque he had worn since he was a pee-wee player. I guess this was proof that Dad was from the old school. Quite simply, he thought a red, white, and blue toque was out of place in the NHL, especially one clamped over the ears of a kid getting the privilege of wearing the red, white, and blue uniform of the Montreal Canadiens. Dad was reminded that Plante considered the toque his good luck charm. Too bad. The crabby old coach was having none of it.

The press blasted Dad in both languages. Baz O'Meara, the veteran sports editor of the *Montreal Star*, wrote that Irvin was going to ruin the kid's career before it began.

To his credit, Plante didn't utter a word of protest. In those days, rookies were thankful for the chance to play, and the one hundred dollars per game that was paid to temporary replacement players. Plante played very well that night and the Canadiens won 4-1.

The next night, in New York, the teams tied at 2-2. Two nights later, the Canadiens defeated Toronto 3-1. The new kid in the crease had played three games in four nights and had given up only four goals. When he returned to the Royals, everyone expected Jacques to resume wearing his toque.

"No more," he told the press. "I don't need it for luck anymore. I won't wear one again."

And he didn't.

A few years later, Plante had to deal with another coach who didn't want him to wear something during games, in this case a protective face mask.

Jacques began wearing a mask in practice. When he asked his coach, Toe Blake, if he could wear it in a game, the answer was no. Blake was sure the mask would hamper Plante's vision, especially when the puck was on the ice near his feet. However, Blake did make one concession.

"If you get a puck in the face, then you can wear it."

In a game in New York, November 1, 1959, Andy Bathgate of the Rangers drilled a shot that hit Plante with a sickening crack, ripping open a vicious cut on the left side of his nose. Seven stitches were needed to close the wound. But while Plante seemed to be an unfortunate victim, his teammates said later he was the happiest person in Madison Square Garden.

That was in the era of the one-goaltender system, so Plante had to return to the game. When he did, he was wearing a mask. Blake may not have been too happy, but a deal was a deal. And hockey history was made.

One of the first celebrities I met after getting into the TV business was former boxing champion Archie Moore, who was in Montreal training for a fight against a local boxer, Robert Cleroux. The fight was eventually called off because of a lack of interest at the box office.

Three years earlier, Moore had defended the Light-heavyweight title at the Forum against Canada's "Fighting Fisherman" Yvon Durelle. Moore had been heavily favoured, but he almost lost his championship in what turned into one of the best fights ever seen in this country. Durelle had the champion down and almost out a couple of times, but old Archie survived and knocked out Durelle that night, and again in a rematch a year later.

Moore and his manager, the legendary Doc Kearns, appeared on CFCF's *Sportsman Club* program with me and my boss, Brian McFarlane. Brian had obtained a tape of the first Moore-Durelle fight and ran it during the interview, complete with the blow-by-blow description used on the telecast.

We were sitting on a couch, with Archie on my left. As the fight unfolded on the studio monitor, he grabbed hold of my arm as he started to point out various things that were happening on the screen. When Durelle was knocking Moore to the canvas for a couple of eight-counts, old Archie's grip got stronger and stronger to the point where he was actually hurting me. I broke my left arm four times as a kid and I had visions of number five that night in the TV studio.

At the height of Durelle's onslaught, Archie stared at the monitor like a man transfixed; suddenly, he said, "Watch here. Watch his head." A few seconds later, Durelle's head snapped backward. Moore, seemingly out on his feet, had nailed him with a stiff right jab.

"That's when I got him. That's when I started to come back."

"Way to go, Champ," I said and he thought I was congratulating him for what was happening on the screen. What I was really happy about was the decreased pressure on my arm as he sat back to watch the end of the fight in a much more relaxed manner.

Archie Moore had experienced a close call, and so had my left arm.

Travel is part of the job when you are a play-by-play broadcaster and I have certainly done my share over the past twenty years. When our son Doug was learning what life with his father was all about, someone asked him where his daddy worked.

"At the airport," was the reply of a three-year-old who had been on many a car ride taking Daddy to the airport.

An enjoyable part of my travel has been the winter trips to sunny California.

One morning, we woke up in Los Angeles to learn that a massive blizzard had buried Montreal. I couldn't resist phoning Wilma and greeting her with, "Hi. I'm going down to have breakfast at the pool. It's gorgeous here today. What's new with you?"

"Go to hell," was her reply as she heard the beginning of my taunting laugh before slamming the phone down in my ear. . . .

While travel can be fun, there are moments when you have to stop and wonder if it really is worth it, especially when your kids are young. I was in Minnesota watching an anniversary show of ABC's *Wide World of Sports* on which the host, Jim McKay, gave a very touching tribute to the families of those who worked on the globe-trotting program.

"They're the real stars of a show like this," he said. "Those of us who have spent too much time away from home, who have said too many goodbyes at too many airports, dedicate this program to those who have had to share our lives this way."

There I was, watching the show in a hotel room in Bloomington, Minnesota, getting choked up thinking of Wilma, Nancy, and Doug back home. But I kept travelling. So did Jim McKay.

My two longest trips were to Austria for CTV to work on the 1967 World Hockey Tournament in Vienna, and the Winter Olympics in Innsbruck, in 1976.

A day or two before the Innsbruck Games began, I went to the town of Seefeld to interview members of Canada's Cross Country Ski team which included the Firth Twins, who had represented our country for several years on the international circuit. That night there was a party for Canadian athletes and media people and, when I walked into the room, Jim Proudfoot of the *Toronto Star* was chatting with the Firths. They were telling Jim how much they enjoyed their life when one of them spotted me coming through the door.

"We get to meet a lot of well-known people," she was saying. Then, pointing at me, she added, "Like him. We met him today. Howie Meeker."

I often tell that story at dinners when describing how those of us who appear on the tube can be victims of mistaken identity. In my case, there's one mistake that leads all the rest. It's the question, "Can I have your autograph, Mr. Gallivan?"

When the Danny and Dick show was front and centre on the CBC Saturday nights, Red Fisher gibed me by writing that I was travelling with the Canadiens hoping to find a city where people didn't call me Danny Gallivan. He wasn't far wrong. Even though Danny seldom appeared on camera in the final few years of his career, and has been retired for a while, his image is still very strong from coast to coast.

I had one particularly bad day in Toronto a few years ago. I was on a hotel elevator, when a fellow passenger asked me, "Aren't you Ernie Afaganis?"

When I assured him I wasn't the popular CBC sportscaster from Edmonton, he replied, "You sure look like him."

A few hours later, I was riding the subway when the chap seated across from me posed a similar question.

"Aren't you Frank Selke Jr. from Montreal?" Again, I pleaded mistaken identity, but I don't think he believed me. What bothered me about that one was that it had been about fifteen years since Frank had hosted *HNIC* out of the Forum, while I had been on the show ever since.

Then there was Torrie Robertson, the hockey player, who greeted me with "Hello, Mr. Hewitt."

Another time, an exuberant, and slightly under-the-weather fan in Buffalo yelled at me, "Hey, you're Dick

McFarlane from Antigonish." At least he had all locations covered: Dick from Montreal, McFarlane from Toronto, and Gallivan from Antigonish.

But in my case the "Danny Gallivans" beat all the rest. The doorman at the Palliser Hotel, in Calgary, made quite a fuss over me as I was getting into a cab on my way to the Saddledome for a game in the 1986 Stanley Cup finals. After a quick exchange of ideas as to what might happen in the game, he ushered me into the taxi and, as he closed the door, signed off with, "Have a nice evening, Mr. Gallivan."

You lose some, but you win some too. CFCF-TV's newscast *Pulse* is a highly rated show. When Brian Mulroney and Ronald Reagan met at the Shamrock Summit, in Quebec City in 1985, a *Pulse* team was there. When Mulroney arrived, reporter Ken Ernhoffer caught the PM getting out of his car and asked him, "What are you going to say to the President when he gets off his plane?"

Mulroney, noticing the CFCF logo on the microphone, replied, "Well, I'll welcome him to Canada on behalf of Dick Irvin, Ron Reusch, and everyone else on *Pulse*."

The folks on our news team were somewhat distressed that the PM had singled out the show's sportscasters by name. The sportscasters wasted no time claiming that it was obvious what part of the program he found the most interesting.

"Everybody's an expert."

I've heard hockey coaches say that when under fire from fans and media, and people in my business often feel that way too. Nit-picking is a hazard of our trade, even from within our own ranks, and I'm no exception.

For example, I agree with the complaint that we don't give the score of the game enough during a play-by-play broadcast. The problem can be related to the old saying, "Time flies when you're having fun." I think I give the score plenty of times, yet listening to some tapes I'll sometimes clock seven or eight minutes between mentions. It doesn't seem like that when you're doing the game, but to a viewer or listener it can be a long time, especially for someone who tuned in just after you gave the score, and has to wait that long before you announce it again.

It would be nice if we said "going to" more often than "gonna," but we don't. Baseball errors are often pronounced "airs." Athletes are constantly setting "new" records, when we all know that every record is a new one. Just like "very" first, which of course every first is. And then there are all those players who have "good speed." Does anyone have "bad speed?"

How many times during a TV sportscast does the announcer say to his viewers, "Watch this," when showing game highlights? And how many viewers are saying right back at him, "What do you think I'm doing, you dummy? I am watching."

There was a time in my early days on *Hockey Night in Canada* when the announcers weren't able to "watch this" when the viewers could. In some U.S. cities proper facilities for instant replays weren't available, so they would run them from the studios in either Toronto or Montreal. While the viewers at home were watching the replay of a goal, the commentator whose job it was to describe the play, knowledgeably of course, was looking at a blank screen. So the director would have to lead him through it by saying things like, "OK, the replay is on and Esposito has the puck at the blue line. There's his pass to Orr. There's Orr's shot, off the goal post, and now Espo is scoring on the rebound." He would be getting his direction from someone 500 miles away and in turn relaying it to the commentator in the booth. They called them "blind replays" and it was a happy day when that particular technical glich was eliminated.

I'm at the stage now where young sportscasters often ask me for advice. The main thing I tell them is to "be yourself," a lesson I learned early in the game. When I joined CFCF, I was thrown onto the air with seasoned veterans like Brian, Jimmy Tapp, and Dean Kaye. Dean was the newscaster on *Pulse* and following one of the first shows we did together, on which I obviously had been trying much too hard to make an impression, he gave me some fatherly advice.

"They're going to tell you to do all kinds of things but, no matter what they say, be yourself. If you're not, the camera will kill you. That lens is powerful. Be yourself, it's the only way to do it."

That's one reason Don Cherry has become a media star. You may agree or you may disagree with him, but with Grapes what you see is what he is, high starched collar and all.

There's one show I've been associated with that has drawn more response from the public than any other. *Hockey Night in Canada*, you say, or perhaps the Olympics, or Montreal Canadiens' broadcasts on the radio? The answer is none of the above. Instead, it's an FM radio program called *Big Band Swing*.

A couple of years ago, David Middleton, the Station Manager, called me in the broadcast booth at the Spectrum in Philadelphia about five minutes before the start of our hockey broadcast.

"How would you like to host a big band show on CFQR?" he asked me. "Two hours, every Saturday night. We'll call it *Big Band Swing*. Think about it and let me know."

I thought about it a lot. David knew that, while I'm not an expert on big bands, we had a pretty good record collection at home and it was my favourite kind of music. I decided to give it a try. A few weeks later, I was nervously introducing a two-hour radio program starring Glenn Miller, Tommy Dorsey, Artie Shaw, and a cast of dozens of other big bands. By the time the second rating of the show came out, it had become the Number One radio program in Montreal on a Saturday night, with 40,000 listeners. Two years later, it was close to 50,000.

The reaction has been unreal. I have received more letters and phone calls and have had more people stop me on the street to talk about *Big Band Swing* than any show I've ever done, including the big Saturday night hockey telecast on the big network. I pick the music, with the help of CFCF's Music Director Chris Brooke, and it's quite a treat to be paid to listen to Benny Goodman.

The music of Miller, Dorsey, Shaw, Goodman, *et al.*, won't disappear as long as there are old guys like me around helping it stay on the air.

It is impossible not to become emotionally involved in some of the events you cover. Two such moments stand out in my memory bank.

In 1973, Montreal financier J. Louis Lévesque sponsored a Ladies' Professional Golf Tournament at the Municipal Course. It was the first LPGA tournament held in Montreal and Lévesque did it as a showcase for Jocelyne Bourassa, a young Quebec golfer who had recently joined the pro tour. There was a lot of pressure on Jocelyne. Had she merely played well and finished with a respectable score, her performance would have been termed a success. But she did more than play well, she played super.

In the final round, Jocelyne needed a birdie on the eighteenth hole to join Judy Rankin and Sandra Haynie in a playoff for the championship. I was working for CTV on the tower behind the eighteenth green. When Jocelyne's approach left her with a thirty foot putt, it seemed too much to expect her to sink it. Donna Caponi, one of the stars of the LPGA, had joined me in the booth following her round. As Jocelyne got set to putt, Donna whispered (golf announcers are supposed to whisper), "Come on Jocelyne." By now everyone was totally keyed up and when the gutsy little Quebecer curled the putt dead centre into the hole, Donna started to cheer, and so did I, completely oblivious to the rule, "No cheering in the broadcast booth."

Jocelyne then won the playoff, but it was somewhat of an anti-climax following her big putt under pressure. That's one I'll never forget.

I was again working for CTV, this time at the 1976 Innsbruck Winter Olympics, when a Soviet athlete gave me another emotional moment in a broadcast booth.

Al McCann and I were broadcasting the closing ceremonies, which featured the usual array of athletes plus a dozen or so eight- and nine-year-old figure skaters, who were on the ice handing out flowers to the Olympians as they paraded around the arena.

The official part of the ceremonies came to an end. And that's always a time of emotion and memories. Then, as the athletes began leaving the arena in a very informal fashion, a huge bear of a man, one of the Soviet cross-country skiers, stopped and picked up a cute little flower girl, hoisting her as high as his arms could reach. He had a marvellous smile on his face and so did she.

What a contrast – the big, burly athlete of the present day whose task was done and the little Austrian girl who might be a skating star in an Olympics of the future. Coming in the final moments of what had been a tremendous Winter Games and an unforgettable time for me, it hit me right in the middle of my heartstrings.

Last Minute to Play in the Third Period

The first week in May, 1988 was a significant one for me. Wilma and I celebrated our twenty-fifth anniversary, I finished writing this book, and I received a phone call from Jiggs McDonald.

Jiggs is the TV play-by-play announcer for the New York Islanders. He works with me and Bob Wilson, the radio voice of the Boston Bruins, on the committee which annually nominates a broadcaster for induction into the Media section of the Hockey Hall of Fame.

"Congratulations," Jiggs began. "It is my pleasant duty to inform you that you are the broadcasters' Hall of Fame nomination for 1988."

"Wait a minute," I replied. "That's not the way it was when we talked about another name for this year."

"That was a smoke screen," Jiggs laughed. "We knew you wouldn't vote for yourself."

It wasn't the first time something like that happened. The previous year, Jiggs and I had pulled the same routine on Bob Wilson when he was nominated. He was right, I wouldn't have voted for myself. But as he said, the majority rules, two votes to one.

Wilma, Nancy, and Doug were there to share the moment, and of course I thought again how great it would have been for my dad to have been part of my hockey broadcasting career. But after I hung up the phone, I found myself thinking mainly of my mother, and what it would have meant for her.

Mother watched and listened through the first fourteen years her son was a sports announcer. At first, she was confused as to why I would want to leave the business world and get into something like that; but, as the years went by, she got a great kick out of what I was doing.

She watched as only a mother could. I might have gone on the air with the most sensational scoop in Canadian sports history, called her right after the show, and she likely would have said, "Your tie was crooked."

As was the case with Dad, I was talking hockey with my mother the night before she died. We were in her apartment watching a TV game between the Maple Leafs and the Pittsburgh Penguins. Syl Apps Jr. was playing for the Penguins. Mother was talking about what a marvellous player his father had been. Syl Apps Sr. was captain of the Maple Leafs during Dad's last few years with the Toronto team.

The next day, December 19, 1974, I drove her to the airport and she flew to Ancaster, Ont., to attend her brother's funeral. That same evening, she was struck down by a car while walking across a main thoroughfare during a snow storm, and was killed instantly.

Mother had a big role in compiling the Irvin family's hockey scrapbook. It had been started by my grandmother. When she passed away in 1932, Mother took over and kept it going through Dad's coaching days with the Leafs and the Canadiens, with help from my sister Fay in later years.

One hockey personality who got a great charge out of going through the scrapbook was former NHL goalie Chico Resch. Chico is a true hockey "collector," always on the lookout for anything of value from the old days, sticks, pucks, sweaters, and the like.

A few years ago, Chico was in Montreal with the New

Jersey Devils. He wasn't going to play that night so instead of taking his afternoon nap, he opted for a visit to our house and a look at the scrapbook. Once he got going, he didn't just look at it, he devoured it.

The afternoon wore on and it was time for me to get back to the Forum for the pre-game TV production meeting.

"Come on Chico, we've got to go," I told him.

"Just a few more minutes," he said, as his devouring continued. "Look at this picture. It's from 1915 and it's so clear. And all these write-ups and old cartoons. This stuff is like gold, Dick . . . like gold."

"Come on Chico," I kept saying, again and again. By the time I pulled him away from the scrapbook and made it to the Forum, the meeting was over.

"Terrible traffic jam on Decarie Boulevard," I mumbled in response to an icy stare from the producer.

Chico loved the scrapbook, but he was distressed by the condition it was in. Over the past several years, I have stripped it of pictures and articles to use on various TV programs and they've never been put back in place.

"Dick, you've got to get the book back in shape. You've got all those pages lying around and you don't want to lose them. That book has meant a lot to your family and your career. You've got to fix it."

Chico is right. The old scrapbook has meant a lot to the Irvin family. It's a big reason I began my broadcasting career twenty-seven years ago and it's a big reason I wrote this book.

One of these days, very soon, I'll fix it.

I'm always looking for links between my dad's career and mine. When the Boston Bruins defeated the Canadiens in the 1988 playoffs, it was the first time that had happened since 1943. When the game was over, I mentioned to Don Cherry that an Irvin had been present both times.

"Dad was coaching the Canadiens in '43, and here I am in the building tonight, forty-five years later."

Don liked that. He liked the fact that the Bruins had beaten the Canadiens even better.

The last game Dad coached for the Toronto Maple Leafs was the one in which the New York Rangers won the Stanley Cup in 1940, and I was there. I'd like to be present the next time they win it, but I don't know if I can hang around that long.

Time marches on, but every once in a while someone comes along to help rekindle memories of Dad. One of my best-remembered was supplied by that famous politician from my native province of Saskatchewan, The Chief himself, John Diefenbaker.

I met John Diefenbaker at the Grey Cup Game in Montreal in 1969. Saskatchewan was playing Ottawa and, on the eve of the game, Wilma and I attended a Saskatchewan rally. We arrived in time to hear Diefenbaker address the faithful and he was in great form, giving a rousing and hilarious pep talk to his fellow westerners.

Before the game the next day, one of his aides spotted me and introduced me to The Chief.

"Are you the son of Dick Irvin, the coach?" he asked.

"Yes sir," I replied. I was somewhat in awe of the legendary Tory from Prince Albert, and there was no doubt who was in charge of the conversation.

"Always thought so. You're from the West aren't you? Didn't you grow up in Regina?"

"Yes sir."

"I trust you're still a westerner today when it comes to the team you'll be cheering for."

"Yes sir."

"Keep up the good work. Your father was a fine man. Make sure you do the kind of a job he'd be proud of."

"Yes sir."

I hope I have.

···················
Acknowledgements

I wish to thank those people who helped me write this book. Don Cherry and Al Strachan gave me some encouraging pep talks that convinced me to start writing.

Michael Barnett of CorpSport International put the project together and contributed his permanently positive attitude from the very beginning.

Stu Hackel kindly read initial outlines of the early chapters and offered valuable advice.

My pick-and-punch typing was transferred into usable form by Carole Robertson, and my wife Wilma.

David Bier, in Montreal, and Joseph Romaine of the Hockey Hall of Fame were very generous with photographs, past and present.

I am grateful to McClelland and Stewart for their interest and support, and especially for assigning Patrick Crean as my editor. Patrick's enthusiasm, guidance, and, above all, his patience with a rookie author extended, I'm sure, far beyond his normal call of duty.

Index